PSYCHOL

REVISI

FOR EDEXCEL

If you're studying for a GCSE in Psychology you'll need a revision guide that tells you everything you need to know. This accessible and interactive book covers all compulsory and all optional topics on the GCSE Edexcel Psychology syllabus introduced in 2017, including development, memory, psychological problems, brain and neuropsychology, social influence and research methods. It summarises the specification material clearly and attractively, enabling you to easily digest and retain the information ready for your exams.

Packed full of revision ideas and techniques designed to help you cement your knowledge, the book includes a number of unique and helpful features, such as:

- Expert tips from an experienced senior examiner to clarify key points and help you avoid making common errors
- Sample exam questions to aid practice
- Active learning tasks, such as key definitions and word gaps
- Double page spreads outlining the studies you need to know, and their strengths and weaknesses
- Coverage of the new compulsory mathematical element which was brought into the specification in 2017

Perfect for revising psychological concepts, theories and studies in relation to the three critical assessment objectives, *Psychology GCSE Revision Guide for Edexcel* is an essential resource for anyone taking a psychology GCSE using the Edexcel specification.

Ali Abbas has 13 years' experience working as a Principal Examiner, which has included responsibility for writing A Level exam papers for Edexcel, and nearly 20 years' teaching experience for the major exam boards at A Level and GCSE. He has been providing training and support to staff and students since 2003 and regularly visits numerous schools and colleges nationally and internationally. Ali has been a Fellow of the Chartered Institute of Educational Assessors (FCIEA) since 2008.

Endorsement Statement

In order to ensure that this resource offers high-quality support for the associated Pearson qualification, it has been through a review process by the awarding body. This process confirms that this resource fully covers the teaching and learning content of the specification or part of a specification at which it is aimed. It also confirms that it demonstrates an appropriate balance between the development of subject skills, knowledge and understanding, in addition to preparation for assessment.

Endorsement does not cover any guidance on assessment activities or processes (e.g. practice questions or advice on how to answer assessment questions), included in the resource nor does it prescribe any particular approach to the teaching or delivery of a related course.

While the publishers have made every attempt to ensure that advice on the qualification and its assessment is accurate the official specification and associated assessment guidance materials are the only authoritative source of information and should always be referred to for definitive guidance.

Pearson examiners have not contributed to any sections in this resource relevant to examination papers for which they have responsibility.

Examiners will not use endorsed resources as a source of material for any assessment set by Pearson.
Endorsement of a resource does not mean that the resource is required to achieve this Pearson qualification, nor does it mean that it is the only suitable material available to support the qualification, and any resource lists produced by the awarding body shall include this and other appropriate resources.

PSYCHOLOGY GCSE REVISION GUIDE FOR EDEXCEL

Ali Abbas

LONDON AND NEW YORK

First published 2019
by Routledge
2 Park Square, Milton Park, Abingdon, Oxon OX14 4RN

and by Routledge
52 Vanderbilt Avenue, New York, NY 10017

Routledge is an imprint of the Taylor & Francis Group, an informa business

British Library Cataloguing-in-Publication Data
A catalogue record for this book is available from the British Library

Library of Congress Cataloging-in-Publication Data
A catalog record for this book has been requested

ISBN: 978-1-138-49409-1 (hbk)
ISBN: 978-1-138-49411-4 (pbk)
ISBN: 978-1-351-02658-1 (ebk)

Typeset in Goudy
by Wearset Ltd, Boldon, Tyne and Wear

Contents

Chapter 1
Development – how did you develop?

This chapter deals with how we develop and its importance in understanding human behaviour. How we develop is tied into various stages which correspond with particular ages, so early brain development occurs in young children, whereas issues surrounding morality will occur later in life. This is determined by what we are born with (our nature) and also how the environment (nurture) influences us.

Rather than by a slow, continuous process of change over time, children's abilities develop in stages. These stages are pre-determined and follow a strict sequence so that a child has to complete one stage before they can progress to the next. Psychologists such as Piaget believed that whatever adults do to speed up the process of change, a child will not 'stage-shift' until they are 'ready' to do so.

Early brain development

A mere 16 days after conception, the foetus's **neural plate** forms. It grows longer and folds onto itself, until that fold morphs into a groove, and that groove turns into the neural tube. Once the neural tube closes, at around week six or week seven of pregnancy, it curves and bulges into three sections, commonly known as the **forebrain**, **midbrain** and **hindbrain**. Just below the hindbrain sits the part that will soon turn into the baby's spinal cord.

Hindbrain parts include the **medulla**, the **cerebellum** and the **pons**. Together, these three structures govern our autonomic or 'automated' body systems, controlling our heart, breathing and sleep patterns. Basically, the hindbrain controls all the things that you want to automatically work without having to think about them. Can you imagine having to remind your heart to beat or consciously adjust your sense of balance? And what if you forgot?

The hindbrain is the oldest part of our brain and is located deep within our head and on top of our spinal cord. Because this was our first and most basic brain (way back before we were cave people), it controls most of our most basic functions. The cerebellum is extremely important for being able to perform everyday voluntary tasks such as walking and writing. It is also essential to being able to stay balanced and upright. It is responsible for movements so that extensive damage of the cerebellum can cause failure to even stand up.

Key terms

Neural plate is the foundation of a baby's brain and spinal cord.
Forebrain means 'last brain', or the most recently developed portion of our brain.
Midbrain serves to relay information between the hindbrain and the forebrain. It acts as the information superhighway connecting these two regions, particularly information coming from the eyes and the ears.
Hindbrain is located at the rear of the skull and is the lowest portion of the brain and includes the medulla, the cerebellum and the pons.
Medulla is where the spinal cord enters the skull. It is responsible for controlling reflex actions such as coughing, sneezing, swallowing, vomiting and breathing.
Cerebellum is two rounded structures located besides the medulla.
Pons serves as the bridge towards the midbrain.

Now test yourself

1. How does the neural plate turn into the neural tube?
2. Which is the oldest part of our brain?
3. Problems with writing are associated with which part of the brain?

The midbrain is the biological equivalent of the Internet; it is a vital aspect of our neural 'information superhighway', which transfers visual and auditory input to the brain and motor (movement) information from the brain. It enables your brain to integrate sensory information from your eyes and ears with your muscle movements, thereby enabling your body to use this information to make fine adjustments to your movements.

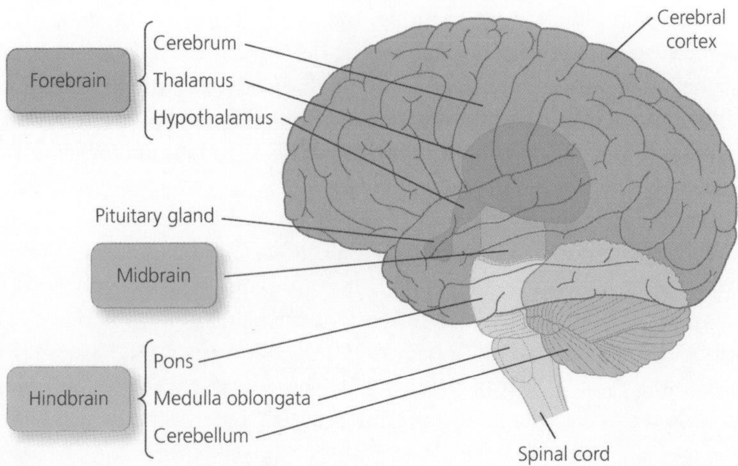

Figure 1.1 Different parts of the brain

The forebrain is considered as the highest region of the brain because it essentially differentiates us humans from the rest of the animal kingdom. This region is also involved in processing complex information; it is the 'supercomputer' of the human body.

Piaget's theory of cognitive development

Jean Piaget became interested in the answers schoolchildren gave whilst he was carrying out some IQ tests with them in his early work as a clinical psychologist. Although he was interviewing them to find out what they knew, he found their mistakes, rather than their correct answers, to be most revealing. Piaget proposed that children give different answers to problems because they think differently to adults. He also noticed how their thinking changed through to adulthood, when they developed a logical approach to solving problems.

Piaget proposed that children pass through four stages as they develop their understanding of the world. At each stage, the child develops certain abilities, which help him to make the transition to the next stage, and Piaget proposed that this happens at roughly the same time for all children, regardless of upbringing.

The sensorimotor stage (0–18 months approx.)

Children have not yet learned to use language and symbols to represent the objects and events in the environment. They know the world only in terms of their own sensory impressions of its sights, sounds, tastes and smells, and their own muscular movements and the effects these movements create.

- Early schemas are reflex actions, e.g. sucking. These are gradually generalised so that all objects are sucked.
- Gradually schemas are combined, e.g. sucking and arm-movement schemas are combined and coordinated into the action of putting the thumb into the mouth.
- By 4–6 months, babies can understand cause and effect as it applies to their own movements. They repeatedly kick at toys hanging over their cots, apparently to make them move.
- At the beginning of the sensorimotor period, the infant has no awareness of anything outside themselves: everything they come into contact with is regarded as part of the child themselves. If you hide an object from a young baby, then it will not search for it; Piaget says this is because the infant has no object concept – when a toy is out of sight, then it does not exist anymore. Gradually, the child develops object permanence – they will search for a missing object and know it exists when it cannot be seen. This develops at around ten months of age.

Now test yourself

4. Suggest how you could test whether a baby has object permanence.
5. How would the baby respond if it lacked object permanence?
6. How would the baby respond if it had object permanence?

Key terms

Schema is a type of mental structure that children use to help organise knowledge of the world.
Sensorimotor is experiencing the world mainly through senses and physical activity.
Object permanence is the ability to appreciate that things exist even when they cannot be seen.

The pre-operational stage (18 months–7 years approx.)

The basic difference between the sensorimotor and the pre-operational stage is that the child now becomes capable of **symbolic representation**.

Another indication of the use of symbolic thought is that the child now engages in **representational play**. They will play 'mummies and daddies' or pretend that a cardboard box is a house. The box represents a house; he and his friend represent mummy and daddy.

This ability to represent something symbolically becomes extended to language. The child now begins to talk and this means that he can represent an object or event by means of words.

Key terms

Symbolic representation means that the child can now represent events in their mind and anticipate events.
Representational play is a form of make-believe play.

Limitations of the pre-operational period

1. EGOCENTRICITY

The child is not capable of understanding that there can be a viewpoint other than their own.

This is demonstrated by the 'three mountains task' (see page 20) and also the following example:

ADULT: Do you have a sister?
GIRL: Yes.
ADULT: What's her name?
GIRL: Susan.
ADULT: Does Susan have a sister?
GIRL: Nope.

Another example of **egocentricity** is **animism**. Young children believe that objects like stones, cars and lakes act intentionally; *they* are alive and have feelings, so everything else must have.

2. LACK OF CONSERVATION

One classic experiment involving **conservation** uses two equal-sized lumps of clay. The experimenter takes one lump and squashes it like a pancake. The question for the child is: 'Is there the same amount here (pointing to the pancake) as there is here (pointing to the ball)?' A preschooler nearly always thinks the amount of clay is different (most think the pancake is bigger).

The child is unable to grasp the fact that the amount of clay remains the same even though the appearance of one lump may change. There are four types of conservation, as follows:

- Conservation of quantity (clay)
- Conservation of length (string)
- Conservation of number (counters)
- Conservation of liquid quantity (beakers of milk)

Why is this called the pre-operational stage? Because the child at this stage cannot perform **operations**. The rules of arithmetic involve operations, which are reversible. For example, a child at the age of five will readily understand that $2+3=5$ but will not appreciate that this process is reversible by subtraction $5-3=2$. The older child who is capable of operational thinking will recognise that addition is reversible by subtraction and division is reversible by multiplication.

3. LACK OF REVERSIBILITY

This is precisely why the pre-operational child cannot conserve: this involves a reversible operation. To understand that water in a tall thin container is still the same in quantity as that in a short, fat beaker from which it came, you must be capable of performing the mental operation of reversibility or mentally pouring the liquid back.

Key terms

Egocentricity means the child is unable to see the world from anything but their own point of view.
Animism is the belief that everything is alive.
Conservation is the ability to understand that some features of an object may change whilst others remain the same.
Operations are thought processes which have the characteristic of being reversible, or can be done backwards.

Now test yourself

7. List the four main features of the pre-operational stage.
8. What are the four types of conservation?

Concrete operational stage (7–12 years, approx.)

The stage of concrete operations is so called because the child needs to manipulate and experiment with real objects in order to solve problems in a logical way. They can arrange a series of boxes in order of size, but would have difficulty solving verbal problems like 'Lisa is taller than Susan, Katy is shorter than Susan. Who is the tallest?'

Concrete operational thinkers are able to solve the problems outlined above because they have the ability to de-centre – to consider more than one aspect of a problem. Therefore, children now show:

- Reduced egocentrism.
- Ability to conserve. These abilities develop in order: first quantity (6–7), then length (7–8), weight (8–10) and volume (11–12). The order of conservations is invariant but children do not go through them all at the same time at the same ages.
- Ability to classify, i.e. grouping objects together logically in terms of their common characteristics. Concrete operational thinkers can also understand that groups can fit into each other, e.g. that one flower is a primrose, another is a buttercup, but both are flowers.
- Seriation. The child can order a series of great length on the basis of more than one dimension, such as height and weight.
- Reversibility. This means that an operation can be regarded as a mental activity, which can be reversed – done backwards, so to speak. The rules of arithmetic involve operations, which are reversible. For example, a child of five will readily understand that $2 + 3 = 5$ but will not appreciate that this process is reversible by subtraction $5 - 3 = 2$. The older child who is capable of operational thinking will recognise that addition is reversible by subtraction and division is reversible by multiplication.

Active learning

Table 1.1 lists six statements concerning the concrete operational stage; three statements are true and three are false. Write true next to the three statements which are true.

Table 1.1 True or false?

The child is capable of abstract thought	
The child becomes less egocentric	
The child acquires reversible thinking	
The child becomes more egocentric	
The child can solve conservation tasks	
The child acquires object permanence	

Formal operational stage (12 years onwards)

This is the most advanced stage, when we become capable of logical, rational thinking.

Table 1.2 Characteristics of the formal operational stage

Characteristic	Example
Hypothetical reasoning: the child is now able to reason about hypothetical problems – what might be, as well as real problems – and think about possibilities as well as actualities.	The third eye problem or the pendulum task – see 'Active learning' below.
Systematic/analytic thinking: the child can now make a systematic search for solutions rather than using trial and error.	'If Kelly is taller than Ali and Ali is taller than Jo, who is tallest?'
Logical problem solving: mental operations are now organised into higher order operations. Higher order operations are ways of using abstract rules to solve a whole class of problems.	What number is 30 less than 2 times itself?
Tendency to philosophise: people in the formal operational stage think about their own thoughts, evaluating them and searching for inconsistencies and fallacies in logic.	A 14-year-old may brood about the following two propositions: 1. God loves humanity. 2. There are many suffering human beings. These two beliefs are incompatible and spur the adolescent to look for ways of resolving the tension created by the inconsistency.

Active learning – testing formal operational thinking

Pendulum task

What factor influences how fast a weight will swing – the weight, the length of string, how hard you push?

You have five attempts: try different weights on different lengths of string and push them whilst the researcher holds the string.

Write down what the participant did on each attempt:

1.

2.

3.

4.

5.

The third eye problem

Children were asked where they would put an extra eye, if they were able to have a third one, and why. Schaffer (1988) reported that, when asked this question, nine-year-olds all suggested that the third eye should be on the forehead. However, 11-year-olds were more inventive – for example, suggesting that a third eye placed on the hand would be useful for seeing round corners.

Piaget's theory application to education

Piaget himself did not apply his theory to education, but other researchers have put Piaget's ideas into practice in the classroom.

The readiness approach – learning should be appropriate for a child's level of development. Children should only be taught certain concepts when they are 'cognitively ready'. For example, we would not give children still in the concrete operational stage tasks that require abstract thought. According to Piaget, children would only be capable of such tasks when they had reached the formal operational stage.

Discovery learning – according to Piaget, cognitive development occurs when our schemas no longer fit the environment, causing a state of **disequilibrium**. When learning, children need to make their own discoveries in order to escape disequilibrium, through a process of **assimilation** and **accommodation**.

The role of the teacher – this should be to facilitate rather than dominate the learning process so children can find things out for themselves. It is the teacher's role to:

- provide suitable materials to match the child's level of development
- set tasks that are challenging enough to put the child into a state of disequilibrium, so children have the opportunity to develop their schemas through a process of assimilation and accommodation
- encourage interaction between children by setting small group work in order to allow the child to de-centre.

The curriculum – if children are capable of understanding different concepts at each stage of development then the curriculum should be tailored so that children encounter new ideas when they can cope with them. Certain concepts should be taught before others; for example, conservation of number, followed by conservation of weight, followed by conservation of volume. New knowledge should be built on pre-existing schemas, which should be expanded through accommodation. Children in the concrete operational stage should, therefore, start with concrete examples before progressing onto more abstract tasks.

Piaget proposed that cognitive development could not be speeded up, because of its dependence on biological maturation.

Piaget's theory application to intelligence

Intelligence is developed through a process of active exploration by the child, where they manipulate objects (and later, ideas) in order to understand their properties. This process is called performing operations. The child's first schemas are based on their own body and are purely automatic (involuntary) reflexes, such as sucking, crying, grasping or kicking, known as body schemas.

After a while, the infant learns to control their body to satisfy their needs more effectively – for example, reaching out and smiling to get attention, leading to a feeding or play session.

Children develop their understanding of the world by the twin processes of **assimilation** and **accommodation**. When a child meets a new situation, they are thrown into a state of disequilibrium. In order to overcome this uncomfortable feeling, they must perform an operation to help increase their knowledge of the situation and overcome it. New information gained from the operation is assimilated (taken on board), and the structure of the child's schemas is accommodated (changed) to make use of the incoming knowledge. Now that the child understands the situation, they feel content again and return to a state of **equilibrium**.

Cognitive development occurs when our schemas no longer fit the environment, causing a state of disequilibrium. **Adaptation** to the environment then occurs through two complementary processes: assimilation and accommodation. Piaget believed that children are instinctively driven or motivated to seek equilibrium. This is why they constantly play with objects and ask questions so that they can develop new schemas that help them understand the world around them.

Key terms

Disequilibrium is an imbalance when encountering information that requires us to develop new schemas.
Assimilation is the process of acquiring new knowledge by relating it to existing knowledge.
Accommodation is the process of changing the way in which the person acts or the way he sees the world.
Equilibrium is when existing schemas are capable of explaining what a child is experiencing, a state of balance.
Adaptation is using the assimilation and accommodation process to understand the world.

Now test yourself

9. What is the purpose of disequilibrium?

Active learning

Imagine a two-year-old child who has formed the schema of 'bird' as an object that flies in the sky. One day she sees her first aeroplane and tries to link it to her schema of 'bird' because this is the only suitable schema she has – this is .... because she is trying to fit something new (the aeroplane) into her existing knowledge.

She then notices the noise, the size and the shape, which do not fit her existing 'bird' schema. If she questions an adult, they will provide a new word and explain the differences between birds and aeroplanes – this is ...., the formation of new schemas ('aeroplane') through which the world is seen.

She is in a state of disequilibrium when ....

She is in a state of equilibrium when ....

Table 1.3 Summary and evaluation of Piaget's four stages

Stage	Key features	Strengths of Piaget's theory	Weaknesses of Piaget's theory
Sensorimotor stage	Reflexive and action schemas, e.g. sucking Totally egocentric Object permanence	Piaget investigated his children's lack of object permanence during this stage by hiding an object from them under a cover. At 0–5 months, an object visibly hidden will not be searched for, even if the child was reaching for it. At eight months, the child will search for a completely hidden object.	Bower and Wishart (1972) offered an object to babies aged 1–4 months, and then turned off the lights as they were about to reach for it. When observed by infra-red camera, the babies were seen to continue reaching for the object despite not seeing it. Bower (1977) tested month-old babies who were shown a toy and then had a screen placed in front of it. The toy was secretly removed from behind the screen and, when the screen itself was taken away, Bower claimed that the babies showed surprise that the toy was not there.
Pre-operational stage	Symbolic representation Egocentricity Animism Lack of conservation	Piaget and Inhelder (1956) demonstrated the egocentrism of pre-operational children with their 'three mountains task'. **Conservation experiments** – Piaget tested for many different types of conservation. The child would fail in each case, since they lacked the necessary operations.	Bryant (1974) argued that the design of many Piagetian tasks made it very difficult for children to give the correct answers. Piaget, he felt, may have over-estimated the language and memory skills of young children. By using slightly different wording of a question, or by using tasks that are more meaningful to the child, different results may be obtained. **Egocentricity** – Hughes (1975) used a design in which a child had to work out where a doll must hide in order not to be seen by a policeman. He demonstrated that three-and-a-half to five-year-olds could de-centre and overcome their egocentrism, if the task made more 'human sense' to them. When these children had to hide a boy doll from two policeman dolls (a task that required them to take into account the perspectives of others but have a good, understandable reason for doing so), they could do this successfully 90 per cent of the time.

continued

Table 1.3 Continued

Stage	Key features	Strengths of Piaget's theory	Weaknesses of Piaget's theory
			Conservation – McGarrigle and Donaldson (1974) demonstrated that pre-operational children of 4–6 years could successfully conserve if they were not misled by demand characteristics into giving the wrong answer ('naughty teddy'). The way the problem is presented may again confuse the child. The conservation experiments were all carried out in a similar way: the child was shown two identical objects (e.g. glasses of water, rows of beads) and agreed that they were the same, then an adult would manipulate one of them (pour the water into a tall thin container, push the beads together, etc.) and then ask the child again whether the two amounts were the same. It has been suggested that the fact that the child was asked twice 'Are they the same?' made them think that the experimenter expected a different answer the second time. Since the experimenter had drawn attention to what he had done, the child may have thought that something special had happened even though it hadn't.
Concrete operational stage	Ability to de-centre Ability to conserve Reversibility	**Conservation** – Piaget conducted many tests of conservation on children in the concrete operational stage and found that their mental operations allowed them to think about problems in new ways. Children now have the ability to understand that some features of an object may change whilst others remain the same.	McGarrigle and Donaldson demonstrate that children can conserve at an earlier age than Piaget suggested. Hughes also found that children had the ability to de-centre at an earlier age than Piaget suggested.

		Ability to de-centre – Piaget and Inhelder demonstrated that children of seven years and over do have the ability to see things from others' point of view (see study in detail on page 20).	
Formal operational stage	Hypothetical reasoning Systematic/analytic thinking Logical problem solving Tendency to philosophise	**Transitive inference tasks** – the child can follow the abstract form of arguments, e.g. 'If A > B > C, then A > C'. They can solve problems, such as 'Edith is fairer than Susan. Edith is darker than Lily. Who is the darkest?' without needing to use dolls or pictures to help them. **Deductive reasoning tasks** – problems are carried out logically and systematically, such as the pendulum task, where the child is given string and a set of weights and is asked to find out what determines the swing.	Piaget seemed to have over-estimated people's formal operational ability – some research has even suggested that only one third of the population actually reach this stage.

Dweck's mindset theory and the effects on learning and development

Your intelligence and other characteristics – where do they come from? Can they change?

People vary in the degree to which they attribute the causes of intelligence and other traits.

Your **mindset** can be defined as either **fixed** or **growth**. A growth mindset is generally seen as more advantageous.

People can have different mindsets towards different aspects of their lives, e.g. a fixed mindset towards their **ability** to do science, but a growth mindset towards their ability to play football.

For individuals with a fixed mindset, receiving feedback is negative – it reveals their limitations. They don't use feedback to learn, since they do not believe that their success depends on their **effort** to learn. Effort is seen as fruitless – if they don't 'get it' then it suggests that they lack the intelligence.

Rather, they believe that success depends on the level of innate ability that they have. Therefore, they dread failure, because it suggests constraints or limits that they will not be able to overcome. These students have a high desire to prove themselves to others – to be seen as smart and avoid looking unintelligent.

Individuals with a growth mindset believe that effort is seen as worthwhile – a path to mastery. Getting things wrong and receiving feedback is positive – it guides further improvement. They are not terrified of failure, because it only signals the need to pay attention, invest effort and practise what is required. They are confident that after such effort they will be able to learn the skill or knowledge, and then to improve their performance.

Key terms

Mindset refers to a view that we hold regarding the nature of intelligent behaviour.

Fixed mindset is a belief that qualities are 'set in stone' – how God made you is basically who you are and these are fixed – not something that can be practised or developed.

Growth mindset is a belief that effort or training can change one's qualities and traits, and success is attributed to learning.

Ability refers to what you can do and are capable of.

Effort refers to your attempt to do something.

Students with a growth mindset see satisfaction coming from the process of learning and often see opportunities to get better.

Fixed mindset teachers see those that are struggling as not being bright or talented in the subject. Growth mindset teachers see struggling students as a challenge – in need of guidance and feedback on how to improve.

If parents or teachers constantly seem to attribute success to inborn abilities, children will come to develop a fixed mindset ('Hassan failed the biology test

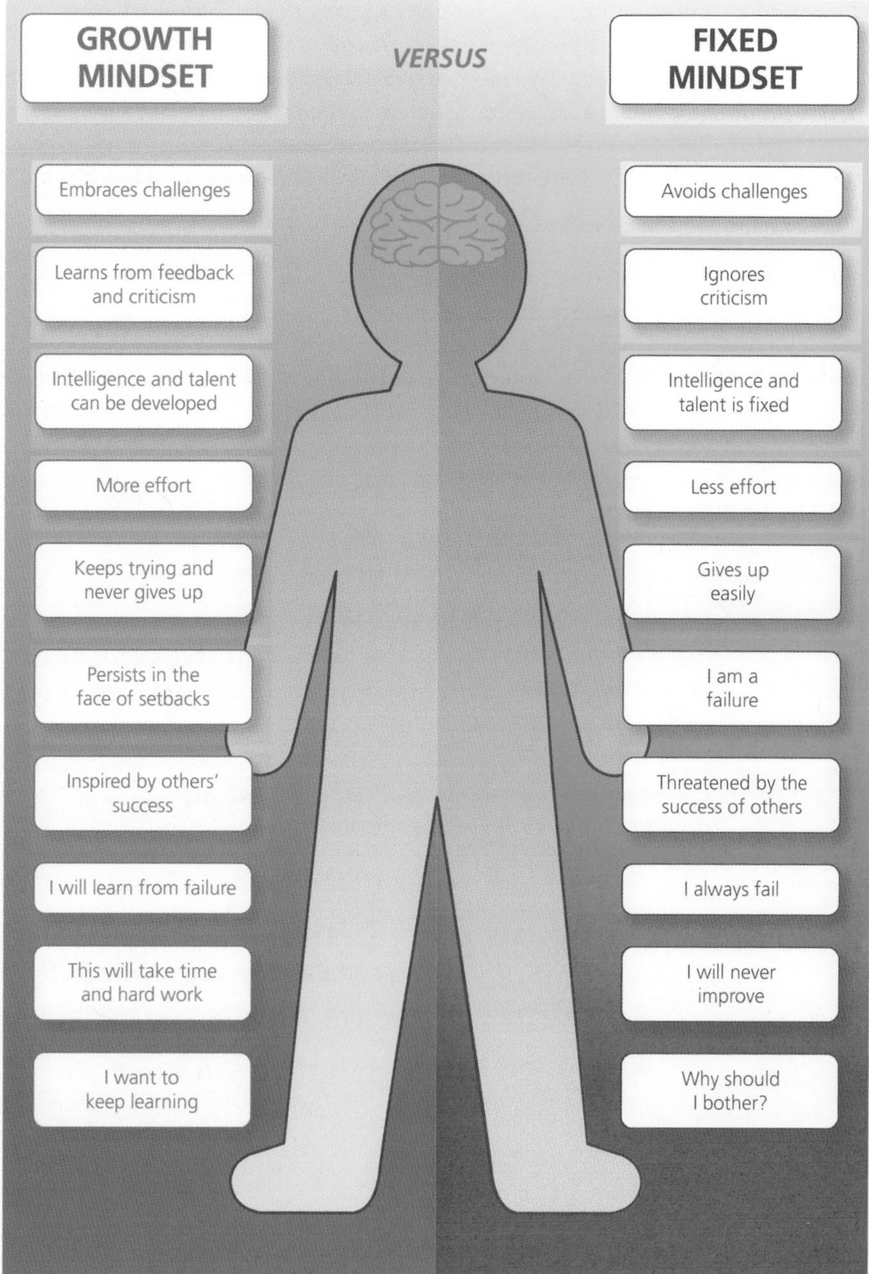

Figure 1.2 Characteristics of a growth versus fixed mindset

because he not very able in that subject'). However, if parents or teachers attribute success to effort and practise, children will be more likely to developed a growth mindset ('Hassan failed the biology test because he did not do his homework, but he will pass the next one because I will make sure he puts in the time and practises').

Dweck believes that the particular mindset a person has is not necessarily permanent. Mindsets can be changed in either direction.

Just by knowing about the two mindsets, people can start thinking and reacting in new, growth-orientated ways. Students benefit from being taught about the brain. Knowledge of how the brain makes new neural connections in response to learning provides them with a model of why effort and mastery-related practices lead to achievement.

Dweck's research has demonstrated the importance of praise that recognises effort. Praise that focuses on practice, study, persistence and good strategies is seen to develop a growth mindset in learners. Her research has shown that praise linked to reinforcing learners about their intelligence or talent is detrimental to their view about their abilities. It reinforces (fixed mindset) ideas that their achievements are a consequence of IQ or other innate ability. It may lead to students worrying that future tests might reveal their shortcomings, and that challenges should be avoided as, again, struggling would demonstrate that they aren't really as smart as their teachers had believed.

Now test yourself

10. Which type of learner will not benefit from feedback?

Strengths and weaknesses of Dweck's mindset theory

What if a student's ability is the same as their effort? What if they have already tried a range of approaches and still failed? Is telling them to put in even greater effort likely to be motivational? Maybe we *can* all be cleverer, but maybe there's also a limit?

The growth mindset as used in most schools is especially problematic for students who can't obtain success even with strong effort and the theory can't explain those students who put in no effort but can still succeed, due to their ability.

The theory has an application to education, and teachers and parents can support students if they put the emphasis on praising effort rather than ability. Instead of telling a child she is smart or talented, they should be praised for her strategies (e.g. 'You found a really good way to do it') or effort (e.g. 'I can see you've been practising' and 'Your hard work has really paid off').

Dweck has lots of evidence to support her theory that growth mindset leads to better grades and that mindset can indeed be taught and can improve performance. However, lots of her evidence has come from experiments carried out in artificial settings which can't be applied to real life. This lack of ecological validity from the supporting evidence therefore undermines her mindset theory.

Willingham's learning theory and the effects on learning and development

Factual knowledge precedes skill

If you watch children on a museum field trip, you'll notice that they stop to look at different paintings and that these differences are due to the children's backgrounds, their personalities, tastes, and so on. The same seems to be true of learning.

Some lessons click with one child and not with another, but not because of something in the way the child learns, but because of the *past knowledge* the child brought to the lesson, their interests, or other factors.

Daniel Willingham proposes that students need facts to think well in school, and that these facts then inform their thinking; having past knowledge increases the speed at which more knowledge can be acquired. Willingham suggests that what someone already knows leaves them more processing power to solve a problem and aids understanding.

Doctors cannot cure an ailment if they do not know how various organs and tissues work. Students remember knowledge longer if they learn it in a meaningful context with which they are familiar. Consider the following example of a teacher's use of a student's past knowledge:

STUDENT: Miss, what does the word 'rivalry' mean?

TEACHER: Well, think about your relationship with your sister. Do you ever compete with her? Do you sometimes fight over something?

STUDENT: Yes. We fight over the TV remote sometimes.

TEACHER: People call that a 'sibling rivalry' – a rivalry is a relationship that involves a lot of tough competition.

STUDENT: Like, maybe, a hockey game?

TEACHER: Absolutely. People often call teams that compete really hard with each other 'rivals'. You play hockey. Which team that you play would you say is your biggest 'rival'?

STUDENT: Probably the Totley All Saints.

TEACHER: So, the Totley All Saints are your 'rival'. That's exactly right.

This teacher has hooked a new word to a concept that the student already had in his mind, a much more successful technique than simply defining the new word for the student. Note that to do so successfully, the teacher had to have a foundation of knowledge about the child's prior experience.

Similarly, teaching younger students that DNA is the shape of a spiral staircase might be appropriate for them, while for older children who have studied geometry, you might say DNA is shaped like a double helix.

Having past knowledge also means we have more time and space in our **working memory** to use mental skills such as problem solving.

A part of working memory is used for making decisions about the information, and working memory is limited. So if we already have past knowledge for things like 'rivalry' in the example above, we don't have to relearn it and this in turn gives working memory more room to breathe.

Key term

Working memory involves different processes that make use of information that comes in through our five senses. Visual information (what we see) is stored and processed separately from sound information (what we hear).

The importance of practice and effort

We need enough working memory to learn new things. Practice is essential as it focuses effort on learning and creates automaticity, which saves room in our limited working memory. For example, riding a bike becomes automatic once you have given it enough practice and effort. This in turn enables us to master knowledge and skills. Varied, repeated rehearsal of information, preferably in a number of different contexts and in a variety of ways, helps to transfer information from short-term memory into long-term memory. More practice leads to better memory. Memory in either the short- or long-term requires ongoing practice.

Practice also means trying to improve. We check our performance, say, for playing the violin, noting errors and thinking of new ways to do it better. However, your handwriting may be pretty bad, despite thousands of hours of writing, because during all of that time you were *not practising* and were just writing to get something on paper. Thus, students are unlikely to practice their writing, but they would practice the violin.

Strategies to support cognitive development

Cognitive development is characterised by the way a child learns, acquires knowledge and interacts with their surrounding environment. Willingham believes it is not about matching the child's supposed learning style to how they are supposed to learn, but rather teachers need to think about the content and what it is about this content that they really want students to understand, and what the best way is to convey that. Within this, teachers need to make sure students are sufficiently challenged to put in enough effort.

Willingham suggests teachers need to understand three factors that are important when students are reading in class: monitoring your understanding, relating the sentences to one another, and relating the sentences to things you already know. In this way, students are taught to become aware of when they do not understand – for example, by formulating what exactly is causing them difficulty. After students read a text, the teacher should ask questions that emphasise the information students should have obtained from their reading.

Strategies to support physical development

Practice and effort are also linked to our physical development. Fine motor skills are small, precise movements, needed for things like holding a pencil or using cutlery, and gross motor skills are larger movements – for example, walking and running. Like any other skill, children need to practise movements regularly to get them right. In order to improve any skill, we need to practice them so they become automatic, or as the new saying goes, 'practice makes permanent'.

Practice requires focusing on the quality of your movements, with less intensity. For example, rather than setting a goal of 12 quick press-ups, instead slow down your movements and focus on practising the parts of the push-up you are struggling with the most. The number of reps doesn't matter; it's the process of learning the details of the exercise that matters. It is this conscious effort that will help develop the motor skill.

Strategies to support social development

Practice requires **self-regulation** – for example, being able to stay focused on revision rather than checking social media on your phone. In this way, you are overcoming the impulse to go on social media and are focusing on something else (revision) which has longer term benefits to you. Higher levels of self-regulation are associated with higher levels of **school readiness**, good attitude to studying and good physical health. Students who are low in self-regulation are at greater risk of persistent disobedience. Parents can increase self-regulation in their children by posing questions using complex sentence structures to develop patience (e.g. 'Why did you burn the dinner but not the cake?'). Parents can also encourage children to be autonomous (independent) and then give support for that autonomy. The factors that improve self-regulation in the home, such as warmth, organisation and predictability, are also seen to be important in classrooms.

Key terms

Self-regulation means being able to control your emotions and behaviour regarding one thing and do something else instead.

School readiness means how prepared you are to go and learn at school on a daily basis.

Strengths and weaknesses of Willingham's learning theory

Willingham's ideas come from many areas of **neuroscience**, memory theory and cognitive development. This means that his ideas are scientifically tested and we can trust his conclusions. Willingham's work can be applied to support teachers and parents to promote a child's development in a positive way. We can take his ideas to help support a child's cognitive, social and physical development.

Willingham did not emphasise the importance of individual differences in learning. What is in someone's genes cannot be changed easily using his strategies. This means that if a child has poor self-regulation passed down from a parent, then no amount of activities will change their behaviour.

Key term

Neuroscience is the study of the role of our brain in muscle movements.

Studies

Piaget and Inhelder (1956): three mountains task

Key Study

Aim

To investigate whether children under the age of seven can see the world from another person's point of view.

Procedure

One hundred participants were used whose ages ranged from four to eight years. All participants were seated at a table upon which was placed a papier mâché model of three mountains. One mountain had snow on the top, one had a house on the top and one had a red cross on the top. The child was allowed to walk around and explore the model. Each child was then seated on one side of the table and a doll was placed at different locations on the model. The child was shown ten pictures of different views of the mountains and asked to choose the one that represented what the doll could see. They also had three pieces of board, shaped and coloured to match each mountain in the model of the three mountains, which they could move and arrange to represent the model.

Results

Piaget and Inhelder noted that children less than seven years old had difficulty with this task. For example, four-year-olds were completely unaware of perspectives different from their own and always chose a picture which matched their view of the model. Six-year-olds showed some awareness, but often chose the wrong picture. Only seven- and eight-year-olds consistently chose the picture that represented the doll's view, showing their ability to de-centre.

Conclusion

After questioning them, Piaget found children below the age of seven suffer from egocentrism – they have great difficulty in seeing the world from the viewpoint of others. They fail to understand that what they see is relative to their own position and instead take it to represent the world as it really is. Children in the concrete operational stage started to show understanding of others' viewpoints. They were seen to select a picture from their own perspective but to turn this towards the doll so that the image could be seen by the doll. This showed the start of an ability to understand that the doll has a different viewpoint. By the end of this stage, children could select pictures that represented the doll, demonstrating that egocentrism had lessened.

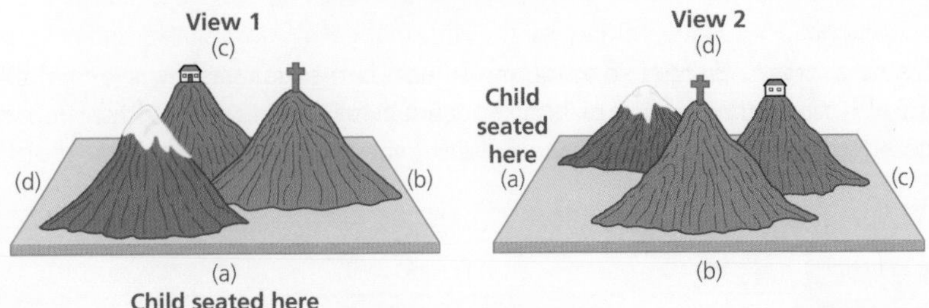

Figure 1.3 Three mountains task perspective

Strengths and weaknesses of the three mountains task

Piaget's tasks have generated considerable research and many of his major principles, like egocentrism, still stand today and have greatly influenced the way children are viewed as active learners. Many researchers have carried out Piaget's experiment exactly as he did and have found similar results, providing further evidence for his theory as well as demonstrating reliability for the three mountains study itself.

When Piaget questioned children about the three mountains task and tried to uncover their reasons for choosing a particular picture, it seemed clear to him that they understood the rationale behind the experiment. Other researchers who have criticised Piaget cannot claim to have done this, i.e. they may have found children under the ages of seven who could de-centre but don't really know why as they were not put through the same level of questioning.

Hughes (1975) used a design in which a child had to work out where a doll must hide in order not to be seen by a policeman. He demonstrated that three-and-a-half to five-year-olds could de-centre and overcame their egocentrism, if the task made more 'human sense' to them. When these children had to hide a boy doll from two policeman dolls (a task that required them to take into account the perspectives of others but had a good, understandable reason for doing so), they could do this successfully 90 per cent of the time. This demonstrates that children under the age of seven can de-centre and are not as egocentric as Piaget claims.

Piaget has also been accused of over-emphasising intellectual development to the exclusion of social and emotional development. The three mountains task demonstrates that a child's perception of adults, the meaning of questions and the importance of a familiar context all affect children's performance.

Gunderson *et al.* (2013): parent praise to 1–3-year-olds predicts children's motivational frameworks five years later

Aim

Does the type of praise from parents affect children? In particular, if the praise is focused around a child's behaviour rather than the child's personality, will this have an impact on their behaviour years later?

Procedure

The researchers videotaped 53 children (29 boys and 24 girls from a mix of different cultures) and their parents during everyday interactions at home. Each family was videotaped three times at 14 months, 26 months and 38 months – and they were videotaped as they went about their everyday activities with their parents. The parents weren't told to do anything in particular – just to go about their daily routines. They didn't know the study was about praise. From the videotapes, the researchers identified instances in which parents praised their children and classified their praise as either **process praise**, **person praise** or other praise.

They then followed up with the children five years later, when they were 7–8 years old, and assessed whether they preferred challenging versus easy tasks, were able to generate strategies for overcoming setbacks, and believed that intelligence and personality are traits that can be developed (as opposed to ones that are unchangeable).

They were asked a series of questions about intelligence and behaviour, such as:

- 'Imagine a kid who believes that you can get smarter and smarter all the time. How much do you agree with him?'
- 'How much would you like to do mazes that are very easy so you can get a lot right?'
- 'How much would you like to do math problems that are very hard so you can learn more about doing math?'
- 'Imagine that a kid you know keeps getting lots and lots wrong on their schoolwork and asks you for your help. What would you say or do?'

Results

Use of praise

The results of the coding of praise utterances are shown in Table 1.4. Praise was measured cumulatively using all three visits. The mean percentage score for each category of praise is shown as a percentage of all utterances by the parent, and as a percentage of all praise comments made by the parents.

Overall, praise of any type was, on average, 3 per cent of all utterances by parents.

Person praise as a percentage of all praise was significantly less at 38 months old than it was at 14 months old, whereas process praise showed no significant change and other praise was significantly higher at 38 months old than 14 months old.

When parents used a larger percentage of process praise, their children reported more positive approaches to challenges and believed that their traits could improve with effort. The link held even after controlling for other variables – like socioeconomic status, children's gender, parents' personal attitudes about ability and the overall amount of praise and verbal interaction children got from their parents.

Table 1.4 Results: coding of praise utterances

Category	Mean % as a total of all utterances	Mean % as a total of praise utterances
Process praise	0.59	18.0
Person praise	0.45	16.0
Other praise	1.97	66.0

However, the other two types of praise (person praise and other praise) and the total amount of praise were not related to children's responses.

In addition, parents of boys used a greater percentage of process praise than parents of girls. Later, boys were more likely to have positive attitudes about academic challenges than girls and to believe that intelligence could be improved. So perhaps, without realising it, some parents are setting up girls for a more helpless 'you've either got it or you don't' mentality.

The results demonstrate that process praise – praise that emphasises children's effort, actions and strategies – predicts children's attitudes towards challenges and their beliefs about trait malleability five years later.

These findings suggest that improving the quality of early parental praise may help children develop the belief that their future success is in their own hands.

Conclusion

It is important to emphasise praise that makes children feel **resilient**. The problem with telling children that they are smart or talented is that they become frightened of failure. They have been labelled and they don't want to do anything to lose that label.

Moreover, children praised for intelligence tend to believe that intelligence is something innate and unchangeable. As a result, these children are rendered helpless by failure. If you fail, you must not be smart. End of story.

Key terms

Process praise emphasises a child's effort, strategies or actions (such as 'you're trying your best', 'good job counting').

Person praise implies that a child possesses a fixed, positive quality ('you're a smart girl', 'you're good at this').

Resilient refers to being able to withstand, or recover quickly from, difficulties.

Strengths and weaknesses of Gunderson *et al*. (2013)

The findings of the study are **correlational** and cannot demonstrate a **causal relation** between process praise and children's behaviour in later life. This means we cannot say for definite that process praise *causes* a child to believe that putting in effort in later life is worthwhile; it is only a link or relationship between the two variables. Other factors could still explain the correlations between parents' use of process praise and children's motivational frameworks, such as parenting style or child **temperament**.

One limitation of any observational study such as this one is the possibility that parents could change their behaviour because they are aware they are being observed. They may have wanted to praise their child in a way they thought might please the observer and so may not be showing their natural behaviour, which reduces the validity of the study.

Another limitation is that the study had a small sample size that was selected to represent the range of the Chicago area in terms of income and race and ethnicity. This means results cannot be generalised to the wider population as the sample is not representative.

The person praise parents give their children when they are young toddlers may differ from the kinds of person praise given to school-aged children and from the kinds of person praise given in experimental studies. Saying 'good girl' to a very young child may be fundamentally different from telling a school-aged child that she is smart.

Key terms

Correlational refers to a link or relationship between two things.

Causal relation means if the occurrence of the first event actually causes the occurrence of the other.

Temperament refers to a person's nature or personality.

Issues and debates

The development of morality

The concept of **morality** revolves around a person's view of good and bad when it comes to intentions, decisions and actions.

Morals are what is considered 'right' and 'wrong' behaviour within society, providing a guide for individuals to follow. It is what many believe is the main principle that allows for improvement in man and civilisation as a whole.

Moral development looks at the appearance, change and understanding of the idea of morality from infancy to adolescence, and eventually towards adulthood.

According to Piaget, children between five and ten years old make moral decisions strictly based on what an authority figure dictates is right and wrong. Rules must be followed exactly and cannot be changed even in the smallest detail, due to fear of punishment. Around age ten, Piaget believed that children base moral decision making on **social cooperation**. Children now believe that rules given by society must be followed as they are for the social good of all, but the child is not yet able to formulate their own individual idea of morality.

During the early teen years, the child's idea of morality is based on **empathy**. Empathy can only occur when the child possesses the ability to take another's perspective or see things from another's point of view.

According to Kohlberg, moral development begins with a child's rather selfish desire to avoid and prevent punishment, to belong to society and to be consistent with what the public views as moral.

Kohlberg's stages of moral development are shown in Table 1.5.

Table 1.5 Kohlberg's stages of moral development

Level 1: pre-conventional morality (up to nine years old)	Punishment orientation and obedience By doing what others say, they can avoid punishment. They begin to see different sides to an issue vs. fully obeying what they are told.
Level 2: conventional morality (most young people and adults)	**Good interpersonal relationships** The individual recognises that being a good person brings him closer to others. **Maintaining social order** The individual now sees that he needs to be a good person in order for society to accept him.
Level 3: post-conventional morality (only 10–15 per cent of people reach this level)	**Individual rights and social contract** The individual now has a concept of basic rights and the right to democracy – that everyone has a say in an issue. **Universal principles** The individual is able to define principles that are most just and fair.

Key terms

Morality is about being able to tell the difference between good and bad behaviour.

Morals are standards of behaviour; principles of right and wrong.

Social cooperation refers to the practice of individuals and groups working in common, with commonly agreed-upon goals and possibly methods, instead of working separately in competition.

Empathy is where an individual tries to understand the decisions others make by gaining knowledge and comprehension of their circumstances.

Exam questions

1. After an accident, Joe is found to have damaged his hindbrain. Explain changes in his behaviour that might occur as a result of this damage. (3)
2. For each statement below, write whether it is true or false in relation to Piaget. (4)

Statement	True or false
With expert help, it is possible for one child to skip one of the stages of development	
The majority of children will not pass through developmental stages	
Formal operational tasks are not as abstract as concrete operational tasks	
Pre-operational children will normally be egocentric	

3. Explain two ways of applying Piaget's theory to education. (4)
4. Write the correct name of the process next to each description below. (3)

Description	Process
Information (in the form of new experiences) is taken in	
Schemas are altered in order to understand new information	
A state of balance is achieved when the child has taken in all of the information that s/he can absorb	

5. John is going to a posh restaurant for the first time and, sitting down at the table, he sees lots of knives, forks and spoons laid out next to his plate. Explain what might happen next using the process of adaptation. (3)

6. Explain the possible advantages of a growth mindset over a fixed mindset. (4)
7. According to Willingham, outline the importance of practice and effort in learning. (4)
8. John is trying to improve his tennis. How can a strategy from Willingham support John to improve his tennis? (3)
9. John feels his job interview did not go well. Explain how his wife may encourage John by praising his efforts so that he does better on his next interview. (3)
10. Outline one similarity and one difference between Piaget's and Kohlberg's theories of moral development. (4)

End of chapter summary

You should now have an understanding of all the points below:

Understand early brain development, including the development of the:

- forebrain
- midbrain
- hindbrain
- cerebellum
- medulla.

Understand the role of education and intelligence, including Piaget's theory of cognitive development, and the four stages of cognitive development, including strengths and weaknesses of the theory:

- sensorimotor
- pre-operational
- concrete operational
- formal operational
- schemas
- assimilation
- accommodation
- equilibrium.

Understand the effects of learning on development using Carol Dweck's mindset theory, including strengths and weaknesses of the theory:

- fixed mindset
- growth mindset
- ability and effort.

Understand the effects of learning on development using Daniel Willingham's learning theory, including strengths and weaknesses of the theory:

- factual knowledge precedes skill
- the importance of practice and effort
- strategies to support cognitive development
- strategies to support physical development
- strategies to support social development.

Understand the aims, procedures and findings (results and conclusions), and strengths and weaknesses of:

- Piaget and Inhelder (1956): three mountains task
- Gunderson *et al.* (2013): parent praise to one- to three-year-olds predicts children's motivational frameworks five years later.

Understand morality issues in psychology and the individual, including:

- the terms 'morality' and 'moral(s)'
- pre-conventional, conventional and post-conventional stages of morality
- the use of content, theories and research drawn from cognitive development to explain development of morality.

Now test yourself answers

1. It grows longer and folds onto itself, until that fold morphs into a groove, and that groove turns into the neural tube.
2. Hindbrain.
3. Cerebellum.
4. Show an object to the baby and then hide it behind your back.
5. Would show no interest and look away/continue playing.
6. Would try and look behind your back or pull your arm holding the object.
7. Egocentrism, animism, lack of conservation and lack of reversibility.
8. Conservation of quantity, length, number and liquid.
9. To help us learn new information by causing an imbalance that requires us to develop new schema.
10. A learner with a fixed mindset.

Chapter 2
Memory – how does your memory work?

This chapter deals with how our memory works, the structure and processes behind it and how it determines our information processing in everyday life. If we know how our memory works, we can help improve it and support others whose memory may not function as well as ours does. How we recall and why we forget are part and parcel of understanding memory.

Have you ever wondered how you manage to remember information for a test? The ability to create new memories, store them for periods of time and recall them when they are needed allows us to learn and interact with the world around us. Consider for a moment how many times a day you rely on your memory to help you function, from remembering how to use your computer to recollecting your password to log in to your online bank account.

Memory is essential to all our lives. Without a memory of the past we cannot operate in the present or think about the future. We would not be able to remember what we did yesterday, what we have done today or what we plan to do tomorrow. Without memory we could not learn anything.

Memory and information processing

The information processing model is used by psychologists to explain how we receive, interpret and respond to information. It describes the flow of information using the terms **input**, **process** and **output**. For example, when we are crossing the road, we are using information processing to get across safely. The road and cars are the 'input', considering when and how safe it is to cross is the 'process' and crossing the road is the 'output'.

Our mind is like an information processor. The major influence on human behaviour and emotion is how the mind processes information and so psychologists compare the human brain to a computer. A computer has input, processing and output. Humans receive information through their senses before it is processed.

Information comes into a computer through a keyboard or software disk. Humans receive information through their senses. The computer then runs programs to process the information. Humans process the information via the central nervous system and the brain. Once the processing is complete, there is output. The computer produces output in the form of a printout or a screen display. A human being produces output using language, body language, emotions and their actions, so their output is more complex.

Key terms

Input is the process of receiving information from the environment from our five senses.
Processing refers to analysing the information we have received and referees the relationship between input and output.
Output is the consequence of the analysis of the input and refers to our response to the input.

There are three major processes involved in memory: encoding, storage and retrieval.

In order to form new memories, information must be changed into a usable form, which occurs through a process known as **encoding**. Once information has been successfully encoded, it must be **stored** in memory for later use. Much of this stored memory lies outside of our awareness most of the time, except when we actually need to use it. The **retrieval** process allows us to bring stored memories into conscious awareness. At any of the three stages of memory, if we fail to encode, store or retrieve the information, forgetting can occur.

Key terms

To store new information we must first transform it into a form capable of being entered into the memory system. The process of forming sensory input into a memory trace is called **encoding**.
When we register an experience, it is held as an exact copy in our **storage**. This holds information long enough to decide whether to process it further. If we do not attend to it, the information is quickly forgotten.
Retrieval refers to the process of accessing stored memories so that they can be used.

If you meet someone for the first time at a party, you need to encode the person's name while you associate their name with their face. Then you need to store this information over time. If you see them a week later, you need to recognise their face and have it serve as a cue to retrieve their name. Any successful act of remembering requires that all three stages be intact.

Memory encoding

The physical and mental environments are much too rich for you to encode all the happenings around you or the internal thoughts you have in response to them. So, an important first principle of encoding is that it is selective: we pay attention to some events in our environment and we ignore others.

When information comes into our memory system (from sensory input), it needs to be changed into a form that the system can cope with, so that it can be stored. Think of this as similar to changing your money into a different currency when you travel from one country to another. For example, a word which is seen (in a book) may be stored if it is changed (encoded) into a sound or a meaning (i.e. semantic processing).

There are three main ways in which information can be encoded:

1. Visual (picture)
2. Acoustic (sound)
3. Semantic (meaning)

For example, how do you remember a telephone number? If you can see the number in your head (picturing it) then you are using visual coding, but if you are repeating it to yourself aloud, you are using acoustic coding (by sound). Semantic encoding refers to the meaning of something, so rather than focusing on the sound or picture we focus on what it means. For example, you know a chair is for sitting on or that a knife and fork are for eating with.

Evidence suggests that the principal coding system in short-term memory (STM) is acoustic coding. When a person is presented with a list of numbers and letters, they will try to hold them in STM by rehearsing them (verbally). Rehearsal is a verbal process, regardless of whether the list of items is presented acoustically (someone reads them out) or visually (on a sheet of paper).

The principal encoding system in long-term memory (LTM) appears to be semantic coding (by meaning). However, information in LTM can also be coded both visually and acoustically.

Memory storage

This concerns the nature of memory stores, i.e. where the information is stored, how long the memory lasts for (**duration**), how much can be stored at any time (**capacity**) and what kind of information is held. The way we store information affects the way we retrieve it. Memories have to be stored somewhere in the brain, so in order to do so, the brain biochemically alters itself and its neural tissue. Just like you might write yourself a note to remind yourself of something, the brain 'writes' a memory trace, changing its own physical composition to do so.

Memory retrieval

This refers to getting information out of storage. If we can't remember something, it may be because we are unable to retrieve it. When we are asked to retrieve something from memory, the differences between STM and LTM become very clear. Psychologists distinguish information that is available in memory from that which is accessible.

Available information is the information that is stored in memory – but precisely how much and what types are stored cannot be known. That is, all we can know is what information we can retrieve – *accessible* information. The assumption is that accessible information represents only a tiny slice of the information available in our brains.

Key terms

Duration refers to how long we can keep the information in our memory, which could be from a couple of seconds, like in our sensory register (see page 37), or forever, like in our long-term memory.

Capacity refers to how much we can hold in our memory, much like a storage box.

Features of short-term and long-term memory

Short-term memory

Short-term memory acts as a scratch-pad for temporary recall of the information under process. For instance, in order to understand this sentence, you need to hold in your mind the beginning of the sentence as you read the rest.

Short-term memory decays rapidly and also has a limited capacity. According to Miller, we can hold between five and nine items (digits, words, etc.) at any given time in our STM (7+/–2). Chunking of information can lead to an increase in the short-term memory capacity. This is the reason why a hyphenated phone number is easier to remember than a single long number. If information is not rehearsed within 15–30 seconds whilst in STM, it is lost due its limited duration.

Active learning

Demonstration of STM capacity

With a partner, one of you read out the sequence of numbers below at a rate of approximately one a second. After you have presented the numbers, your partner is to read them back to you. Make a note of how far you get before you make a mistake and then swap over.

346
7395
98213
203948
2547676
24216789
163705857
7565556789
36772568423
431135427657
7336585066364
90868524611677
227667863421168
8325366784525647
32765904678257268

This exercise demonstrates the limited nature of STM when there is no time for rehearsal and consolidation. Miller (1956) used the word *chunk* to refer to a discrete piece of information. So when attempting to remember an unrelated string of letters (in this case, numbers), each constitutes one chunk of information.

However, STM's capacity can be enlarged if separate pieces of information are combined into a larger piece of information. This is an example of **chunking**. For example, a phone number can be easily remembered if it is chunked together, such as 01709-814-341, as opposed to 01709814341.

Key term

Chunking involves reducing long strings of information that can be difficult to remember to shorter, more manageable chunks.

Long-term memory

Long-term memory is intended for storage of information over a long time. Information from short-term memory is transferred to it after a few seconds. Unlike in short-term memory, there is little decay. The capacity of long-term memory could be unlimited, the main constraint on recall being **accessibility** rather than **availability**. The term long-term memory refers to the unlimited capacity memory store that can hold information for an entire lifetime. In addition, there are different types of memories that can be stored in LTM: **procedural memory, semantic memory, declarative memory** and **episodic memory**.

Key terms

Availability refers to the storage of the memory; **accessibility** refers to its retrieval. If a memory is available, it means that it is stored somewhere in your memory system. Accessibility is about how well you can get at that memory, which is generally easier when prompted.
Procedural memory is knowledge of *how* to do things, such as the procedure for riding a bike or swimming.
Semantic memory is knowledge of what things mean, such as knowing that a chair is for sitting on.
Declarative memory is knowledge of things/factual information, such as 'I can declare that the capital of France is Paris'.
Episodic memory includes episodes/experiences in your life, such as your first holiday abroad.

Now test yourself

1. What are the differences between STM and LTM in terms of capacity and duration?

Retrograde and anterograde amnesia

Amnesia is the general term for a condition in which memory is disturbed or lost, to a much greater extent than simple everyday forgetting or absent-mindedness. Amnesia may occur as a result of damage to the brain through physical injury.

There are two main types of amnesia, called **retrograde** and **anterograde amnesia**.

Key terms

Amnesia is the loss of memory, usually through injury, but can be caused by psychological problems, like too much stress.
Retrograde amnesia is when patients are unable to remember events before the injury that led to amnesia, so a person's pre-existing memories are forgotten.
Anterograde amnesia is when patients may be able to recall events from before the injury, but are unable to store new information after it. The ability to memorise new things is lost because data does not transfer successfully from short-term memory into long-term memory.

Anterograde amnesia is the more common of the two types. Sometimes both types of amnesia occur together, called total or global amnesia.

Anterograde amnesia is the loss of the ability to create new memories. Sufferers may, therefore, repeat comments or questions several times, for example, or fail to recognise people they met just minutes before. New information is processed normally, but almost immediately forgotten, never making it into the regions of the brain where long-term memories are stored. Sufferers of anterograde amnesia usually only lose declarative memory (the recollection of facts), but they retain non-declarative or procedural memory (the learning of skills). For instance, they may be able to remember talking on the phone or riding a bicycle, but they may not remember what they had eaten for lunch earlier that day.

Retrograde amnesia is a form of amnesia where someone is unable to recall events that occurred before the injury that caused the amnesia, even though they may be able to memorise new things that occur after the start of the amnesia. The patient may remember words and general knowledge (such as who their country's leader is, how everyday objects work, colours, etc.) but not specific events in their lives. Procedural memories of knowing how to do things, such as riding a bike, are not affected at all. Those with retrograde amnesia have more easily accessible memories than events occurring just prior to the trauma, and the events nearest in time to the event that caused the memory loss may never be recovered.

Studies of brain-damaged patients with amnesia

Although it is very rare for anyone to experience permanent amnesia, the worst case of amnesia ever recorded is that of the British musician Clive Wearing, who suffered damage to his brain. Because the damage was to a part of his brain called the **hippocampus**, which has a vital role in laying down memories, he is completely unable to form lasting new long-term memories, and his memory is therefore limited to a short-term memory of between 7 and 30 seconds, to the extent that he will greet his wife like a long-lost friend even if she only left to go into the kitchen 30 seconds before. When his wife walks into the room, he feels he is seeing her for the first time. If she leaves the room for a short while and then re-enters, he sees her for the first time again. It is like living with snapshots of time. However, Wearing still recalls how to play the piano and conduct a choir, despite having no recollection of having received a musical education, because his procedural memory was not damaged by the virus that caused the brain damage.

In another case, H.M. underwent an operation for epilepsy, and his hippocampus was removed on both sides of the brain. He had severe amnesia, in that he had difficulty in laying down new memories, even though he could remember things from before the operation. He could not transfer information to long-term memory. From this sort of study, it has been concluded that the hippocampus is needed for memories to be transferred to long-term memory, or at least to some permanent store. Such evidence also supports that claim that there is a short-term and a long-term memory.

Cases of anterograde amnesia such as H.M. or Clive Wearing provide strong evidence for the distinction between STM and LTM, because brain damage can affect one store and not the other. H.M. and Clive Wearing both had a normal STM, but were unable to transfer information into LTM.

Key term

Hippocampus refers to an area of the brain required to transfer memories from short-term memory to long-term memory.

Reconstructive memory

Schemas are a product of our experiences, starting from a very early age, and can be adjusted or refined throughout our lives. For instance, as young children, we may encounter pet cats. We recognise the typical characteristics of these animals (e.g. furry, walk on four legs and have whiskers around their mouths) and gradually create in our minds a schema of a cat. The next time we see an animal, we will use the schema to identify it as being a cat: if it resembles our schema, we consider it to be a cat. But if we see a dog barking instead of purring like a cat does, the animal does not conform to our schema and we do not consider it to be a cat. Schemas also affect the way in which memories are encoded and retrieved, supporting the theory that our memories are **reconstructive**.

Key terms

A **schema** is a package of knowledge that helps organise and interpret information. Schemas can be useful because they allow us to take short-cuts in interpreting the vast amount of information that is available in our environment.

Reconstructive memory is the act of remembering something using a number of factors, such as emotion, imagination, and semantic and episodic memory.

Bartlett was the first to recognise that memory can be seen as a reconstructive process. Information we already have stored affects the remembering of other events. People frequently add/delete details to make new information more consistent with their conception of the world.

Bartlett's view of memory is 'an imaginative reconstruction' of our experience; as well as organising incoming material, we also impose meaning upon it.

One of the techniques Bartlett used was **serial reproduction**. Bartlett believed interpretation plays a large and largely unrecognised role in the remembering of stories and past events. We reconstruct the past by trying to fit it into our existing schema and the more difficult this is, the more likely elements are forgotten or distortions are made.

Memory does not work like a video recording, but is changed when we recall it; coding and retrieval depend on how well an event is processed, meaning that our memories of an event are often incomplete, as we only recall the important points. Memory is more of an imaginative reconstruction of past events influenced by how we encode, store and retrieve information.

Reconstructive memory suggests that, in the absence of all information, we fill in the gaps to make more sense of what is happening using our existing schemas. This means that our memories are a combination of specific traces encoded at the time of the event, along with our knowledge, expectations, beliefs and experiences of such an event.

Retrieval of stored memories thus involves an active process of reconstruction using a range of information. The schemas might fill in the gaps in our memory, known as **confabulation**, which is when information is added to fill in the gaps to make a story make sense.

Key terms

Serial reproduction is a method which duplicates the process by which rumours/gossip are spread/passed on from generation to generation.

Confabulation is a memory error in which a person confuses imagined or made-up scenarios with actual memories.

Strengths and weaknesses of reconstructive memory

This theory simply describes that memory is reconstructive rather than explaining how. It says that memory is active and uses schemas, but does not say how memory is active.

Reconstructive memory is vague about how schemas work and where they are located. Other theories, such as the multi-store model, describe the processes at work in rehearsing, retrieving and recalling.

The theory can be applied to the testimony of eyewitnesses, who are often heavily relied upon in court in the absence of other evidence; these testimonies have been found to be unreliable in a large number of cases. Research has found no link at all between a person's certainty that their memory is accurate and the actual accuracy of their memory.

Supporting evidence for memory being reconstructive can be found in Bartlett's own research, 'War of the Ghosts', in that participants distorted the story on recall to fit in with their existing schemas. The more unusual aspects of the story were left out or changed to fit in with their cultural norm, which supports this theory.

The reconstructive memory model makes predicting behaviour difficult and a good explanation for memory should make prediction possible for it to have **credibility**. The reconstructive model of memory does not predict how experiences or emotions can affect memories but simply gives principles of how reconstruction may work.

Key term

Credibility refers to the trustworthiness, believability and reliability of information.

The multi-store model of memory

We receive information from the environment through our senses, which is automatically stored briefly in a **sensory register**. It is the sensory register that enables you to remember sensory stimuli after your exposure to the stimuli has ended.

Key term

The **sensory register** is your immediate memory that takes in information through your five senses (sight, hearing, smell, taste and touch) and holds it for no more than a few seconds.

For example, when you are walking to school in the morning, you will see various buildings, different types and colours of cars, and other people on their way to work. All this information will be taken in by your five senses but you will tend to ignore most of it because it is impossible to pay attention to all of the stimuli you are exposed to.

However, anything that you do pay attention to, such as your friend's dad on his way to work, becomes part of your sensory register. These and other sensory experiences that you attend to enter your sensory register and allow you to remember them after you leave the scene.

There are two main parts of the sensory register which take in most of the stimuli you are exposed to: **visual memory**, also called iconic memory, and **auditory memory**, also called echoic memory. You also have sensory registers for touch (tactile memory), smell (olfactory memory) and taste (gustatory memory).

Key terms

Visual memory holds images we see for less than a second before it fades.
Auditory memory holds sound for a little longer, a few seconds.

Any information that has been paid attention to in our sensory register is transferred into out short-term memory and thereafter rehearsal determines the fate of this information. Rehearsal is seen as a key process as it not only keeps information in STM, but is also responsible for transferring it to LTM.

Material in the sensory register that is paid attention to is coded in STM, and information in STM that is sufficiently rehearsed is coded in LTM. The multi-store model (Atkinson and Shiffrin, 1968) suggests we receive information from the environment through our five senses, which is automatically stored briefly in our sensory register, the duration of which is up to two seconds. It has a large capacity as it needs to encode all types of sensory experience.

The STM works mostly by acoustic encoding; whereas the LTM uses all types of encoding but favours semantic.

Support for the multi-store model of memory comes from free recall experiments and studies of brain-damaged patients.

In free recall experiments, subjects are given a number of words (for example, 20) in succession to remember and are then asked to recall them in any order ('free recall'). The results reliably fall into a pattern known as the **serial position curve**. The curve consists of **primary** and **recency effects** and **asymptote**.

This experiment supports the multi-store model of memory.

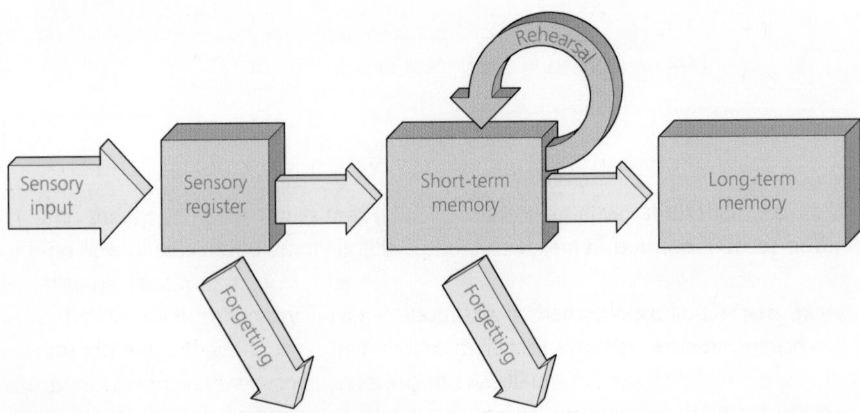

Figure 2.1 The multi-store model of memory

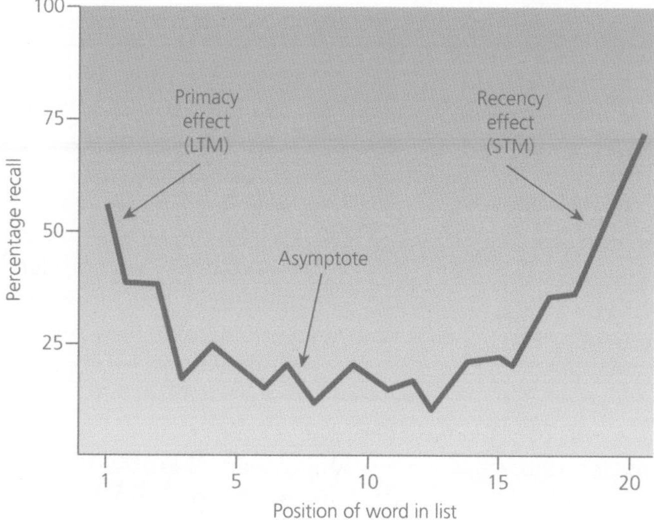

Figure 2.2 A serial position curve

Key terms

A **serial position curve** shows the tendency of a person to recall the first and last items in a series best, and the middle items worst.

Primacy effect is when participants recall the first words of the list well, which indicates that the first words entered short-term memory and had time to be rehearsed and passed on to long-term memory before the STM capacity was reached. The primacy effect, therefore, involves recall from long-term memory.

Recency effect is when participants recall those items from the end of the list first, and tend to get more of these correct, since the items at the end of the list were the last to enter STM and were not displaced by further items.

Asymptote means the middle portion items of the list are remembered less well than those at the beginning and the end. This is probably because the increasing number of items fills the limited capacity of the STM and these later items are unable to be properly rehearsed and transferred to LTM before they are displaced.

Findings from studies investigating the primacy and recency effects have shown that there *is* a STM and a LTM. This is because words from the top of the list were rehearsed over and over and went from STM to LTM. And those words at the bottom of the list were the most recent and were actually in STM so were easier to recall. The words in the middle were forgotten as, by the time they got to be rehearsed, the STM was already full (7 +/– 2).

Now test yourself

2. What is the function of rehearsal?
3. What is the difference between the primacy and the recency effect?
4. Why are you more likely to forget the words in the middle of the list?
5. Explain how amnesia patients can be evidence for the multi-store model.
6. A student revising for exams could read their notes over and over again. Is this a good way of learning material? Explain your answer.
7. Which types of long-term memory does Clive Wearing still have?
8. What does this tell us about the long-term memory store in the multi-store model?

Active learning

The capacity of STM is .... We can increase this capacity by .... The duration of STM is .... We can increase this by ....

The capacity of LTM is .... The duration of LTM is ....

Information is encoded into short-term memory ....

infinite *forever* *acoustically* *7 +/– 2*

rehearsal *chunking* *15–30 seconds*

Strengths and weaknesses of the multi-store model

Rehearsal of information alone does not necessarily lead to better recall. Craik and Watkins (1973) asked participants to rehearse a number of certain words from a list. They found that recall was unrelated to both duration in STM and the number of times words were rehearsed.

Lab studies using free recall experiments provide empirical evidence for the model. Findings from the serial position effect, i.e. the primacy and recency effects, have shown that performance on certain memory tasks can be explained in terms of a STM and LTM distinction.

Studies of brain-damaged patients provide strong evidence for the distinction between STM and LTM because brain damage can affect one store and not the other. Patients regularly show deficiencies in one store and normal functioning in the other.

Clive Wearing has demonstrated that the separate stores within the multi-store model must actually exist as he suffers from anterograde amnesia and cannot transfer information from STM to LTM.

However, he still has some types of LTM working, such as procedural (playing the piano) and semantic (knowing what a knife and fork is for) LTM, so the model does not differentiate enough between different types of LTM and instead lumps all the different types of LTM together as if they were effectively all the same.

Studies

Bartlett (1932): War of the Ghosts

Key Study

Aim

To investigate how memory of a story is affected by previous knowledge or reconstructed based on our existing schema.

Bartlett predicted that memory is reconstructive and that we store and retrieve information according to our own culture that we live in. He wanted to see if cultural background and unfamiliarity with a text would lead to distortion of memory when the story was recalled.

Procedure

Bartlett performed a study where he used repeated reproduction, which is a technique where participants hear a story or see a drawing and (the same participants) are told to reproduce it after a short time and then to do so again repeatedly over a period of days, weeks, months or years. He also used serial reproduction, where this time different participants are used in the story recall. So a participant will retell the story to someone else, who will then retell it again to someone else, a bit like Chinese whispers.

The story Bartlett used was a Native American legend called *The War of the Ghosts*. For the participants, who were all British, the story was filled with unknown names and concepts, and the way it was told to them also felt a little strange.

Findings

Bartlett found that participants changed the story as they tried to remember it – a process called distortion. Bartlett found that there were three patterns of distortion that took place.

Assimilation: details were unconsciously changed to fit the norms of British culture, such as using 'boat' instead of 'canoe' or 'fishing' instead of 'hunting'.

Levelling: the story also became shorter with each retelling as participants tended to leave out anything unfamiliar from the story.

Sharpening: participants also tended to change the order of the story in order to make sense of it using terms more familiar to the culture of the participants. They also added detail and/or emotions.

The participants overall remembered the main themes in the story but changed the unfamiliar elements to match their own cultural expectations so that the story remained a coherent whole, although changed.

Key terms

The participants **assimilated** the story so it became more consistent with the participants' own cultural expectations.
Levelling refers to leaving out information which is seen as not important.
Sharpening refers to changing the order of a story and also adding detail and/or emotions in order to make sense of it using terms more familiar to the culture of the participants.

The original story is shown in Part 1.

The story as recalled by a student 20 hours after reading the original is shown in Part 2.

Part 3 shows the story as recalled by a man with an extraordinary memory, called VP, over a period of one year.

Part 1: original story

One night two young men from Egulac went down to the river to hunt seals, and while they were there it became foggy and calm. Then they heard war-cries, and they thought: 'Maybe this is a war-party.' They escaped to the shore, and hid behind a log. Now canoes came up, and they heard the noise of paddles, and saw one canoe coming up to them. There were five men in the canoe, and they said:

'What do you think? We wish to take you along. We are going up the river to make war on the people.'

One of the young men said: 'I have no arrows.'

'Arrows are in the canoe', they said.

'I will not go along. I might be killed. My relatives do not know where I have gone. But you', he said, turning to the other, 'may go with them.'

So one of the young men went, but the other returned home.

And the warriors went up on the river to a town on the other side of Kalama. The people came down to the water, and they began to fight, and many were killed. But presently the young man heard one of the warriors say: 'Quick, let us go home; that Indian has been hit.' Now he thought: 'Oh, they are ghosts.' He did not feel sick, but they said he had been shot.

So, the canoes went back to Egulac, and the young man went ashore to his house, and made a fire. And he told everybody and said: 'Behold I accompanied the ghosts, and we went to fight. Many of our fellows were killed, and many of those who attacked us were killed. They said I was hit, and I did not feel sick.'

He told it all, and then he became quiet. When the sun rose he fell down. Something black came out of his mouth. His face became contorted. The people jumped up and cried.

He was dead.

Part 2

Two men from Edulac went fishing. While thus occupied by the river they heard a noise in the distance.

'It sounds like a cry', said one, and presently there appeared some in canoes who invited them to join the party on their adventure. One of the young men refused to go, on the ground of family ties, but the other offered to go.

'But there are no arrows', he said

'The arrows are in the boat', was the reply.

He thereupon took his place, while his friend returned home. The party paddled up the river to Kaloma, and began to land on the banks of the river. The enemy came rushing upon them, and some sharp fighting ensued. Presently someone was injured, and the cry was raised that the enemy were ghosts.

The party returned down the stream, and the young man arrived home feeling none the worse for his experience. The next morning at dawn he endeavoured to recount his adventures. While he was talking something black issued from his mouth. Suddenly he uttered a cry and fell down. His friends gathered around him.

But he was dead.

Part 3

One day two young men from Egliac went down to the river to hunt seals. While there, it suddenly became very foggy and quiet, and they became scared and rowed ashore and hid behind a log. Soon they heard the sound of paddles in the water and canoes approaching. One of the canoes, with five men in it, paddled ashore and one of the men said: 'What do you think? Let us go up-river and make war against the people.'

'I cannot go with you', said one of the young men. 'My relatives do not know where I have gone. Besides, I might get killed. But he', said he, turning to the other young man, 'will go with you'. So one of the young men returned to his village, and the other went up-river with the war-party.

They went to a point beyond Kalama, and the people came down to the river to fight them, and they fought. Soon, the young man heard someone say: 'This Indian has been wounded' – 'Maybe they are ghosts', he thought, because he felt perfectly OK. The war party suggested leaving, and they left, and the young man went back to his village.

There he lit a fire in front of his abode, sat down to await the sunrise, and told his story to the villagers. 'I went with a war-party to make war with the people. There was fierce fighting and many were killed, and many were wounded. They said I was wounded, but I did not feel a thing. Maybe they were ghosts.'

He had told it all, and when the sun came up, he gave a little cry. Something black came out of his mouth. He fell over. He was dead.

Strengths and weaknesses of the War of the Ghosts

The study was performed in a laboratory and can be criticised for its lack of ecological validity. Also the folk tale is written in an unusual style and contained strange words and concepts so is not representative of everyday memory tasks.

The methodology used in the study was not rigorously controlled. Participants did not receive standardised instructions, and participants read the story in their own time and they even recalled the story at different time intervals. This means some of the distortions could be due to participants' guessing or other demand characteristics, such as wanting to make the story more entertaining.

Bartlett's study was important at the time in that it pointed towards the possibility of studying cognitive processes like memory scientifically and the research resulted in support for schema theory and the theory of reconstructive memory, which have been useful theories in understanding human memory and social cognition. Bartlett is now recognised as one of the first cognitive psychologists.

Peterson and Peterson (1959): short-term retention of individual verbal items

Aim

To investigate the duration of short-term memory and provide support for the multi-store model.

Procedure

A laboratory experiment was conducted in which 24 psychology students had to recall trigrams (meaningless three-consonant syllables – for example, THG, XWV).

To prevent rehearsal (practice), participants were asked to count backwards in threes or fours from a specified random number at different intervals (3, 6, 9, 12, 15 or 18 seconds) until they saw a red light appear and then they were asked to recall the letters. This is known as the Brown Peterson technique. The function of this retention interval (counting backwards) is to act as a distracter task to prevent rehearsal. At the end of the time period (3, 6, 9, 12, 15 or 18 seconds), participants tried to recall the trigram.

Findings

The longer the interval delay, the fewer trigrams were recalled. Participants were able to recall 80 per cent of trigrams after a three-second delay. However, after 18 seconds, less than 10 per cent of trigrams were recalled correctly.

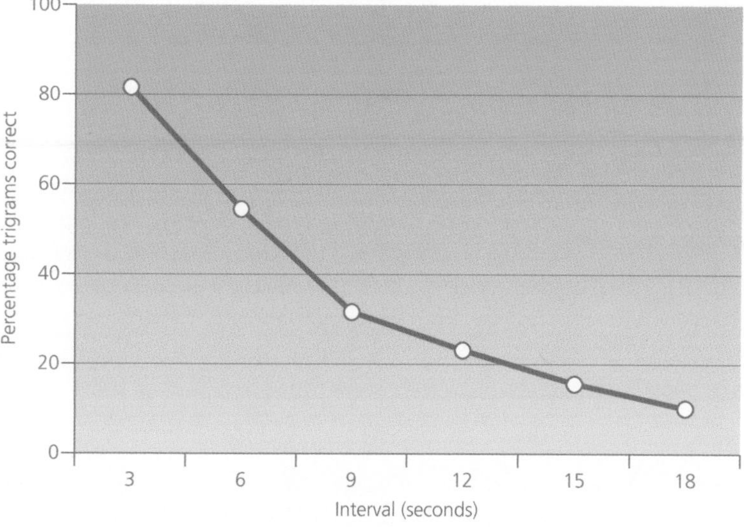

Figure 2.3 Findings from Peterson and Peterson (1959)

Conclusion

Peterson and Peterson concluded that short-term memory has a limited duration of approximately 18 seconds. Furthermore, the results show that if we are unable to rehearse information, it will not be passed to long-term memory, providing further support for the multi-store model and the idea of discrete components. It is thought that this information is lost from short-term memory from trace decay (where your memory starts to naturally fade over time). The results of the study also show that short-term memory is different from long-term memory in terms of duration.

Strengths and weaknesses of Peterson and Peterson (1959)

Peterson and Peterson used a sample of 24 psychology students, which is an issue for two reasons. First, the psychology students may have encountered the multi-store model of memory previously and therefore may have demonstrated demand characteristics by changing their behaviour to assist the experimenter, which reduces validity. Participants may try to behave in some way that they perceive as being helpful to the researcher.

Second, the memory of psychology students may be different to that of other people, especially if they had previously studied strategies for memory improvement. As a result, we are unable to generalise the results of this study to non-psychology students.

Furthermore, it could be argued that Peterson and Peterson's study has low levels of ecological validity. In this study, participants were asked to recall three-letter trigrams, which is unlike anything people would want to memorise in their everyday lives. As a result, we are unable to apply these results to everyday examples of memory and are unable to conclude if the duration of short-term memory may be longer for more important information, e.g. memorising a phone number.

However, Peterson and Peterson's study was highly controlled and took place in a laboratory at Indiana University. As a result, Peterson and Peterson had a high degree of control by eliminating noise and using fixed timings for participants to count backwards, which makes their procedure easy to replicate.

Issues and debates

The reductionism and holism debate

There are many different types of **reductionism**.

Physiological reductionism, for example, argues that all behaviour and experiences can be explained by (or reduced to) biological factors, such as hormones or the nervous system. So, for example, being aggressive may be due to having too much of a certain hormone called testosterone.

Genetic reductionism reduces all causes of behaviour to genetic inheritance, such as your phobia of heights being passed down from one of your parents to you.

Social reductionism argues that all behaviour and experiences can be explained simply by the effect of groups on the individual. So you may be prejudiced against someone simply because your friends are causing you to be prejudiced.

The criticism of reductionist arguments is that they are too simplistic because they ignore the complexities of human behaviour and experience. Behaviour often has a number of different causes and to reduce the possible explanations to one level (such as in the three examples above) can only provide a limited understanding. It's too simple to reduce your aggressive behaviour to one hormone or your phobia to one gene.

However, an advantage of the reductionist view is that, by breaking down behaviour such as aggression to its smaller parts, it may be possible to understand the whole. This type of single-mindedness has led to some great discoveries in psychology, as it has in the 'natural' sciences.

Holism has a different way of examining behaviour and aims to explain behaviour as links or interactions between different things and does not reduce behaviour to one cause.

For example, a watch is made up of many component parts, such as its face, strap, internal cogs, etc. However, all these parts come together to tell the time – the purpose of the watch is missed unless you see the whole put together.

Similarly, imagine you had never seen an aeroplane before and in front of you were placed all its component parts, engine, wings, tail, etc. Would you know that it was an aeroplane? No, you would not, which just demonstrates that we need to see the bigger picture and how all the bits interact with each other, which is the holistic viewpoint.

Holism considers several levels of explanation for behaviour to have a better understanding of the problem. For example, holism would explain a phobia of heights as caused by a number of factors interacting with each other, such as having a bad experience on a ride alongside humiliation from friends, never having experienced high rollercoasters in childhood and possibly a biological predisposition to be scared.

The holism/reductionism debate in psychology refers to whether it is more appropriate to study behaviour by breaking it down into small component parts or to study many interacting and complex aspects of behaviour as a whole.

A holistic theory takes into account all the ingredients that may contribute to behaviour and accepts that they all play a role in the specific outcomes. Such theories are more realistic and representative of human behaviour but do not establish any causation.

How reductionism and holism can be applied to memory

Studying memory in a laboratory is not the same as studying memory in the real world so by reducing memory to just one factor, such as rehearsal, ignores the importance of the environment and other variables which can affect how we remember.

A reductionist approach means breaking up areas of memory, giving less importance to the interconnections between parts of the brain, in favour of individual parts responsible for memory.

Atkinson and Shiffrin's (1968) multi-store model of memory was a reductionist account of how memory works. This could be classified as 'machine reductionism', as the brain is likened to a computer. Reductionist explanations can therefore play only a limited role in understanding memory. However, reducing behaviour to a form that can be studied is productive. This is indeed useful when trying to understand how our memory works.

Peterson and Peterson's memory research involves learning nonsense syllables or trigrams. This is a simplification of real-world memory tasks and the findings are mistakenly generalised to memory in general. The study tries to reduce our complex memory structure to tasks involving simple three-letter words.

Similarly, those suffering from amnesia, such as Clive Wearing or H.M., have their illness simply reduced to damage to a specific part of the brain, namely the hippocampus. This is sure to play a part in their amnesia of course but it rules out other factors from the environment.

If memory is studied in the real world, findings may be different. Bartlett's work on schemas demonstrates the importance of a holistic approach to explaining memory. Our schemas are formed by different life experiences and how these interact with each other to form new memories and experiences. We don't just reconstruct our memory based on one single factor; our memories are made up of a mixture of factors, such as emotions and experiences. The War of the Ghosts study shows how the story changes from person to person based upon the participants' own individual schema, culture and experiences. It is the combination of these factors and others that makes them retell the story in the way they do and not just solely due to a solitary part of the brain.

Key terms

Reductionism is the argument that we can explain behaviour and experiences by reference to only one factor, such as physiology or learning.
Holism is the opposite of reductionism and refers to any approach that emphasises the whole rather than their smaller parts. In other words, 'the whole is greater than the sum of its parts'.

Now test yourself

9. What is the difference between physiological and social reductionism?
10. Do amnesiac patients such as H.M. demonstrate that memory is reductionist or holistic?

Exam questions

1. Describe what is meant by storage and retrieval stages of memory. (4)
2. Kazim banged his head against the cupboard and can no longer recall anything from before his injury. Which type of amnesia is he suffering from? (1)
3. Describe the features of short-term memory. (2)
4. Explain the difference between duration and capacity; you must refer to either STM or LTM in your answer. (4)
5. Explain why Bartlett believed memory was reconstructive. (3)
6. Give two weaknesses of the study by Peterson and Peterson (1959). (4)
7. During a shopping trip, John is only able to recall the last three items from his shopping list of 12 items. Explain why John is only able to recall the last three items. (3)
8. During a lesson, the teacher nearly falls over the desk; one student claims he is just clumsy, but another student believes it was no accident and the teacher was tripped.

   Using reconstructive memory, explain the difference between the students' accounts of what happened. (4)

End of chapter summary

You should now have an understanding of all the points below:

Know the structure and process of memory and information processing:

- input
- processing
- output
- encoding
- storage
- retrieval.

Understand the features of short-term and long-term memory, including:

- duration
- capacity.

Understand retrograde and anterograde amnesia, including:

- the term 'retrograde amnesia'
- the term 'anterograde amnesia'
- the symptoms of retrograde amnesia
- the symptoms of anterograde amnesia.

Understand the active process of memory through the theory of reconstructive memory (Bartlett, 1932), including strengths and weaknesses of the theory:

- how schemas are formed
- how schemas influence memory.

Understand the structure and process of memory through the multi-store model of memory (Atkinson and Shiffrin, 1968), including strengths and weaknesses of the theory:

- sensory register
- the capacity of short-term memory
- the duration of short-term memory
- the capacity of long-term memory
- the duration of long-term memory
- role of attention in memory
- role of rehearsal in memory.

Understand the aims, procedures and findings (results and conclusions), and strengths and weaknesses of:

- Bartlett (1932): War of the Ghosts
- Peterson and Peterson (1959): short-term retention of individual verbal items.

Understand the reductionism and holism debate, including:

- the terms 'reductionism' and 'reductionist'
- the terms 'holism' and 'holistic'
- the use of content, theories and research drawn from human memory to explain the reductionism and holism debate.

Now test yourself answers

1. STM has a capacity of 7 +/–2 and duration of 15–30 seconds. LTM has an infinite capacity and duration.
2. To maintain information by repeating it again and again so it transfers from STM to LTM.
3. The primacy effect is when participants recall the first few words at the top of a word list as information has been transferred from STM to LTM through rehearsal, and the recency effect is the ability to recall the final few words from a list as these are still in the STM upon recall.
4. You are more likely to forget the words in the middle of the list as the STM starts to get full (reaches capacity) so these words don't reach LTM.
5. Amnesia patients provide strong evidence for the STM and LTM distinction, as brain damage can affect one store and not the other.
6. No, as they need to actually semantically understand what they are rehearsing.
7. Procedural and semantic memories are strong, with some elements of declarative and episodic for older memories.
8. That there is more than one type of LTM which needs to be acknowledged.
9. Physiological reductionism argues that all behaviour and experiences can be explained by biological factors and social reductionism argues that all behaviour and experiences can be explained simply by the effect of groups on the individual.
10. Reductionist, as his memory loss is reduced to damage to his hippocampus.

Chapter 3

Psychological problems – how would psychological problems affect you?

This chapter deals with what happens to you if you have a mental health problem. It is important to investigate this as in today's society so many people suffer from mental health problems and numbers are still rising. Understanding the causes of **unipolar depression** and **addiction** can in turn help improve the quality of life of those suffering as we can develop appropriate treatments for their disorders.

Key terms

Unipolar depression is a mood disorder which is seen as a constant disturbance to mood, whereas bipolar disorder involves fluctuations between moods of manic depression (very low mood swings) and mania (very high mood swings).

Addiction is a physical or psychological need for a habit-forming substance, such as a drug or alcohol.

Unipolar depression

Depression is an example of a disorder which can affect mood. The disorder prevents the individual from leading a normal life, at work, socially or within their family.

Symptoms and features of unipolar depression

Depression can exist in patients as an episode, lasting for a few months, and that may never return, or it can be a condition that returns periodically, or it can last a lifetime. Depression is the most common form of mental disorder, with an estimated 120 million people worldwide suffering from it, with an estimated 3.5 million sufferers in the UK.

Common symptoms of depression are reduced concentration, lack of self-esteem, pessimism, disturbed sleeping and eating habits, and sometimes ideas of self-harm. A general loss of interest and increased tiredness are the most typical symptoms and patients may complain of 'feeling nothing'.

There is a gender difference as women are more likely to be diagnosed with depression than men, with some studies estimating that a woman is 2–3 times more likely to become clinically depressed than a man.

Depression affects all age groups but tends to occur more in young people than older people. Saluja *et al.* (2004) found that depression was statistically more likely to start in early adolescence.

Depression is found in all cultures, with most showing a range of between 8 and 12 per cent of the population suffering from the disorder (Andrade and Caraveo, 2003) although a big difference emerges between the USA at 17 per cent and Japan at just 3 per cent.

Now test yourself

1. What is the difference between unipolar and bipolar depression?

How the incidence of depression changes over time

Seligman (1973) referred to depression as the 'common cold' of psychiatry because of its frequency of diagnosis. In 1985, 10 per cent of people had no-one to discuss important matters with; by 2004, that number had grown to 25 per cent – one out of every four people.

The National Ambulatory Medical Care Survey (NAMCS) found that the number of people diagnosed with depression has increased by 450 per cent since 1987. For every person who took an antidepressant in 1987, there are now more than five.

According to the British Psychological Society figures, a staggering 9 million people in Britain reported feelings of depression to their GP in 1998.

The proportion of 15/16-year-olds reporting that they frequently feel anxious or depressed has doubled in the last 30 years, from 1 in 30 to 2 in 30 for boys and 1 in 10 to 2 in 10 for girls.

A study of national trends in depression among adolescents and young adults published in the journal *Pediatrics* found that the prevalence of teens who reported a **major depressive episode (MDE)** in the previous 12 months jumped from 8.7 per cent in 2005 to 11.5 per cent in 2014. That's a 37 per cent increase.

Key term

Major depressive episode (MDE) is defined as a period of at least two weeks of low mood that is present in most situations. Symptoms include low self-esteem, loss of interest in normally enjoyable activities and problems with sleep, energy and concentration.

How depression affects individuals and society

People who suffer from any form of depression usually live shorter lives – those with depression may die 25 years sooner than the average person, possibly due to a link between depression and heart disease and other stress-related illnesses. This is thought to be due to both the physical and the social side effects of depression.

The physical effects of depression impact the brain, heart and other parts of the body. A decrease in brain volume is one of the most disturbing side effects of depression. Fortunately, antidepressants appear to be able to reverse this brain volume loss. Long-term depression is also known to negatively impact the heart. Depression causes an inappropriate release of adrenaline, which, over time, damages the cardiovascular system. An increase in artery and blood vessel stress is a further health effect of depression. This can increase the risk of blood clots and heart attack.

There is a reason that employers focus on positive energy in the workplace. They know it generates loyalty and makes for a more pleasant work environment. Because of this, an obvious lack of motivation and a 'downer' personality is thought to lower performance of the operation as a whole. If your co-workers don't know or understand that you are depressed, the fatigue and inability to enjoy interactions can be misinterpreted as disappointment in them or the job itself. This is especially so when you are normally a person with 'positive energy'.

The results can be avoidance by other workers. They don't want to catch what you have and may even feel emotionally drained themselves when dealing with you. In the extreme, the depressed person may just not feel the job is worth it and either quit or arrange to get fired.

Depression can put a real stress on friendships. Since part of the relationship is enjoyment of one another's company, when that is missing, the friendship can break down. The friendship can quickly turn into a cycle of dumping your problems on your friend in a one-way fashion that drains all the life out of the relationship. Friends may avoid you or cut interactions short if they sense you are 'going there'.

Now test yourself

2. According to the proportion of 15/16-year-olds, which group feels more anxious or depressed – boys or girls?
3. What does the term 'prevalence' mean?
4. The release of which hormone can cause blood clots and a possible heart attack?

Genes as an explanation of unipolar depression

The first attempt at identifying specific genes for depression was by Egeland *et al.* (1987), who researched 81 members of the Amish community of Pennsylvania.

Four families within the community showed a much higher than expected incidence of depression. Of the 81 studied, 14 were diagnosed with the disorder and all had abnormalities on the tip of chromosome 11. This caused particular interest at the time since this location is adjacent to genes known to be involved in the production of serotonin.

Nemeroff (1998) has implicated a gene on the X chromosome. Recent research has also suggested a possible link with genes on seven other chromosomes alongside chromosome 11, which clearly makes it genetically complex!

Research led by King's College London in 2011 discovered the first solid evidence that genetic variations on chromosome 3 may cause depression. The findings have been replicated concurrently by another group from Washington University. The study led by King's presents the results of ten years of work from the Depression Network project of over 800 families with recurrent depression. Scientists believe that as many as 40 per cent of those with depression can trace it to a genetic link. Environmental and other factors make up the other 60 per cent.

Psychologists look for genetic explanations to support the argument that depression is biologically determined. One of the best ways to do this is to study identical twins. Researchers focus on the study of identical twins (**monozygotic** or MZ twins) because they share 100 per cent of their genes. The results are then compared with findings from pairs who are less genetically alike, i.e. non-identical twins (**dizygotic** or DZ twins).

Psychologists look at twins to see what behaviour they share by looking at **concordance rates.**

Key terms

Monozygotic twins are split from one egg and one sperm after fertilisation.
Dizygotic twins are from two different eggs and two different sperms.
Concordance rate is the likelihood that, if one twin has a certain trait, the other twin will also have the same trait.

If an individual persistently has episodes of depression, a genetic factor may be suspected. Several family and twin studies are reported that show concordance rates between 30 and 40 per cent, which is higher than would occur by chance. Gershon (1990) reviewed ten family studies and found that concordance rates of unipolar depression in first-degree relatives (i.e. a parent, sibling or child) ranged between 7 and 30 per cent.

Clearly there are environmental factors involved in depression. A negative environment acting on a person genetically predisposed to depression has more of an impact than a similar environment acting on a person without that predisposition. Kendler *et al.* (1995) found the highest levels of depression in those scoring high on negative life events and having the genetic predisposition.

Now test yourself

5. Genes known to be involved in the production of serotonin are located near which chromosome?

Strengths and weaknesses of the genetic explanation

McGuffin *et al.* (1996) found 46 per cent concordance in MZ twins compared with 20 per cent in DZ twins in a total of 109 twin pairs, with no evidence of the effect of shared environment. This suggests depression is more likely to be genetic as the MZ twins share more genes than the DZ twins.

Adoption studies have shown that the biological parents of adopted children who develop depression were eight times more likely than the adopted parents to have suffered from depression, which suggests the role of nature over nurture (Wender *et al.*, 1986).

There is lots of genetic evidence, but those with shared genes normally also share the same environment. Depression is not entirely genetic since no studies have shown a 100 per cent concordance rate between MZ twins! Genetics seems to be a risk factor but not a whole explanation, and environmental factors such as death in the family or losing one's job must have a part to play.

Even if genetic factors do play a part in the origins of unipolar depression, it is not clear what the precise mechanism is that is transmitted. Without knowing the specific genes involved, it is impossible to understand how they code biological structures and functions that produce the symptoms of depression.

Cognitive theory as an explanation of unipolar depression

Cognitive theory takes the view that dysfunctional behaviour is the result of irrational or faulty thinking.

Beck (1976) argues that patients with unipolar depression have lower self-esteem and are high in self-blame.

The first part of Beck's cognitive model of depression is the **cognitive triad**. These are negative views of the self (feeling inadequate), negative views of the world (feeling defeated) and negative views of the future (believing that your suffering will continue). A sufferer of depression tends to think life will always be that way for them, and that nothing can improve: this comes from the 'future' aspect.

The second part of the model looks at **cognitive errors**. Beck described this as the faulty thought patterns. The 'downside' is over-estimated so that the most pessimistic conclusion possible is reached when in a situation.

Schemas make up the final part of the model. A generalised negative belief outlook makes someone susceptible to depression. A new situation is interpreted through the use of a person's appropriate existing schemas, including self-schemas. The way to beat depression according to the cognitive model is to change the maladaptive thought interpretations by allowing for alternative thoughts and interpretations of events. If evidence is presented that there are other interpretations, an individual can change their thinking.

Key terms

Cognitive triad includes three areas where there are negative automatic thoughts.
Cognitive errors are where an individual gives selective attention to the negative side of a situation, always ignoring the positive aspects.

Now test yourself

6. What is meant by the term dysfunctional behaviour?

Strengths and weaknesses of the cognitive theory explanation for unipolar depression

The most powerful support for the validity of the theory must be that it has led to the most successful treatments for depression. These include Ellis' rational emotive therapy (RET), which encourages patients to recognise their negative thoughts and replace them with more realistic outlooks.

Lewinsohn *et al.* (2001) assessed teenagers with no existing history of depression and measured their level of negative thinking. A year later, those scoring highest for negative thinking were the ones most likely to be diagnosed with major depression.

Cognitive explanations are associated with successful therapies for depression.

Butler and Beck (2000) reviewed 14 separate studies investigating the effectiveness of Beck's cognitive therapy and concluded that about 80 per cent of adults benefited from the therapy.

McIntosh and Fischer (2000) believe cognitive theory to be unnecessarily complex. Rather than the triad of self, world and future, they suggest that only self is necessary, as all other negative thoughts then arise from this.

The theory can be criticised for being reductionist as it states that if an individual thinks in a negative way/has negative automatic thoughts, then they are likely to develop disorders such as depression. This ignores the fact that biological research has indicated that depression can be down to low levels of the **neurotransmitter serotonin** and, therefore, the cognitive approach can be seen to be too simplistic.

Key terms

Neurotransmitters are chemical messengers within the brain that allow the communication between nerve cells.
Serotonin is a neurotransmitter involved in the transmission of nerve impulses.

Cognitive behavioural therapy as a treatment for unipolar depression

The rationale behind all cognitive behavioural therapies (CBTs) is that thoughts (cognitions) interact with and have an enormous influence on emotions and behaviour. When these thoughts are persistently negative and irrational, they can result in unipolar depression. If a person's problems arise from the fact that they think in abnormal or faulty ways, then it follows that the best way to remove behavioural and emotional symptoms is by helping the client to alter the way they think. A number of different forms of therapy have been put forward. One of the therapies used most often is RET (rational emotive therapy), which is a form of CBT put forward by Ellis (1991).

A – **Activating event** – an unpleasant experience
B – **Beliefs** – the negative thoughts as a result of A
C – **Consequence** – the negative thoughts and actions caused by A and B

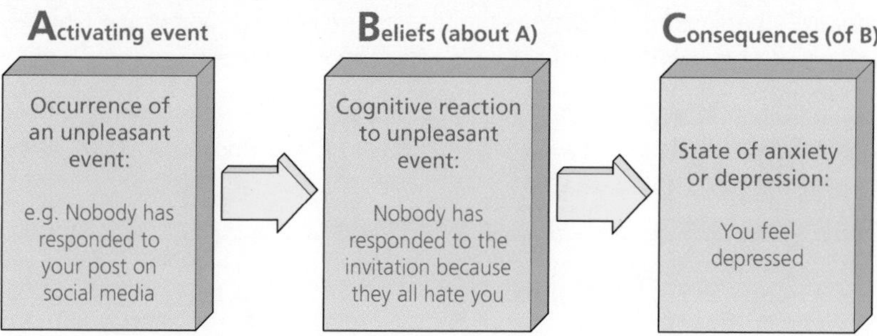

Figure 3.1 Ellis's ABC model

Ellis believes that it is not the activating event (A) that causes negative emotional and behavioural consequences (C), but rather that a person interprets these events unrealistically and therefore has an irrational belief system (B) that helps cause the consequences (C).

The idea is that the client identifies their own unhelpful beliefs and proves them wrong. As a result, their beliefs begin to change. After irrational beliefs have been identified, the therapist will often work with the client in challenging the negative thoughts on the basis of evidence from the client's experience by re-interpreting it in a more realistic light. Clients are then taught to replace their flawed and illogical beliefs with more realistic ones. In other words, they develop a dispute belief system (D).

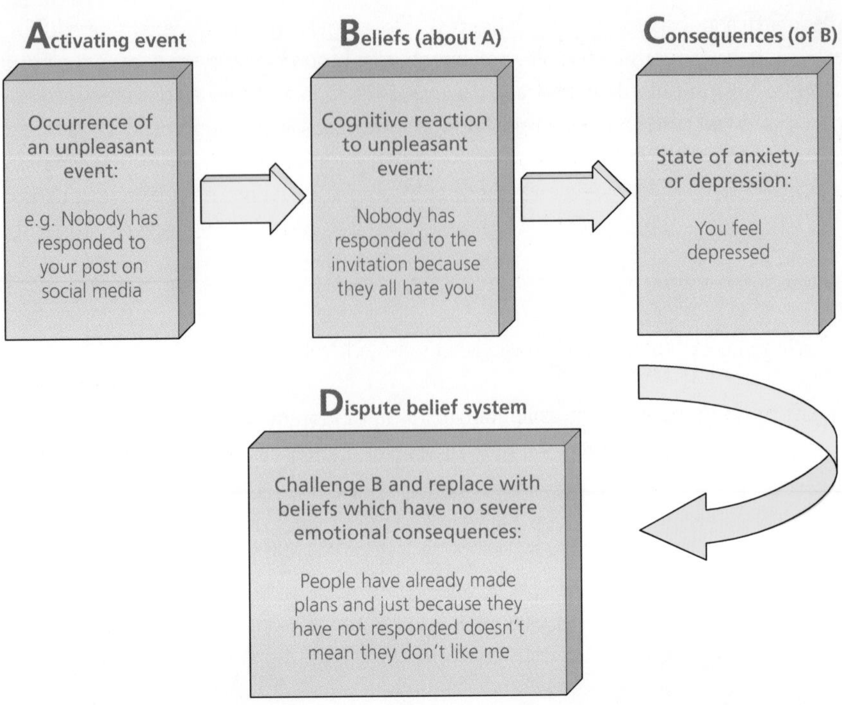

Figure 3.2 The dispute belief system

Active learning

Make your own ABC diagram for other possible reasons that might lead to depression, such as failing a driving test or being fired from work. Now add D to challenge B in your example.

Strengths and weaknesses of CBT as a treatment for unipolar depression

The therapy does try to convince people that they are capable of changing their lives for the better, that they are in control, because they can change their thinking, so it offers the potential for positive psychological change.

Levine and Wetzel (1986) suggest that the relapse rate of mentally depressed people treated by this method is half that of the relapse rate of individuals treated with medication. Hollon *et al.* (2001) demonstrated this remarkable superiority of CBT over medication and discovered that, within a year after treatment, 81 per cent of individuals receiving medication relapsed, whereas only 25 per cent of patients treated by CBT relapsed.

There are ethical issues as the underlying assumptions of this approach may be seen as blaming the individual for his or her maladaptive thinking, which raises issues around labelling and responsibility.

Sanders and Wills (2005) claim clients report an understanding of the principles of cognitive therapy, but cannot seem to apply that understanding in a way that promotes real change. So they are never fully able to challenge B with D as they are unable to alter their thinking, even though they are aware that they need to in order to get better.

Drug therapy as a treatment for unipolar depression

Antidepressants are used to treat depression and lower levels of **noradrenaline**. One of the functions of serotonin is to regulate the other neurotransmitters. Without the regulation provided by serotonin, erratic brain functioning and thinking patterns occur. Low levels of serotonin produce low levels of noradrenaline and evidence suggests that low levels of noradrenaline cause depression. Dopamine is also related to feelings of alertness, motivation and attention, and so it is suggested low levels of dopamine similarly are linked to depression.

Most antidepressants are believed to be equally effective in equivalent therapeutic doses. There is usually a 2–6-week period before the full effect is seen.

Having been released into the synapse, serotonin and noradrenaline are quickly broken down by the enzyme monoamine oxidase. To block the action of this enzyme, **monoamine oxidase inhibitors (MAOIs)** can be used, which can help with depression.

Now test yourself

7. What's the link between serotonin, noradrenaline and depression?

Key terms

Antidepressants usually work by increasing the levels of serotonin in the brain, since some of the symptoms of depression come about due to low levels of serotonin.

Noradrenaline is a neurotransmitter needed for alertness, energy and attention to life.

Monoamine oxidase inhibitors (MAOIs) prevent the action of monoamine oxidase so result in higher levels of serotonin and noradrenaline in the synapse. The increased noradrenaline activity leads to a reduction in depressive symptoms.

Tricyclics block the re-uptake of serotonin and noradrenaline so result in more of the chemical being available in the synapse for a longer period of time.

Selective serotonin re-uptake inhibitors (SSRIs) work in a similar way to tricyclics. By far the most famous of these is Prozac.

Serotonin and noradrenaline re-uptake inhibitors (SNRIs) are also effective for people with anxiety disorders or obsessive compulsive disorder (OCD). They have similar side effects to SSRIs.

Key terms

Tricyclics are so called because of their three carbon ring structure and are linked to arousal and improved mood.

Selective serotonin re-uptake inhibitors (SSRIs) inhibit re-uptake but only impact on serotonin pathways, so leaving the serotonin to have an enhanced effect on the neuron.

Serotonin and noradrenaline re-uptake inhibitors (SNRIs) work in a similar way to SSRIs and prevent the re-uptake of noradrenaline (norepinephrine) and leave the other neurotransmitters unaffected.

Strengths and weaknesses of drug therapy as a treatment for unipolar depression

The 2005 World Health Organisation report pointed to a large number of studies showing that antidepressants are effective for depression in adults. Antidepressants are often used as a starting point in therapy to help boost mood so that other therapies like CBT can be used later if necessary.

The MAOIs are reasonably effective in reducing depression, but they do produce various side effects, such as blocking the production of monoamine oxidase in the liver, leading to high blood pressure.

The tricyclics are less dangerous than the MAOIs, but they can impair driving to a dangerous extent, and other side effects include dry mouth and constipation.

Depressed patients taking SSRIs are less likely to suffer from dry mouth and constipation than those taking tricyclics, and it is harder to overdose on SSRIs. However, SSRIs conflict with some other forms of medication, and Prozac is reported to have severe effects in some people, including suicidal thoughts where none were experienced previously.

Karp and Frank (1995) carried out a review article on the effectiveness of drug therapy in treating depressed women. Meta-analysis (combined analysis) of nine pieces of research featuring a total of 520 women with depression showed that adding cognitive therapy to drug therapy was no more effective than merely prescribing antidepressants. This suggests that drug therapy for depression is sufficient treatment for depression without other components.

Addiction

Addiction is a state that results when a person takes a drug such as alcohol or nicotine, which can be enjoyable, but the sustained use of which becomes uncontrollable and interferes with normal life.

Now test yourself

8. Addiction can be defined as 'a repetitive habit pattern that increases the risk of disease and/or associated personal and social problems'. True or false?

Symptoms and features of addiction

Addiction falls under one of the categories in the International Classification of Diseases (ICD-10) and is classified as a dependence disorder.

Drugs alter the way a person thinks, feels and behaves. Repeated use leads to **physical dependence** because the individual believes they cannot manage without it. An individual may feel compulsion to keep taking drugs in order to avoid withdrawal symptoms and to feel normal.

Physical addiction or **tolerance** is a biological state in which the body adapts to the presence of a drug so that the drug no longer has the same effect, and steadily requires larger amounts to mimic the effects originally produced by lesser doses. Neurons become accustomed to operating with an elevated level of neurotransmitters so their sensitivity to the chemicals in the synapse decreases. It therefore takes more of the substance to produce the same reaction in the neurons as experienced earlier on.

The drug causes feelings of satisfaction that motivate the user to continue to take the drug to produce feelings of pleasure and/or to avoid withdrawal symptoms. With **psychological dependence**, the drug is psychologically necessary for normal functioning. An individual may feel compelled to take a substance even when they are not physically dependent on it. It becomes a compulsion to take a drug for the pleasant effects it has, such as feelings of exhilaration or self-confidence. It may lead to misuse, as compulsion can result in uncontrolled drug taking.

Key terms

Physical dependence refers to a physical need for the drug because the body has adapted to the high amounts of certain chemicals and cannot operate normally without them.

Tolerance results in more and more of the substance being needed for it to have the same effect. It refers to the way the body continues to adapt to a substance.

Psychological dependence refers to the need to take a drug not for physical reasons but for psychological reasons, such as support and feeling calmer.

Withdrawal is the term for physical symptoms that arise upon reduction, or removal, of the drug that the user has become dependent on. As the brain tries to work normally, it has to compensate for the lack of the drug it has got used to working with.

The individual experiences physically painful and unpleasant symptoms as the effects of the drug wear off. These may include vomiting, shaking, headaches and convulsions, although these effects vary from drug to drug. Withdrawal symptoms for heroin include sweating, insomnia, muscle cramps and 'itchy blood'.

Key term

Withdrawal is the term for miserable symptoms that are experienced when someone stops using a substance on which they have become physically or psychologically dependent.

How the incidence of addiction changes over time

Addiction is an evolving concept. Previous classification systems required physical withdrawal symptoms to be present to define something as dependence. There has now been a shift away from the term 'dependence' to 'addiction', which is an all-encompassing term.

A century ago, addicts were believed to be morally degenerate. There was no formal treatment available because addiction was not viewed as a disease. Addicts would instead be locked away in asylums or imprisoned because of their behaviour and lack of self-control. Many of these people would end up going through withdrawal without being in a safe, controlled environment, and this was torturous.

In the 1950s, people believed that drug abuse was still a problem among the lower socioeconomic groups. As soldiers returned home from World War II with addiction problems, people turned the other cheek because they felt the soldiers had fought for their country and their drug use was justifiable. No treatment centres were available, aside from psychiatric centres associated with hospitals.

It wasn't until the 1960s that the attitude towards addiction started to change. This was an era where drug use was part of many anti-war protests, civil rights movements, peace festivals and riots. Our understanding of addiction grew, and alcoholism was officially declared a disease. By the 1970s, lawmakers were recommending treatment rather than criminal prosecution. According to the National Institute of Health, the last three decades have brought a lot of success in understanding the risks, mechanisms and consequences of addiction. We now understand that addiction is a complex brain disease, and it can take a long time to repair all the brain circuits and end drug-seeking behaviour. Thankfully, more therapies are available to help recovering addicts get to the root of their problem and manage temptation.

There has also been a shift to client-centred care, rather than focusing on the physical side of addiction. Treatment centres are taking into account the total person: mind, body and spirit.

How addiction affects individuals and society

Drug taking which leads to drug abuse is a major public health problem that impacts society on multiple levels. Directly or indirectly, every community is affected by drug abuse and addiction, as is every family. Responsibilities, such as work and family, suddenly become affected and users may not even be aware that their behaviour is out of control and causing difficulties for themselves and others.

People who are addicted very often turn to crime as a means of paying for their addiction. This can involve stealing or fraud to obtain the funds necessary to bankroll their addiction. This can start with stealing from one's partner, family or friends but can spread to include stealing from their employer. The majority of crime committed in the UK is usually drug-related. Burglary, muggings, robberies, etc. are all ways of funding an addiction and the more serious the addiction the greater the chance of these being accompanied by violence.

There are also the costs of policing, drug addiction help lines, support groups and rehab clinics. Indirectly there is lost revenue in the form of tax and national insurance contributions each time an addict loses their job or is unable to work. This means a drop in revenue for the Treasury and an increase in welfare benefits, e.g. unemployment benefit.

Employers are affected if any of their employees develop an addiction. The employee concerned may have changed from a smart, punctual and efficient worker to someone who is late for work, has neglected their appearance and personal hygiene and is displaying poor behaviour. This results in that employee losing their job, which then impacts upon their home and family life. Loss of their job means a reduction in income, especially if they are the main breadwinner, and puts a strain on relationships. It can then lead to marriage breakdown or divorce.

If a child or young person is suffering from an addiction then this will impact upon their schooling, relationships with other children and their home life. One such effect of this is truanting from school. This can happen if the child is addicted or if they have a parent who is an addict and neglects to care for them. It is hard for a child or young person to resist the temptation of alcohol, cigarettes or drugs. A desire to be part of the gang or to try 'forbidden fruit' as a means of growing up can very quickly lead to addiction. Addiction tends to occur much more quickly in a young person than in an adult.

They may show signs of anti-social behaviour and unexplained absences from school. Their concentration will be poor and motivation will have dropped. They may be spending inordinate amounts of time in their room or, on the other hand, be staying out most of the night and with people that you don't know.

If you have a situation in which one half of a couple is an addict then this can cause untold hardship for the other half. The person who is addicted may have changed from a previously easy-going personality to one who is prone to mood swings, violent outbursts, secrecy and other forms of extreme behaviour. This is difficult for their partner to deal with and is even worse if there are children involved. It is both distressing and confusing for children to see one parent (or even both parents) exhibit signs of their addiction.

Now test yourself

9. In which decade did attitudes towards addiction finally change?

Genes as an explanation of addiction

Many factors determine the likelihood that someone will become an addict; it isn't just down to a single gene. Researchers often look at DNA sequences in large families searching for pieces of DNA that are shared among individuals affected by addiction, comparing them against those that are not addicted. However, because people have complex and varied lives, researchers often look to animal models, such as mice, to learn more about the genetics of addiction. Because the reward pathway (a pleasure centre in the brain) – and many of the genes that underlie it – functions in much the same way in mice as it does in people, mice are leading the way in identifying addiction genes. When researchers discover a gene that plays a role in addiction in a mouse, they can then identify the counterpart gene in humans by looking for similar DNA sequences. For example, mice lacking the serotonin receptor gene Htr1b are more attracted to cocaine and alcohol.

Similarly the A1 allele of the dopamine receptor gene DRD2 is more common in people addicted to alcohol or cocaine.

Schinka *et al.* (2002) claimed that the mu-opioid gene seems to give an increased risk for addiction to alcohol and nicotine. Numerous laboratory studies have supported this view, where mice without the mu-opioid receptor did not drink alcohol even after they had been trained to drink it in other circumstances. Schinka *et al.* (2002) also found that alcoholics lacked a form of the mu-opioid gene compared with the non-alcoholics in the study.

Most studies looking at alcoholism have determined that children born from alcoholic parents who are adopted into non-alcoholic families have a three- to four-fold increase in the rate of alcoholism over the rest of the population. Indeed, children born and raised by alcoholic parents have an even greater rate of alcoholism. This was further supported by the APA (2008), which suggested a certain type of dopamine receptor, known as D2, might someday be used to predict whether someone will become addicted to alcohol, cocaine and heroin. Brain imaging suggests that people with fewer D2 receptors are more likely to become addicted than those with many of the receptors – and how many of these receptors people have is, in part, genetically determined.

Strengths and weaknesses of the genetic explanation of addiction

McGue (1999) found a concordance rate of 50–60 per cent for alcohol addiction, and Agrawal and Lynskey (2006) found a concordance rate of 45–79 per cent for addiction to illicit drugs. This means that just over half of the factors that cause addiction to alcohol are genetic in origin, as are half to three-quarters of the factors causing addiction to illegal drugs.

More recent research by Wendy Slutske (2010) has looked at the concordance rates of MZ and DZ twins in relation to gambling addiction. She studied nearly 5,000 individuals and found that the concordance rate for MZ twins was double the concordance rate for DZ twins.

Understanding the role of genetic variation in addiction can also help inform treatments. The effectiveness of medication varies from person to person, depending on their genetic make-up. In the future, genetic tests could be used to determine which medications are likely to be most effective based on an individual's genetic profile.

Genes alone cannot explain addiction; we cannot become addicted to any action or chemical if we never engage in that action or take the chemical. We need to be in the right environment to be exposed to the drug. For example, Saudi Arabians are not likely to become alcoholic since alcohol is not freely available in Saudi Arabia.

Learning theory as an explanation of addiction

Learning theorists believe that there is a psychological explanation for drug addiction and that addiction is behaviour, rather than a disease. It is learned behaviour which can be unlearned.

Classical conditioning and addiction

Classical conditioning is the suggestion that feelings can come from stimuli that are paired.

- The process starts with an unconditioned stimulus (UCS) that automatically provokes an unconditioned response (UCR). The stimulus and the response are called unconditioned because the response is bound to happen.
- The UCS is then paired (+) with a neutral stimulus (NS). It is called a neutral stimulus because at this stage it does not produce the response. The UCS still gives the UCR as before.
- After a few pairings, the NS on its own produces the response, which now becomes a conditioned stimulus (CS) and the response now becomes a conditioned response (CR).

So if substance misuse gives pleasure, which will be an automatic response because it is biological, then anything associated with the substance misuse will also give pleasure. For example, drug equipment, such as syringes, or even the place the individual associates with substance misuse can trigger the pleasure response. This conditioning makes a relapse after successful treatment a possibility – because when someone is exposed to things or people linked to the substance misuse then they might experience the pleasure feelings again, which may trigger a desire to abuse the drug again.

Active learning

UCS	UCR
UCS + NS	UCR
CS	CR

Fill in the classical conditioning diagram above using the following terms:

syringes, drug, pleasure

Operant conditioning and addiction

Operant conditioning is the belief that behaviour is repeated if there is a reward and stopped if there is punishment. A reward can be positive, such as gaining pleasure, or negative, such as removing pain or a problem.

Positive reinforcement can also explain why a user can be addicted to a drug even when they are aware of the unpleasant risks. These risks are long term, whereas the effects of positive reinforcement are short term. Therefore, a heroin user is more powerfully affected by the immediate rewards than by the delayed consequences of withdrawal or imprisonment.

Drugs that are injected or smoked pass very quickly into the brain and therefore have an almost instant pleasurable effect. Their reinforcing properties therefore are particularly powerful as the user is learning the association between the drug-taking behaviour and the positively reinforcing experience of desired feelings.

Although positive reinforcement can explain the early stages of drug taking, the concept of **negative reinforcement** can be used to explain the maintenance of drug taking. Dependent users may be reinforced to continue using a drug in order to avoid the unpleasant withdrawal symptoms, such as nausea, anxiety and depression. For example, as the effects of heroin wear off, it can be very unpleasant for the user, who then learns that taking more of the heroin has the effect of removing these unpleasant experiences. Drugs can be taken to remove the unpleasant feelings of withdrawal. After the drug has been taken for a little while, it is more likely that the abuse is maintained through negative reinforcement, because taking the drug removes withdrawal symptoms.

Social learning and addiction

Social learning theory is the explanation that learning is through observing role models, particularly those that a person identifies with and who are similar to them, and then imitating their behaviour.

Social learning theory puts forward the idea of modelling, which is where behaviour is observed when watching a model, and then the behaviour is remembered and imitated. There are features of modelling, such as observing the behaviour, paying attention to it, being able to perform it and being motivated to perform the behaviour.

This means that if substance misuse is learned through social learning then it is likely that the role model is someone similar to the individual, who can be identified with, that there is motivation to carry out the behaviour and that the observed behaviour is attended to and remembered.

An important feature of social learning theory is vicarious learning. At first smoking seems to be an unpleasant experience and social learning theory can explain why, therefore, it is continued with. The idea is that seeing family and friends enjoying smoking would be getting reward vicariously (i.e. through another person) and would lead a person to continue to smoke. **Vicarious reinforcement** suggests that people persist in a behaviour they see rewarded because they expect reward in the future.

It is suggested that for social learning of substance misuse to take place depends on the amount of exposure to peers who abuse drugs compared to exposure to peers who do not. The frequency of drug use amongst peers is also important, as well as the age of the individual and peers. Younger adolescents are more susceptible than older adolescents.

Akers (1992) has pointed out that television might have a role in promoting substance abuse by providing role models for children. High-status people exert a stronger influence on behaviour than low-status people so it is important that those with high status act responsibly – depending on what is considered 'responsible' in a particular culture.

Key terms

Classical conditioning means learning through association.
Operant conditioning refers to learning through the consequences of our actions.
Positive reinforcement refers to getting a reward for a desired behaviour.
Negative reinforcement refers to the strengthening of behaviour by removing something unpleasant.
Social learning theory refers to learning through observation and imitation.
Vicarious reinforcement is our tendency to imitate behaviours for which others are being rewarded.

Now test yourself

10. Ash becomes addicted to nicotine because she sees her dad smoking at home every day. This addiction can be explained best by which theory?

Strengths and weaknesses of the learning theory explanation of addiction

Research support comes from a study on US soldiers in the Vietnam War. The soldiers became addicted to heroin while in Vietnam and experienced withdrawal symptoms whilst there, but when back in the USA they were far less likely to relapse because the sights and sounds they had associated with heroin were not present.

There is also an implication for treatment. If certain environmental cues (sights and sounds) make relapse more likely, then a treatment programme aimed at exposing the addict to those sights and sounds but without any opportunity to carry out the addicted behaviour will lead to successful treatment (stimulus discrimination).

Because conditioning does not require free will or conscious awareness, it explains why addicts continue to take a drug even though they know it is harmful and that they do not really want to take it. It also explains why addicts may neglect themselves (such as not eating) as the primary drive to take the drug becomes a priority over other drives, such as eating.

Research support comes from DiBlasio and Benda (1993), who found that adolescents who smoked associated themselves with other smokers, and were more likely to conform to the social norm of a smoking group. Treatment can therefore be based on teaching individuals the skills necessary to avoid social influence (Botvin, 2000).

It is hard to show a definite link between observation and learning because there are often many factors involved. For example, if it is said that family members act as role models because alcohol abuse tends to run in families, the difficulty is that genes are also handed down through families.

It is hard to test social learning theory for validity because of the many factors involved in behaviour such as drug misuse. It is difficult to pick out behaviour that is modelled and then reproduced without considering other explanations. This theory suggests that commencing drug taking depends on social learning but this is not always the case – drug abuse can occur in isolation from other users, and against the social norms.

Cognitive behavioural therapy as a treatment for addiction

Individuals using cognitive behavioural therapy (CBT) learn to identify and correct problematic behaviours by applying a range of different skills that can be used to stop addiction. CBT was first used to treat alcohol and later heroin addiction, and has two main components: **functional analysis** and **skills training**. With functional analysis, working together, the therapist and the patient try to identify the thoughts, feelings and circumstances of the patient before and after they drank or used heroin. This helps the patient determine the risks that are likely to lead to a relapse. Functional analysis can also give the person insight into why they drink or use heroin in the first place and identify situations in which the person has coping difficulties.

Skills training focuses on someone who is at the point where they need professional treatment for their addiction. Chances are they are using alcohol or heroin as their main means of coping with their problems. The goal is to get the person to learn or relearn better coping skills. The therapist tries to help the individual unlearn old habits and learn to develop healthier skills and habits. CBT tries to educate the alcohol or heroin addict to change the way they think about their addiction and to learn new ways to cope with the situations and circumstances that led to their drinking or drug episodes in the past.

Specific techniques include exploring the positive and negative consequences of continued drug use, self-monitoring to recognise cravings early and identify situations that might put one at risk for use, and developing strategies for coping with cravings and avoiding those high-risk situations. Research indicates that the skills individuals learn through cognitive behavioural approaches remain after the completion of treatment. Current research focuses on how to produce even more powerful effects by combining CBT with medications for drug abuse and with other types of behavioural therapies.

Key terms

Functional analysis is when the therapist looks for causes that may have triggered the addiction.

Skills training is putting the emphasis on the addict to try and implement ways to control their addiction.

Strengths and weaknesses of CBT as a treatment for addiction

CBT does try to convince people that they are capable of changing their lives for the better, that they are in control, because they can change their thinking, so it offers the potential for positive psychological change.

It focuses on re-training your thoughts and altering your behaviours, in order to make changes to how you feel. Skills you learn in CBT are useful, practical and helpful strategies that can be incorporated into everyday life to help you cope better with future stresses and difficulties, even after the treatment has finished.

There are ethical issues as the underlying assumptions of CBT may be seen as blaming the individual for his or her abnormal thinking, which raises issues around labelling and responsibility.

To benefit from CBT, you need to commit yourself to the process. A therapist can help and advise you, but they cannot make your problems go away without your cooperation. Attending regular CBT sessions and carrying out any extra work between sessions can take up a lot of time.

Some critics argue that because CBT only addresses current problems and focuses on specific issues, it does not address the possible underlying, older causes of why individuals started drinking alcohol or taking drugs in the first place.

CBT focuses on the individual's capacity to change themselves (their thoughts, feelings and behaviours), and does not address wider problems in systems or families that often have a significant impact on an individual's health and well-being.

Drug therapy as a treatment for addiction

Medications help suppress withdrawal symptoms during a process called **detoxification**. Detoxification is not in itself 'treatment', but only the first step in the process. Patients who do not receive any further treatment after detoxification usually resume their drug use.

Patients can use medications to help re-establish normal brain function and decrease cravings. People who use more than one drug, which is very common, need treatment for all of the substances they use.

Medications are available for treatment of nicotine, alcohol and heroin addiction. Scientists are developing other medications to treat cocaine and cannabis addiction.

Bupropion, commonly prescribed for depression, also reduces nicotine cravings and withdrawal symptoms in adult smokers.

Disulfiram prevents the production of an enzyme involved in the absorption of alcohol, causing an unpleasant reaction if alcohol is consumed after taking the medication.

Detoxification is done in a controlled, supervised setting in which medications relieve symptoms, and the process usually takes four to seven days. Complications associated with the withdrawal from alcohol may occur, such as delirium tremens (DTs), which could be fatal.

Methadone is an opiate which replaces heroin at the synapse and removes withdrawal symptoms. The idea is that methadone is enough to take away painful withdrawal symptoms, which helps the individual to give up the drug. One reason for continuing to use heroin is to get rid of withdrawal symptoms, which is negative reinforcement (getting rid of something unpleasant). So without the withdrawal symptoms, giving up the drug is more likely. Methadone has been used since 1964 and is prescribed officially. It is a maintenance programme, which means it is a way of controlling heroin addiction. Methadone does not affect normal functioning – those taking it are not 'drugged'.

It is given orally, making it safer than an injection of heroin. It lasts longer, about 24 hours, and so avoids the fluctuations of the rush of euphoria followed by withdrawal effects experienced with heroin. Methadone also blocks the effects of heroin at the synapse and so if heroin is also taken it will not produce its euphoric effects. Addicts are assessed and prescribed a daily dose of methadone. Initially, the addict must drink the dose under supervision of a pharmacist. When considered trustworthy, they are allowed to take some doses home to self-administer. Once the treatment has stabilised, detoxification can begin. The amount of methadone is slowly reduced over time. Medical checks are undertaken regularly to monitor the dosage and to carry out urine tests to check that no other drugs are being taken. Drug treatment is the main way of treating heroin dependence.

Key term

Detoxification is the process of removing chemicals and toxins from within the addict.

Strengths and weaknesses of drug therapy as a treatment for addiction

When a patient is given drugs to help treat addiction, they can take it instantly, which induces instant gratification on their part as they will begin to feel the benefits of treatment rather quickly, which provides a short-term as well as long-term solution through constant usage. A placebo effect can also take place here, which is not necessarily a negative effect, as the patient will believe that the drug will have positive effects, which in turn causes them to feel as though they are being alleviated from their addiction. Drug therapy is also an easy way to treat addiction as patients only need to take a pill each day, or whatever their dose is at that time. This also gives them their independence back as they become responsible for helping themselves get better and move on with their life.

There are some disadvantages to drug therapy, such as greater potential for unexpected or serious negative side effects (e.g. disulfiram can make some individuals very ill).

Drug therapy can be quite expensive, particularly when it requires medical supervision. Some forms of therapy are done in a hospital or residential treatment setting, adding further to the overall cost.

Many patients on methadone need treatment for at least two years, and the longer they stay on the programme the more successful it seems to be. Some studies suggest that 85 per cent stay on methadone for 12 months. So this is not a short treatment, which has cost implications.

Methadone is highly addictive and has many side effects, such as dry mouth, fatigue and weight gain. There are also some ethical objections to heroin users being given drugs as treatment, partly because it will lead to withdrawal symptoms itself when the individual tries to stop using it.

Caspi *et al.* (2003): influence of life stress on depression: moderation by a polymorphism in the 5-HTT gene

There has long been the suspicion that at least a part of the cause of depression is genetic, and researchers have begun to identify some genes which could play a role in the process. We have two sets of each gene in our bodies (one from each parent). Different versions of the same gene are called **alleles** (so, for example, in the genes which code for eye colour, one allele may code for brown eyes, and another allele may code for blue eyes).

Caspi *et al.* (2003) was one of these studies, looking at the effect of possessing different types (alleles) of the 5-HTT gene, which is known to be important in the production and use of the neurotransmitter serotonin.

Aim

To investigate whether the 5-HTT gene is linked to a higher or lower risk of depression in an individual. The researchers expected that people with one type of genetic pattern would show depression following stress to a greater extent than people with a different type of genetic pattern.

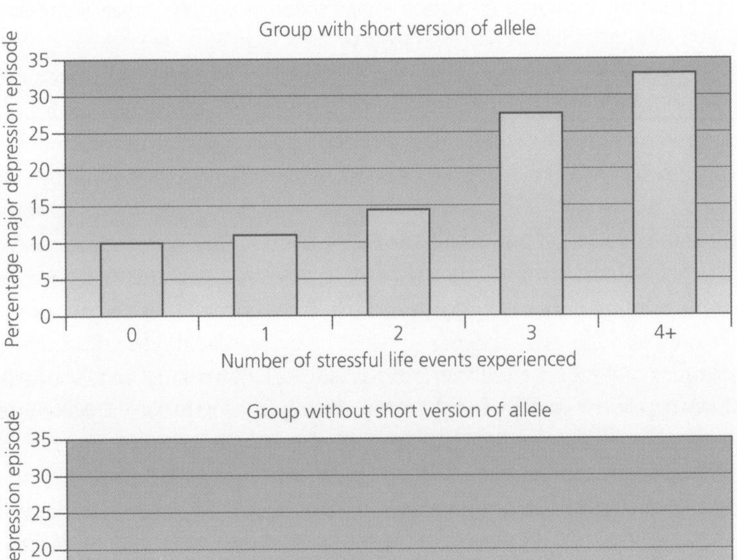

Figure 3.3 Findings from Caspi *et al.* (2003)

Method

Caspi used a **longitudinal study** to test whether genetics might lead individuals to suffer from depression as a result of environmental stress. The researchers focused on the 5-HTT gene because serotonin is known to be important in depression, and because selective serotonin re-uptake inhibitors (SSRIs) have been shown to be effective in treating depression.

847 participants were split into three groups, depending on the length of the alleles on their 5-HTT transporter gene.

Group 1 – two short alleles
Group 2 – one short and one long allele
Group 3 – two long alleles

Stressful life events occurring after the twenty-first birthday and before the twenty-sixth birthday were assessed using a life-history calendar. Past-year depression was assessed using a diagnostic interview schedule. A correlation was tested for between stressful life events and depression, between the length of the alleles and depression and an interaction between perceived stress and the length of the alleles. A further test was done to see if life events could predict an increase in depression over time among individuals with one or two short alleles.

Results

As you can see in Figure 3.3, as the number of stressful experiences the participants reported increased from 0 to 4, depression also significantly increased for the participants with the short version of the gene (top panel). But for the participants who did not have a short allele, increasing stress did not increase depression (bottom panel). Furthermore, for the participants who experienced four stressors over the past five years, 33 per cent of the participants who carried the short version of the gene became depressed, whereas only 17 per cent of participants who did not have the short version did.

Conclusion

While there is no direct relation between short alleles on the 5-HTT gene and depression, there is a relationship between these and incidences of stress and subsequent depression. The long alleles seem to protect against suffering depression as a result of stress.

Key terms

An **allele** is an alternative form of a gene (one member of a pair) that is located at a specific position on a specific chromosome.
A **longitudinal study** is an observational research method in which data is gathered for the same subjects repeatedly over a period of time.

Strengths and weaknesses of Caspi *et al.* (2003)

This was a very large cohort of males and females, and age was controlled in order to isolate the variable of number of stressful life events between the ages of 21 and 26. It was a natural experiment, with the naturally occurring independent variable being the length of the alleles. If the results are replicated, this would suggest high reliability.

Gene action is highly complex, and actions of other genes could not be controlled. While the stressful life events were standardised as employment, financial, housing, health and relationship, whether or not a participant experienced a certain event as stressful is highly personal.

The symptoms of depression were self-reported, which can be unreliable as individuals will differ in reporting their symptoms of depression. Some may inflate their symptoms whilst others may under-estimate them due to the subjective nature of self-reports.

The study showed a correlation between the presence of a 5-HTT short allele and depression but it is not possible to establish a cause–effect relationship. Genes contribute, to some extent, to behavioural traits and disorders but it is not clear how environmental factors influence genes. Environmental factors were included in the study (stressful events) but there is no evidence against the idea that it could be the stressful events (environmental factors) that made people depressed.

Young (2007): cognitive behavioural therapy with Internet addicts: treatment outcome and implications

Research has shown those who suffer from Internet addiction feel a sense of displacement when online and are unable to manage central aspects of their lives due to their growing preoccupation with being online. They start to miss important deadlines at work, spend less time with their family and slowly withdraw from their normal routines. Researchers have suggested using cognitive behavioural therapy (CBT) as the treatment of choice for Internet addiction.

Aim

To assess the usefulness and application of CBT in cases of Internet addiction. In particular, to examine client perceptions towards the therapy and assess targeted goals most associated with Internet addiction.

Procedure

Participants were 114 clients (65 male and 49 female) with mean ages of 38 years (males) and 46 years (females); 84 per cent were Caucasian, 5 per cent were African-American and 11 per cent were of Asian descent. All participants were seen through the Center for Online Addiction in the USA and were screened using the Internet Addiction Test (IAT). The IAT examines symptoms of Internet addiction, such as a user's ability to control online use and the extent of hiding or lying about online use. A client outcome questionnaire was administered after the third, eighth and twelfth online sessions and upon a six-month follow-up. Questions rated how effective counselling was at helping clients' achieve targeted treatment goals associated with Internet addiction recovery. Questions assessed motivation to quit abusing the Internet and ability to control online use amongst others.

Questions were rated along a five-point Likert scale (0=not at all; 5=extremely helpful) and assessed the quality of the counselling relationship, such as:

- 'Rate your ability to develop a supportive therapist–client relationship.'
- 'Rate the overall quality of the counselling environment.'
- 'Rate the overall quality of the counselling relationship.'

Questions also assessed the nature of the presenting problem and related outcome goals. such as:

- 'Rate how effective online counselling was at motivating you to abstain from abusing the Internet.'
- 'Rate your ability to control your computer use.'
- 'Rate how your ability to function in offline relationships has improved.'

To determine the validity and reliability of the questionnaire, a pilot test was carried out by other independent CBT experts.

Results

Table 3.1 Mean rating of some of the target goals from the client outcome questionnaire

Goal	Session 3	Session 8	Session 12	Post six months
Motivation to stop using online apps	4.22	3.96	4.54	4.36
Time management in using online apps	3.95	4.06	4.33	4.22
Relationship function	2.95	3.66	4.42	3.99

The table above shows the mean rating of some of the target goals from the client outcome questionnaire.

Conclusion

Results suggest that the majority of clients showed continuous improvement by the third session, effective symptom management by the eighth and twelfth sessions, and overall improved symptom maintenance upon six-month follow up. Specifically, clients were able to maintain motivation to quit abusing the Internet and improve online time management most effectively early in the counselling process. Upon six-month follow-up, most clients were able to maintain symptom management and continued recovery.

Strengths and weaknesses of Young (2007)

As this study relied upon self-reported data to gauge changes in online behaviour, the results may be biased. Self-reports may be inaccurate, so future studies should include that the reports be verified by relatives or friends close to the client to ensure greater reliability of self-reported data.

It addresses issues for those who may just want therapy online rather than face to face and so in this respect may actually encourage more individuals to access therapy than would have previously done so with more traditional types of therapy.

As the same standardised questionnaire was administered after the third, eighth and twelfth online sessions and upon a six-month follow-up, we can measure its reliability. All participants were given the same questions and same rating scale so the study can be said to have consistency and ease of replication.

The study identified a number of different types of Internet addiction but did not investigate the breakdown for each type of addiction and only focused on the therapy goals. Future studies should also examine if treatment differences exist using CBT to determine if outcomes vary along each type of addiction.

Issues and debates

The nature–nurture debate

Does an addiction begin due to a signal from the genes? Or does an addiction begin due to something a person encounters in their environment?

Supporters of the nature argument assume what is innate (things we are born with) is more influential than nurture (such as experience or the environment). So a male feels masculine because of his XY chromosomes rather than his upbringing. They believe the genes which we inherit from our parents determine who we are. MZ twins share 100 per cent of their genes, DZ twins share about 50 per cent of their genes, and it is assumed that twin pairs share the same environment. Therefore, if MZ twins are more alike than DZ twins, this must be due to genes.

Supporters of the nurture side of the argument believe humans are born as blank slates. We are all born identical and everything about us is shaped by our interactions with the environment. So depending on how you were brought up, you could end up a genius, an artist or a criminal. Everything about our personality – our intelligence, our shyness, our sense of humour, our aggression, etc. is 'programmed' into us by the world around us. There are many different influences on our behaviour (parents, friends, school, the media, etc.). The reason for individual differences amongst people is that everybody has a different set of environmental stimuli which shape their behaviour.

Psychological problems to explain the nature–nurture debate

The difficulty with addiction genes is that there are so many different genes at work in an addiction. There is not one specific gene that could be amended or removed to lower addiction risk. There are many different types of genes all working together that can influence whether someone starts using, likes using and continues to use.

Most of those steps are required in the path to an addiction. Genes may play a role in smoothing that path.

Dopamine, twin studies, adoption studies, all of these go a long way towards understanding addiction. However, what about adopted children of alcoholics who don't become alcoholics? Obviously, our environment has a role as well. If one child is raised in a house where addiction is rife, and one is raised never seeing a drug in their life, it is obvious who's more likely to be an addict. After all, you can't be an addict if you never get high and to get high, you need access to drugs, which means there have to be drugs in your environment.

This leads to another problem when it comes to 'inheriting' addiction. If you are raised by drug addicts, you might become one just by seeing so many drugs, as learning theories would dictate. When this is the case, it is not easy to tell whether nature or nurture was the decisive factor. There have also been cases of addiction/abuse where a change in environment was able to make all the problems go away. In the 1960s–1970s, thousands of soldiers in Vietnam became heroin addicts. They were experiencing traumatic events, plus Vietnam was a major producer of opium and heroin. However, when they returned to the United States (and a different environment), most veterans were able to clean up.

Some people experience a form of trauma while they are growing up. They live in chaotic households in which they feel as though they are in danger most or all of the time. They are worried, concerned and fearful, and they bring those feelings with them into adulthood. As they grow up, these children have higher rates of substance use and abuse. They use these substances as a form of self-medication, and in time, they could develop physical and psychological dependence issues on those substances. This is a nurture issue. These children do not develop addictions due to their genes. They are developing addictions due to an experience they have endured and survived.

Exam questions

1. With reference to either depression or addiction, explain how the incidence of mental health problems changes over time. (4)
2. With reference to either depression or addiction, explain how mental health problems may have a negative effect on individuals. (4)
3. Ben has been prescribed a course of antidepressants to help with his depression but wants to know more about how they will help him get better. Describe how antidepressants will improve Ben's mental health. (4)

4. Jim is about to go through CBT for his addiction to alcohol. His therapist believes Jim's alcohol addiction may have started due to him losing his job a few years ago. Describe how the therapist might use functional analysis to determine Jim's addiction. (4)

5. Linda suffers from depression and has struggled to prepare for her job interview as she believes she is not suited for the job and is wasting her time in even applying for it. Assess how far Beck's cognitive theory could explain Linda's depression. (9)

6. Joanne has been discussing her nicotine addiction with her friends. Alison believes Joanne smokes because both her parents do, whereas Amanda believes it is due to work pressures and the job Joanne is in. Assess how far genes and learning theories of addiction can explain Joanne's addiction. (9)

7. Explain how the study by Caspi *et al.* (2003) has increased our understanding of why stressful life events lead to depression in some people but not others. (3)

8. Compare the genetic explanation of depression with the genetic explanation of addiction. (6)

9. Outline the difference between physical and psychological dependence. (2)

10. Outline one strength and one weakness of the social learning theory explanation for addiction. (4)

End of chapter summary

You should now have an understanding of all the points below:

Understand the two mental health problems, unipolar depression and addiction, including:

- the symptoms and features according to the International Classification of Diseases (ICD) of depression and addiction
- how the incidence of mental health problems changes over time
- how mental health problems affect individuals and society
- the influence of genes as an explanation, including strengths and weaknesses of the explanation
- the use of cognitive theory as an explanation of depression, including strengths and weaknesses of the explanation
- the use of learning theory as an explanation of addiction, including strengths and weaknesses of the explanation
- the use of cognitive behavioural therapy (CBT) as a treatment, including strengths and weaknesses of the therapy
- the use of drugs as a treatment, including strengths and weaknesses of the treatment.

Understand the aims, procedures and findings (results and conclusions), and strengths and weaknesses of:

- Caspi *et al.* (2003): influence of life stress on depression: moderation by a polymorphism in the 5-HTT gene
- Young (2007): cognitive behavioural therapy with Internet addicts: treatment outcomes and implications.

Understand the nature and nurture debate, including:

- the term 'nature'
- the term 'nurture'
- the use of content, theories and research drawn from psychological problems to explain the nature and nurture debate.

Now test yourself answers

1. Unipolar depression is a constant mood disorder, whereas bipolar disorder involves fluctuations between high and low moods.
2. Girls.
3. Prevalence means how widespread or common something is.
4. Adrenaline.
5. Chromosome 11.
6. Abnormal behaviour which deviates from what is expected in society.
7. Low levels of serotonin produce low levels of noradrenaline and low levels of noradrenaline cause depression.
8. True.
9. 1960s.
10. Social learning theory.

Chapter 4
The brain and neuropsychology – how does your brain affect you?

This chapter deals with understanding the structure and function of the brain. Our brain is the most important and complex organ in our body and controls everything we do; without it, we would simply not function. Brain damage is directly linked to what we can and cannot do and provides an understanding of which parts of the brain control which bits of our behaviour.

The structure of the brain

The human brain contains about 100 billion neurons and weighs about three pounds. It controls our organs and flashes messages out to all the other parts of the body. All of our thoughts and feelings are also controlled by the brain. The brain and spinal cord make up the **central nervous system.**

The **cerebrum** is divided into four sections, which are the **frontal lobe, parietal lobe, occipital lobe**, and the **temporal lobe.**

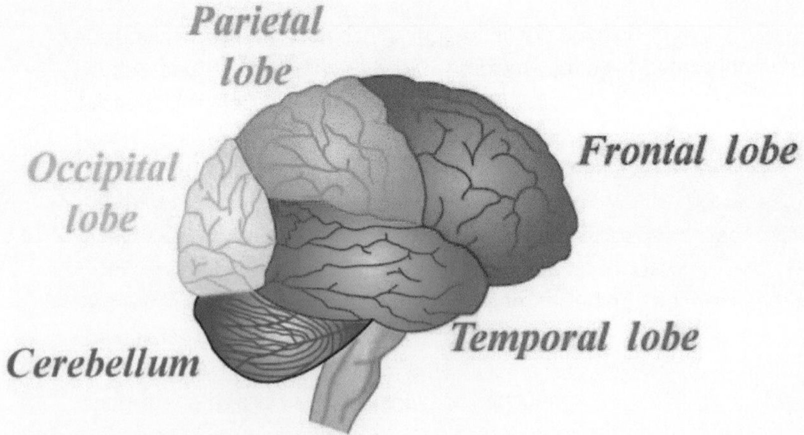

Figure 4.1 The structure of the brain

The **cerebellum** is a region of the brain that plays an important role in motor control. Like the cerebrum, the cerebellum is covered by cortex and consists of two hemispheres, each of which is divided into lobes.

Key terms

The **central nervous system** consists of the brain and spinal cord, which relay messages to the rest of the body.
The **cerebrum** is the largest part of the human brain and deals with higher levels of processing.
The **frontal lobe** is located at the front part of the brain.
The **parietal lobe** is located at the back of the frontal lobe and on top of the temporal lobe.
The **occipital lobe** is located at the very back part of the brain.
The **temporal lobe** is located at the sides, just below the temple.
The **cerebellum** is located at the posterior base of the brain.

The functions of the brain

Frontal lobe

We use our frontal lobe daily to make decisions, such as what to eat or drink for breakfast. It is involved in the control of voluntary movement and is necessary for being able to speak fluently and meaningfully. The most important portion of the frontal lobe is the prefrontal cortex.

Parietal lobe

The parietal lobe is involved in attention and motor control, in processing spatial location and in perceiving pain, touch and temperature. The parietal lobe is where information such as taste, temperature and touch are processed. If this area is damaged, we would not be able to feel sensations of touch.

Temporal lobe

The temporal lobe is located just above the ears and is involved in hearing, language processing and memory. Damage to the temporal lobe leads to failure to store new information and problems in understanding what others are saying to us. It receives sensory information such as sounds and speech from the ears and is key to being able to understand meaningful speech.

Occipital lobe

The occipital lobe is involved in processing visual information, such as colour, shape and motion. The visual cortex is located in this lobe and any damage here may cause blindness. The occipital lobe is important for being able to correctly understand what your eyes are seeing. These lobes have to be very fast to process the rapid information that our eyes are sending.

Cerebellum

The cerebellum is extremely important for being able to perform everyday voluntary tasks, such as walking and writing. It is also essential for being able to stay balanced and upright. Damage to it causes problems with balance and maintaining proper muscle coordination.

Now test yourself

1. Which two parts of the brain deal with movement?

Lateralisation of function in the hemispheres

Asymmetrical function

Our brain is divided into two **hemispheres**, which are connected to each other by the **corpus callosum**. These two hemispheres receive sensory inputs from the opposite side of our body. In other words, the left hemisphere processes information coming from the right side of the body, while the right hemisphere processes information coming from the left side of the body. The two hemispheres of the brain are connected to each other by a bundle of axons, called the corpus callosum. This connection allows the left and the right hemispheres to communicate and integrate information with each other.

The brain is **asymmetrical** and the split-brain design allows us to process many things at once. We owe our ability to multi-task to the hemispheric design of the brain. Like the human brain, many modern computers come with essentially two hemispheres, or dual core processors. When one processor is busy checking email, the other can be scanning for viruses. This is equivalent to how brain hemispheres work.

Key terms

Hemispheres represent each half of our brain.
The **corpus callosum** allows communication between the two hemispheres of the brain and is responsible for transmitting neural messages between them.
Asymmetrical means both hemispheres do not mirror each other exactly in terms of structure and function.

Role of left and right hemispheres

Lateralisation of brain function means that there are certain mental jobs that are mainly specialised to either the left or right hemisphere.

The left hemisphere handles tasks such as language, reading, writing, speaking, and arithmetic reasoning and understanding. Studies show that when we speak or do arithmetic calculations, activity increases in our left hemisphere.

The right hemisphere of our brain excels in visual perception, understanding spatial relationships, and recognising patterns, music and emotional expressions. People with damage to the right brain sometimes have difficulty recognising themselves in the mirror. Unlike the left hemisphere, our right hemisphere tends to process information as a whole.

Key term

Lateralisation means that there are certain mental processes that are specialised to one side or the other of our brains.

Lateralisation as an explanation of sex differences

Male brains are thought to be more lateralised than female brains. This means that, for certain activities, males use one hemisphere whereas women use both hemispheres. Males tend to use the right side of their brains more, whereas women use both sides equally.

In tasks needing spatial ability (e.g. map-reading, maze performance) in males the right hemisphere is shown to have high levels of activity, but in females both hemispheres are activated during spatial tasks. Females are better at some activities that require using both sides of the brain at the same time, such as understanding body language. This would also explain why it is thought that women can multi-task better than men.

Strengths and weaknesses of lateralisation as an explanation of sex differences between males and females

Research by Verma *et al.* (2013) revealed differences in the brain connectivity between the sexes. In women, most of the connections go between left and right across the two hemispheres, while in men most of the connections go between the front and the back of the brain. Verma states that, because the female connections link the left hemisphere, which is associated with logical thinking, with the right, which is linked with intuition, this could help to explain why women tend to do better than men at intuitive tasks.

Cutting and Clements (2006) confirmed that men and women do indeed use different parts of their brains when processing both language and visuospatial information. Distinct differences were evident between 30 male and female participants using an fMRI scan. During the language task, females showed more activation in both hemispheres than males, who were more left lateralised. The opposite pattern was found for the visuospatial task, with males showing more activation than females, whose activations were more right lateralised.

Lateralisation does not take into account other factors, such as culture. In countries that subscribe less strongly to gender-stereotyped beliefs about ability, women tend to perform better at science. These kinds of findings remind us that over-simplifying and over-generalising sex differences to just our brain structure is too limiting.

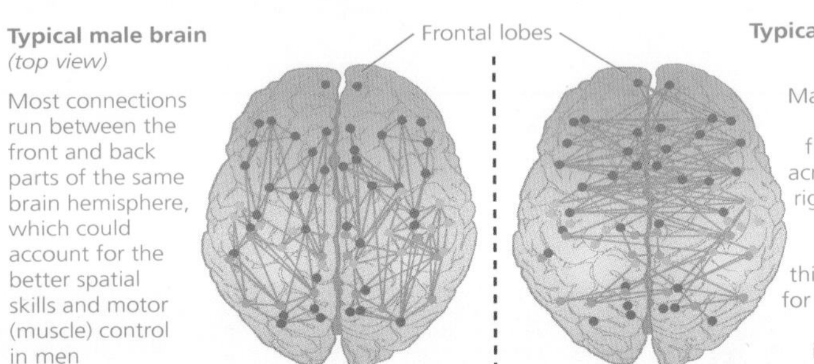

Figure 4.2 The male and female brain

Now test yourself

2. What would having symmetrical hemispheres in the brain mean?
3. Which hemisphere deals with map reading?

Neurons, synapses and the role of the central nervous system

Connecting to the central nervous system (CNS) are neurons that serve the body; these are either **sensory** or **motor neurons**. One important pathway running between the body and brain carrying messages both inwards and outwards is the spinal cord.

Key terms

Motor neurons carry information about movement out from the brain.

Sensory neurons carry sensory information inward to the CNS.

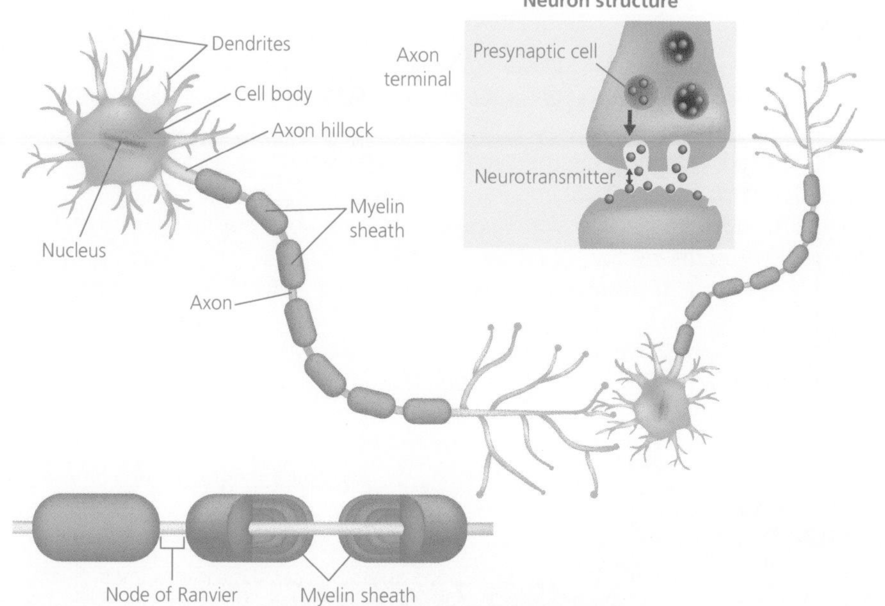

Figure 4.3 The structure of a neuron and synaptic transmission

Therefore, the role of the CNS is one of decision making and coordination. For simple reactions, such as touching a hot iron and moving your hand away, the spinal cord alone can generate a response. When information is more detailed or decision making more complex, however, the brain takes over the processing role. The brain communicates with the rest of the body through the nerve cells in the nervous system, telling different parts of the body what to do.

Neurons communicate with one another through **synapses**, where **neurotransmitters** are released and passed from the **axon terminal** to the **dendrite** of the receiving neuron. This allows the brain to process thoughts and memories. The neurotransmitter travels across the gap between the two neurons (the synapse) and upon reaching the other side attaches itself to receptor sites on the surface of the target neuron, like a key in a lock. The receptors sites are unique to each type of neurotransmitter and are shaped so that only one neurotransmitter can fit into them.

Synaptic transmission occurs when information is transmitted from the **axon** of the first neuron (presynaptic neuron) to the dendrites or cell body of the second neuron (postsynaptic neuron) by discharge of neurotransmitters. Neurotransmitters are stored in small containers (vesicles) located in knoblike structures (terminal buttons) on the axon tips.

The axon of the presynaptic neuron does not actually touch the dendrites of the postsynaptic neuron and is separated from them by a space called the synaptic cleft. Most of the released neurotransmitters bind with molecules at special sites, receptors, on the dendrites of the postsynaptic neuron. Molecules of the neurotransmitter that do not bind to receptors in the postsynaptic neuron are taken up again by the presynaptic neuron, a process called re-uptake.

Key terms

Synapses are small junctions (gaps) between neurons.

Neurotransmitters are chemical messengers that act between the neurons in the brain.

Axon terminals are the hair-like ends of the axon which pass information on to another neuron.

Dendrites are extensions that receive messages from other neurons to take to the cell body.

Synaptic transmission refers to how the nervous system transmits information across a 'synaptic gap' (the physical gap between nerve cells) from one neuron to another.

An **axon** is the part of the neuron that takes information away from the cell body towards the axon terminals.

Now test yourself

4. What connects the brain and the body and helps carry messages inwards and outwards?

Active learning

Match the terms below with the definitions A–F in the table:

Central nervous system (CNS) *Synapse* *Receptor*
Neuron *Neurotransmitter* *Brain lateralisation*

A – These are on the dendrites where the neurotransmitters are received. If the neurotransmitter 'fits', then the message is passed on; if it doesn't 'fit', the message is blocked.	**B** – These are cells that receive and transmit messages, passing the message from cell to cell through the brain. At one end, there are dendrites. From the nucleus, there is a long extension called an axon.
C – This is made up of the brain and spinal cord. It communicates with the rest of the body through the nerve cells in the nervous system, both receiving messages from the senses and telling different parts of the body what to do.	**D** – This is the extent to which each hemisphere of the brain is structurally different and is involved in different activities.
E – These are small gaps between neurons where neurotransmitters are released from the axon terminal of one neuron and are received at the receptor on the dendrite of the next neuron.	**F** – These are chemical messengers that act between the neurons in the brain. When a neuron is excited, it releases these into the synapse. If enough of them are received by the dendrites of the next neuron, it becomes excited.

The impact of neurological damage

Neurological damage can occur to nerves in your brain and spinal cord. Damage may cause an inability to sense chest pain, such as angina or heart attack, and can lead to disorders including epilepsy, Alzheimer's, Parkinson's disease and agnosia.

Visual agnosia is a rare condition characterised by the inability to recognise familiar objects, usually due to a lesion on the parietal and temporal lobes. These regions of the brain also store memories and are responsible for object association. If you have this condition, you can still think, speak and interact with the world. The following symptoms are typical of someone suffering from visual agnosia:

- Affected individuals will be unable to copy, draw or identify common objects such as a television.
- However, objects may be identified by touch, sound and/or smell. For example, affected individuals may not be able to identify a set of keys by sight, but can identify them upon holding them in their hands.
- They may not be able to recognise that pictures of the same object from different angles are of the same object.
- They may be unable to recognise the colour of an object.

The term **prosopagnosia** comes from the Greek words for 'face' and 'lack of knowledge'. Also known as face blindness, it is the inability to recognise faces, including one's own face. Other aspects of visual processing and decision making remain intact. The specific part of the brain associated with prosopagnosia is the fusiform gyrus, known for activating in response to seeing faces. Prosopagnosia often affects people from birth and is usually a problem a person has for most or all of their life.

The following symptoms are typical of someone suffering from prosopagnosia:

- Affected individuals will be unable to recognise family members, partners or friends.
- They may cope by using alternative strategies, such as remembering the way they walk, or their hairstyle, voice or clothing. These types of compensation strategies don't always work, particularly when meeting someone at a place or time where/when they are not used to seeing that person.
- They may avoid social interaction and develop a fear of social situations.
- They may also have difficulty forming relationships or experience problems with their career.
- Inability to recognise certain facial expressions, judge a person's age or gender, or follow a person's gaze.
- Following the plot of films or television programmes can be almost impossible because characters aren't recognisable.

Now test yourself

5. Someone who does not recognise their own car parked in a new road may be suffering from which condition?
6. Someone who wrongly sells cigarettes to an underage child may be suffering from which condition?

Key terms

Neurological damage refers to damage to our nervous system.
Visual agnosia is an inability to recognise objects using our eyes.
Prosopagnosia is a cognitive disorder of facial perception.

The impact of damage to the prefrontal cortex

The prefrontal cortex processes feelings of empathy, shame, compassion and guilt. Damage to this part of the brain causes a reduced ability for social emotions but leaves logical reasoning intact.

Scientists at the University of Iowa (1999) investigated two adults who suffered prefrontal cortex damage when they were very young children. These two individuals had severe behavioural problems, including impaired decision-making ability and defective moral reasoning.

The scientists found that these two people had normal intelligence, language skills, maths and problem-solving ability. However, they had problems with learning the rules and strategies of tests. For example, if they were given different rewards for selecting cards from four different decks of cards, they could not learn which deck of cards gave them the best reward.

The researchers also asked the subjects about real-life situations involving dilemmas and conflicts. The subjects were asked what would be the right thing to do if a man had to steal a drug to save his wife's life. The subjects were also asked about what they would do if two people disagreed on which TV show to watch. Both subjects failed to come up with solutions to these problems and could not even identify the problems in the situations. The scientists estimated that the subjects had the moral reasoning of ten-year-old children.

Studies

Damasio *et al.* (1994): the return of Phineas Gage: clues about the brain from the skull of a famous patient

People who suffer brain damage through accident, illness or injury have provided evidence of the effect of damage in different parts of the brain. For example, in 1848, an explosion whilst constructing a railway blew a metal rod through the face, skull and brain of Phineas Gage. He was stunned but regained full consciousness immediately and was able to talk and even walk with the help of his fellow workers. The 3 cm wide, 109 cm long metal rod landed 30 yards away. His personality subsequently changed as he became more impulsive and irritable and less responsible. His use of language was so shocking that women were advised not to stay long in his presence. His employers, who had once described Gage as their most 'efficient and capable man in their employment' now had to dismiss him due to his change in personality. Gage began to wander from one place to the next and was never able to hold down a job. He died 12 years after his original injury.

Aim

Using advanced technology that was not available to Gage's doctors at the time, Damasio *et al.* looked to create a 3D representation of Gage's skull to see where the iron rod may have passed through his skull and which parts of his brain were affected. This in turn would help Damasio *et al.* understand the changes in Gage's personality by seeing which parts of the brain had been damaged.

Method

Gage's skull, which had been kept at Harvard University, was photographed in order to provide an x-ray giving precise measurements, which could then be used to build a 3D replica model of his skull. This included possible entry and exit holes where the rod may have passed through. The reconstruction was painstakingly carried out using other evidence about possible infections Gage might have developed as the rod struck him. There were no antibiotics as these had not yet been developed so any damage to certain parts of his brain would have resulted in massive infection, which would not have been treatable back then and so would have resulted in his death. The researchers could therefore rule out the rod passing through these areas of his brain. Similarly, evidence from which of his teeth were missing based on the rod's trajectory gave important clues as to the angle it took when passing through his face. For example, they found his molar socket was still intact, although some of the tooth was missing. They narrowed possible routes down to five and, after comparing these five with normal brains, chose one as the most likely trajectory the rod would have taken.

Results

The researchers believed the most likely damage would have been through both the right and the left hemispheres of the frontal lobe in Gage's brain, and also, that no other areas of the brain other than the frontal lobe were affected by the accident. The rod would have passed through his left eye socket, damaging most of the white matter in his left hemisphere, resulting in loss in ability to pass messages via the neurons in this area. As the rod passed through his frontal lobes, it caused most damage on impact to the **ventromedial region**.

Conclusion

The researchers believed the changes in Gage's personality were down to damage to his ventromedial region, which deals with emotions and impulses, which he was no longer able to control.

Key term

The **ventromedial region** deals with risk, fear and self-control.

Strengths and weaknesses of Damasio *et al.* (1994)

Damasio *et al.* also had 12 other patients with similar brain damage in the frontal lobe. They displayed the same kinds of problems with emotions and impulses as Gage. This gives the results of this particular study some reliability as the findings were reinforced by these 12 other patients, suggesting there is a link between damage to the frontal lobes and negative emotional behaviour.

The findings give an insight into the effects that may emerge from accidents. Analysing and closely recording behaviour through case studies like Phineas Gage and others gives a better insight into specific characteristics and behavioural patterns of those individuals who may damage their frontal lobes in the future. This in turn has implications for treatment for these individuals and even supporting family members with knowledge about why a loved one has developed sudden changes in personality.

One of the main criticisms is that the data collected cannot necessarily be generalised to the wider population. Cases like this on one person do not reflect others and may just be unique to Phineas Gage. Cases of brain damage are quite minimal, and it is extremely rare to find people with the exact same parts of the brain affected.

Although modern technology was used, we are still talking about a replication from a skull originally damaged over 150 years ago. This means the researchers are still making best guesses as to what exactly happened, and we can never be fully sure that their conclusions are accurate, which lowers the validity of the study.

Sperry (1968): hemisphere deconnection and unity in conscious awareness

Epileptic seizures are caused by millions of brain cells firing excessively. Many of these seizures can involve both hemispheres and it was noticed by surgeons that if the hemispheres were separated, the seizures could be contained in one half of the brain, thereby causing less damage to the person.

Aim

Roger Sperry wanted to determine whether there are differences between the two hemispheres of human brains. He aimed to investigate the effects of hemisphere **deconnection** and to show that each hemisphere has its own conscious awareness and memory.

Procedure

Sperry used a laboratory and an independent measures design. The independent variable was whether the individual had a split brain or not. The dependent variable was that individual's performance on a number of tasks. All 11 participants suffered from epilepsy and had previously undergone surgery to deal with their condition. The surgery involved the corpus callosum being cut, resulting in the two hemispheres being deconnected (split). Sperry got the participants to carry out a number of visual and tactile tasks.

In the visual task, a picture was presented to either the left or right visual field and the participant had to simply describe what they saw. If a person is looking straight forward, everything to the left of their nose is the left visual field and everything to the right is their right visual field. An image was projected very quickly (one-tenth of a second) to the patient's left visual field (which is processed by the right hemisphere) or the right visual field (which is processed by the left hemisphere). When information is presented to one hemisphere in a split-brain patient, the information is not transferred to the other hemisphere (as the corpus callosum is cut). In a 'normal' brain, the corpus callosum would immediately share information between both hemispheres, giving a complete picture of the visual world.

For example, the word 'key' was projected so that it was only processed by the participant's right visual field (processed by the left hemisphere) and then the same, or different, image could be projected to the left visual field (processed by the right hemisphere).

In the tactile test, an object (which was out of sight) was placed in the patient's left or right hand and they had to either describe what they felt, or select a similar object from a series of alternate objects.

Results

Visual stimuli

When an object is displayed in the right visual field (thus processed in the left hemisphere), participants can describe it well in speech and writing. However, when an object is displayed in the left visual field (thus processed in the right hemisphere), participants struggled to say what they had seen.

Tactile stimuli

For objects placed in the right hand (thus processed in the left hemisphere), participants described the object clearly in both speech and writing.

For objects placed in the left hand (thus processed in the right hemisphere), participants made wild guesses and seemed unaware of the object in their hand.

When an object was displayed in the left visual field (thus processed in the right hemisphere), participants were able to draw it.

Conclusion

The research highlights a number of key differences between the two hemispheres and that they can work well independently of each other. Split-brain patients have a lack of cross-integration, where the second hemisphere does not know what the first hemisphere has been doing. The left hemisphere is dominant in terms of speech and language and the right hemisphere is dominant in terms of visual-motor tasks.

Now test yourself

7. Explain why spilt-brain patients cannot transfer information across both hemispheres.
8. Why did Sperry not need to create a control group for his study?

Key terms

Epileptic seizures can result in uncontrollable movements and eventually a loss of consciousness.
Deconnection refers to cutting the corpus callosum to separate any communication between the right and left hemisphere.

Strengths and weaknesses of Sperry (1968)

The **control group** used by Sperry were people with no history of epileptic seizures, so they could be seen as an inappropriate group to use as a comparison. As the split-brain patients suffered from epilepsy, it could be argued that it may have caused unique changes in the brain which could have influenced the results, so a more appropriate control group would have been people who had a history of epilepsy but had not had the split-brain procedure.

The data gathered from the split-brain research came from the patients being tested under artificial conditions, so it suffers from ecological validity. The findings would be unlikely to be found in a real-life situation because a person with a severed corpus callosum who had both eyes would be able to compensate for such a loss. Therefore, findings cannot be generalised to how split-brain patients function in everyday tasks.

The tasks were carried out in laboratory conditions, using specialised equipment and highly standardised procedures – for example, giving the same tasks to each participant and using standardised equipment. This has helped to enable the research to be checked for reliability. The same procedure has been used on a number of split-brain patients and the results on the left hemisphere being dominant for language has been found to be consistent.

The image was projected extremely quickly (one-tenth of a second) to one or both visual fields. This meant that the split-brain patients would not have time to move their eyes across the image and so the visual information would only be processed by one visual field (and one hemisphere) at a time, therefore increasing the internal validity of the research.

Key term

Control group refers to a comparison group who act as a benchmark against what is being tested.

Now test yourself

9. Sperry used standardised equipment and procedures. What does the term 'standardised' mean?

Issues and debates

How psychology has changed over time

Psychologists have developed a variety of techniques to study the brain so that they can better predict, control and explain behaviour. In the 1800s, Franz Gall devised an early method known as **phrenology**, and although it never produced significant results, it did set the stage for later methods of identifying the functions of particular parts of the brain.

In the 1930s, **prefrontal lobotomy** was discovered, which made violent or extremely emotional mental patients calm. This was, for a time, popular in treating severe behaviour problems. However, studies showed that prefrontal lobotomy had negative side effects: lobotomy patients showed little emotion and had trouble solving problems. Because of these side effects, and because of the ethical implications in cutting out part of the brain, lobotomies are no longer performed to treat mental disorders.

Electrical stimulation of the human brain was discovered next by Penfield (1975), who used brain stimulation to locate malfunctioning areas of the brain. His purpose was to find the areas of the brain causing a type of epilepsy in which a number of neurons begin to fire wildly. When the area was located, the malfunctioning part was removed.

The late 1970s and early 1980s then led to further advances, with CAT, PET and MRI scanning, which are still being used today.

A CAT (computer assisted tomography) scan is a cross-sectional image created by taking traditional x-ray images from many different directions and then using a computer to calculate the shapes and positions of objects blocking the x-rays. CAT scans were impossible before the availability of the modern computer.

The positron emission tomography (PET) technique allows scientists to view brain activity while the subject is engaged in a mental activity. The subject is given an injection of radioactive glucose. The PET scan records the areas of the brain that are actively utilising the radioactive glucose for energy.

Magnetic resonance imaging (MRI) uses magnetic fields to study chemical activity of brain cells. The magnetic field causes the nuclei of the brain cells to line up. This allows scientists to measure brain activity in subjects engaged in mental activity.

Now test yourself

10. Why are lobotomies no longer performed?

Key terms

Phrenology involved looking at bumps on people's skulls and tried to relate them to various behavioural characteristics.

Prefrontal lobotomy was the term given to disconnecting the frontal lobes from the rest of the brain.

Exam questions

1. Sakina fell down the stairs as she was not concentrating on what she was holding and has suffered damage to her right hemisphere. What tasks might Sakina now struggle with? (4)
2. Hassan keeps complaining of headaches and problems with his vision. After a scan it is found that there is damage to the lobe which is located at the very back of his brain. Which lobe is likely to have been damaged? (1)
3. Outline the main differences between visual agnosia and prosopagnosia. (4)
4. Mr and Mrs Wileman are planning a day out to the seaside and are arguing over who should drive and who should make the snacks whilst getting the kids ready. Using your knowledge of sex differences in brain lateralisation, explain who should do each task and why. (4)
5. Explain one improvement that could be made to the study by Sperry on spilt brains. (2)
6. Give one strength and one weakness of the study by Damasio *et al.* on Phineas Gage. (4)
7. Explain one extraneous variable from the study by Sperry which may have affected the validity of the findings. (2)
8. Imagine you are a participant in the study by Sperry. Describe one of the tasks you would have been asked to do. (3)
9. With reference to at least three methods of studying the brain, assess how the study of psychology has changed over time. (9)

End of chapter summary

You should now have an understanding of all the points below:

Know the structure and function of the brain, including:

- temporal lobe
- occipital lobe
- frontal lobe
- parietal lobe
- cerebellum.

Understand the lateralisation of function in the hemispheres, including:

- asymmetrical function
- role of the left hemisphere
- role of the right hemisphere
- role of the corpus callosum
- strengths and weaknesses of lateralisation as an explanation of sex differences between males and females.

Know what neurons and synapses are, including:

- function of neurotransmitters
- synaptic functioning
- how neurons and synapses interact
- the role of the central nervous system.

Understand the impact of neurological damage on cognitions and behaviour, including:

- the term 'visual agnosia'
- the term 'prosopagnosia'
- the symptoms of visual agnosia
- the symptoms of prosopagnosia
- the impact of damage to the prefrontal cortex.

Understand the aims, procedures and findings (results and conclusions), and strengths and weaknesses of:

- Damasio *et al.* (1994): the return of Phineas Gage: clues about the brain from the skull of a famous patient
- Sperry (1968): hemisphere deconnection and unity in conscious awareness.

Understand how psychology has changed over time, including:

- the use of content, theories and research drawn from studying the brain to explain how psychology has changed over time.

Now test yourself answers

1. Frontal lobe and cerebellum.
2. Both hemispheres would be exactly the same in terms of structure and function.
3. Right hemisphere.
4. The spinal cord.
5. Visual agnosia.
6. Prosopagnosia.
7. The information is not transferred to the other hemisphere (as the corpus callosum is cut).
8. Because we already know how the normal brain functions in people who don't have a split brain.
9. Standardised means the same.
10. As we now have more effective methods, such as CAT, PET and MRI to study the brain.

Chapter 5
Social influence – how do others affect you?

This chapter deals with how others influence us and how groups and individuals can alter our behaviour. We tend to believe that we make our own decisions and that we are fully in control of all we do; however, we conform and obey due to the presence of others.

Social influence is defined as 'all those processes through which a person or group influences the opinions, attitudes, behaviours and values of another person or group'. When we change what we believe, or how we behave, after observing the attitudes or actions of others, we are making this change because of social influence. It is a process of changing our attitudes, values and behaviours in response to the attitudes and behaviours of others.

Obedience, conformity, deindividuation and bystander effect

Obedience is where the individual gives up their free will and hands it over to an authority figure by doing what they say, even if they do not believe that what they are doing is correct. It is different from conformity because with conformity there is usually no direct instruction to conform – we just do. Also, we usually conform to our peer group, not to a higher authority.

Conformity is a process by which people's beliefs or behaviours are influenced by others within a group. Conformity can have either good or bad effects on people, from driving safely on the correct side of the road, to harmful drug or alcohol abuse.

Compliance is when the person conforms publicly (out loud) with the views or behaviours of the group, but continues privately to disagree. For example, a person may laugh at a joke that others are laughing at while privately not finding it very funny. Their personal views do not change.

Internalisation is the deepest level of conformity. When the views of the group are internalised, they are taken on at a deep and permanent level and become part of the person's own way of viewing the world. For example, a university student who becomes a vegetarian while sharing a flat with animal rights activists may keep those views and continue to be a vegetarian for the rest of their life.

Informational social influence is when we look to others to see what response they will give, and assume that theirs is the correct response. If everyone else gives the same response, we assume they must all be correct. We are looking for information, because we have none. We are most likely to use informational social influence when a situation is ambiguous and we are uncertain about what to do so are more likely to depend on others for the answer, especially if they are an expert.

Normative social influence is when we know that their answer/behaviour is wrong, but we go along with it anyway. We are conforming to the group norm – behaviour which is showed by all members of a group and which we must show if we want to be accepted by that group. Normative social influence usually results in public compliance, doing or saying something without believing in it.

Deindividuation is when people lose their sense of individual identity. Most individuals would normally refrain from aggression because they do not want to be held to blame for their actions – but in situations such as crowds, social restraints and personal responsibility are perceived to be lessened, so displays of aggressive behaviour occur. Deindividuation can lead to a loosening up of an individual's self-restraint, and is used to explain some types of mob behaviours, such as rioting and lynching.

It can be said that, because of normative social influence, deindividuation causes people to unquestioningly follow group norms instead of personal norms, which sometimes leads individuals to display aggressive behaviour.

The cause for social psychologists to begin to study how bystanders react during emergency situations was due to the famous case of Kitty Genovese, who was attacked and murdered in front of her Queens, New York apartment in 1964. Kitty's unfortunate attack lasted 45 minutes and was witnessed by 38 residents, who did not assist by calling police or trying to stop her attacker. Kitty's death helped establish the **bystander effect**.

Key terms

Obedience can be defined as following the rules set by a recognised authority, who may punish you for disobedience.

Conformity involves changing your behaviour or belief in order to fit in with others.

Compliance is the lowest level of conformity. Here a person changes their public behaviour, the way they act, but not their private beliefs.

Internalisation is when a person adopts the viewpoints and attitudes of a group and makes them their own because they believe the group's viewpoint.

Informational social influence refers to situations in which we conform to others because we do not know the right answer.

Normative social influence refers to situations in which we conform because we do not want to stand out from the crowd and need to feel normal.

Deindividuation can be described as a psychological state in which a person has a reduced sense of individuality and personal responsibility, due to the anonymity of being in a crowd of people.

Bystander effect is where individuals are less likely to offer help to a victim when other people are present.

Now test yourself

1. Which form of social influence involves following authority figures?
2. People often turn to experts for help as they have more knowledge. Which type of social influence is this?
3. The witnesses to the murder of Kitty Genovese were displaying which type of social influence?

Personal factors affecting bystander intervention

Empathy

We are more likely to help others we empathise with as it will remove the unpleasant feeling we are having watching them suffer. It reduces our levels of stress and allows us to avoid any feelings of guilt that might arise through not helping.

Similarity

We are more likely to feel empathy if we are similar to the person who is suffering – the greater the similarity the greater the empathy, and vice versa. It makes it easier to identify with the person in need, i.e. 'it could be happening to me'.

Mood

Generally, those in a good mood are more likely to help than those in a bad mood. When we feel good after succeeding in a given task, we are more likely to try and help those who failed in the same task. Similarly, if we hear good news or are just enjoying the weather, we are more likely to feel optimistic towards others and help them. Conversely, if we are in a bad mood, we tend to direct all our energy and attention inwards towards us rather than outwards towards helping others.

Competence

Our ability to help others and whether we feel we can or not also determines our actions. Someone who is trained in first aid is more likely to help than someone who has no training. Similarly, we are aware that other people are present and may be afraid of being evaluated negatively if they react (fear of social blunders).

Now test yourself

4. Megan feels she is not able to give assistance to the person who has collapsed. Which personal factor is this an example of?

Situational factors affecting bystander intervention

Diffusion of responsibility

Diffusion of responsibility implies that bystanders do not react because they feel that other bystanders will respond to the emergency situation and give appropriate assistance. This phenomenon only requires one bystander and increases in larger groups and decreases in smaller groups.

Pluralistic ignorance relates to our reaction to the incident by calculating other onlookers' responses to the incident. If the bystander sees others not helping, then they will not help either, because they assume that the other onlookers think it is not an emergency. This misconception of others' values causes the group members to act in ways that differ from what they believe in. Pluralistic ignorance is an error in our estimation of the beliefs of other people. We guess at the group members' beliefs and norms based upon our observations, and our guess is wrong.

Attention

According to Latane and Darley, we tend to go through the stages below, which will determine whether we help or not:

1. Notice the situation (if you are in a hurry, you may not even see what is happening).
2. Interpret the situation as an emergency (e.g. people screaming or asking for help, which could also be interpreted as a family quarrel, which is none of your business).
3. Accept some personal responsibility for helping even though other people are present.
4. Consider how to help (based on how competent you think you are).
5. Decide how to help (based on observing how others are helping).

If a bystander stops at any one of these steps, they are less likely to provide help. Most stop at stage 3 and decide it is not our responsibility.

Now test yourself

5. According to Latane and Darley, if we do not think the situation is an emergency, are we more or less likely to help?

Key terms

Diffusion of responsibility is a phenomenon related to the bystander's sense of responsibility to aid, and decreases when there are more witnesses present.

Pluralistic ignorance relates to our interpretation of the situation on how others are interpreting the situation.

Conformity to majority influence

Researchers have tried to discover if there are personality types which are more likely to conform or indeed whether it is the situation that causes an individual to conform.

Personal factors affecting conformity

Rotter (1966) refers to individual differences in how we see the world: this is called the **locus of control**. It refers to the way we see the world and our ability to control what happens to us. There are two extremes – we are likely to lie somewhere between them.

Internal locus of control – these people believe they can control their lives and succeed in difficult and stressful situations. They believe they can influence events in their life, e.g. a promotion at work is due to their hard work!

External locus of control – these people believe things happen to them; they focus on fate and luck. This person may think that they got a promotion at work because their boss was in a good mood, or their star signs were positive that day.

Key terms

Locus of control relates to our interpretation of how much control we have in our lives.
Those with an **internal locus of control** feel they are responsible for the events that happen to them.
Those with an **external locus of control** see the things that happen to them throughout their lives as caused by other people or events.

Situational factors affecting conformity

Asch carried out a number of important experiments investigating conformity in the 1950s. He wanted to investigate whether people would conform to the majority in situations where an answer was obvious. In Asch's original classic study (1951), there were 5–7 participants per group. Each group was presented with a standard line and three comparison lines. Participants had to say aloud which comparison line matched the standard line in length. In each group, there was only one true participant; the remaining six were **confederates**. The confederates were told to give the incorrect answer on 12 out of 18 trials. True participants conformed on 32 per cent of the critical trials where confederates gave the wrong answers. Additionally, 75 per cent of the sample conformed to the majority on at least one trial.

Size of the majority

Asch altered the number of confederates to see what might happen. The larger the number of confederates, the more people conformed, but only up to a certain point.

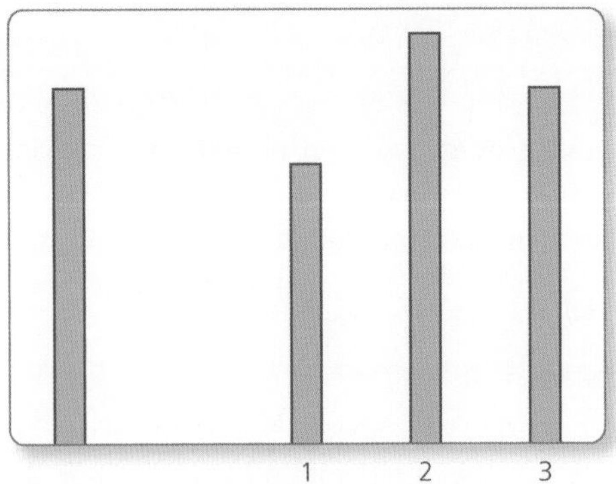

Figure 5.1 The lines used in Asch's conformity experiment

With just one other confederate in the group, conformity was 3 per cent, with two others it increased to 13 per cent, and with three or more it was 32 per cent. However, conformity did not increase much after the group size was about four. Because conformity does not seem to increase in groups larger than four, this is considered the optimal group size.

Unanimity

A person is more likely to conform when all members of the group agree and give the same answer. When one other person in the group gave a different answer from the others, and the group answer was not unanimous, conformity dropped. Asch (1951) found that even the presence of just one confederate going against the majority choice can reduce conformity as much as 80 per cent.

Task difficulty

When the task was made more difficult by making the lines more similar in length, it was harder to judge the correct answer and conformity increased. When we are uncertain, it seems we look to others for confirmation.

Key term

A **confederate** is an actor, or stooge, who has been asked to behave in a certain way in the study by the researcher to see how the real participants react.

Now test yourself

6. What was the percentage of Asch's participants that never gave the wrong answer?
7. What did Asch find was the optimal group size?

Obedience to authority

Milgram conducted a series of classic experiments to investigate how obedient participants would be when following orders which would mean breaking their moral code and harming another person.

Participants were introduced to 'Mr Wallace' (an actor) and were assigned to roles of either 'teacher' or 'learner'. The study was fixed so that Mr Wallace was always the learner and the participant was always the teacher. Mr Wallace was strapped into a shock generator and the teacher and learner were placed either side of a screen so that they could hear but not see each other. The participants asked the learner questions and were told to administer electric shocks of increasing voltage, up to 450 volts each time he made an error. (No shocks were administered, and no harm came to Mr Wallace, although the real participant was not aware of this.) The experimenter was in the room overseeing the operation and was dressed in a white lab coat. When the 'learner' started to make errors and the 'teacher' began to worry, the experimenter used 'prods' which reminded them of the need to continue.

All of the participants gave Mr Wallace at least 300 volts (more volts than you would achieve from the mains supply in Britain). Sixty-five per cent gave the maximum 450 volts to an apparently dead Mr Wallace. Most participants were obviously distressed by the task and some wept and begged in distress, obviously believing that they had killed Mr Wallace. When interviewed, the participants explained that they did not feel that they were able to stop when the experimenter ordered then to continue. The study clearly shows the power of authority over our behaviour.

Now test yourself

8. What percentage of Milgram's participants went all the way to 300 volts?

Personal factors affecting obedience

Authoritarian personality

Psychologists questioned whether the obedience in Milgram's study occurred due to situational factors, for example, uniform and location, or dispositional factors, such as a particular personality characteristic.

Adorno *et al.* (1950) felt that personality rather than situation could explain obedience. He proposed that there was such a thing as an **authoritarian personality**.

One of the various characteristics of the authoritarian personality is that the individual is hostile to those who are of inferior status, but obedient of people with high status.

Elms and Milgram (1966) wanted to see if the obedient participants in Milgram's research were more likely to display authoritarian personality traits, in comparison to disobedient participants. Their sample consisted of 20 obedient participants, who administered the full 450 volts, and 20 disobedient participants, who refused to continue. Each participant completed Adorno's **F scale**, to measure their level of authoritarian personality.

Elms and Milgram found that the obedient participants scored higher on the F scale in comparison to disobedient participants. In addition, the results revealed that obedient participants were less close to their fathers during childhood and admired the experimenter in Milgram's experiment, which was the opposite for disobedient participants.

Key terms

Those with an **authoritarian personality** favour strictness and admire authority figures.

The **F scale** (F stands for fascist) was a questionnaire used by Adorno to measure how much of an authoritarian personality someone has.

Situational factors affecting obedience

Proximity of learner

Because the learner was in another room and could not be seen, it was easier for the teacher to ignore their pain. Even though they could hear his cries of pain, they could not actually see him, which made it a case of out of sight, out of mind.

Proximity of the authority figure

People are more likely to obey an authority figure who is nearby. In Milgram's study, the experimenter was in the same room as the participant. If the authority figure is distant, it is easier to resist their orders. When the experimenter instructed and prompted the teacher by telephone from another room, obedience fell to 20.5 per cent. Many participants cheated and missed out shocks or gave less voltage than ordered to by the experimenter.

Legitimate authority figure

Milgram's experimenter (Mr Williams) wore a laboratory coat, which was a symbol of scientific expertise, giving him a high status. But when the experimenter dressed in everyday clothes as part of one of Milgram's variation experiments, obedience was very low. The uniform of the authority figure can give them high status, which makes us want to obey them.

Lack of social support

The teachers had no-one to support them. They had two people making demands: the experimenter asking them to continue, and the learner asking them to stop. With no-one to help them decide what to do, it is easier just to obey the higher authority.

Prestigious university

Milgram's obedience experiment was conducted at Yale, a prestigious university in America. The high status of the university gave the study credibility and respect in the eyes of the participants, thus making them more likely to obey. When Milgram moved his experiment to a set of rundown offices rather than the impressive Yale University, obedience dropped to 47.5 per cent. This suggests that status of location affects obedience.

Now test yourself

9. Why would the location be a factor in explaining why participants obeyed in Milgram's study?
10. When the experimenter instructed the teacher by telephone, obedience fell to 20.5 per cent. How much of a drop is this from the percentage in Milgram's original experiment?

Active learning

Explaining the results of Milgram's obedience studies – why people obey

Draw an arrow from each factor to the appropriate definition.

Buffers make it easier for you to obey	Anything (e.g. the wall) that prevents those who obey from being aware of the full impact of their actions
Prods/prompts	Participants both drew lots at the start so had an equal chance of being teacher or learner
Slippery slope	Generator switches only went up in small increments (15 volts) so participants found it easier to obey
Personal responsibility	Many participants asked whose responsibility it was if the learner was harmed and showed visible relief when the experimenter took responsibility
Seen as a fair experiment	'You must continue, the experiment requires that you continue'

The behaviour of crowds

When people are alone, their behaviour can be different to when they are part of a crowd, and sometimes this change in behaviour can even lead to violence. However, in situations where people are acting positively, such as at music concerts, the likelihood of **pro-social behaviour** occurring is high. This is because, when there are large numbers of people acting in a pro-social way, the behaviour may be repeated. Pro-social behaviours are those intended to help other people. In the music concert example, we want everyone to have a good time and so act in a peaceful way that looks after the welfare of others through pro-social behaviour.

According to deindividuation, the anonymity and excitement of the crowd make individuals lose a sense of individual identity. As a result, crowd members cease to evaluate themselves, and may become irrational and irresponsible. All of this makes the crowd fickle, explosive and prone to anti-normative and disinhibited behaviour. Zimbardo sees people in crowds as being anonymous, with lessened awareness of individuality and a reduced sense of guilt, or fear of punishment. The bigger the crowd, the more this will be the case. The loss of individuality relieves the individual of moral restraints, and they become submerged within the group and capable of **anti-social behaviour**.

Crowds give you the opportunity to hide and also allow you to share the blame, reducing the sense of individual responsibility. Uniforms and war paint also help hide your true identity. Even sunglasses can support aggressive attitudes as they hide the eyes, a very important part of the individual.

Views like these have given crowds a bad name and those in authority may treat all crowds as having a mob mentality. This may have contributed to the Hillsborough disaster, which occurred at the ground of Sheffield Wednesday Football Club on 15 April 1989. Mismanagement by police and officials allowed thousands of Liverpool supporters into already overcrowded pens, a fatal mistake that 'directly followed from a [false] interpretation by South Yorkshire Police that they were dealing with a violent crowd pitch invasion, rather than a problem of safety and overcrowding'. As a result, the pens became terribly overcrowded, with no means of escape due to perimeter fencing set up to prevent pitch invasions. The resulting crush cost the lives of 96 people and resulted in 730 injured.

Key terms

Pro-social behaviour is characterised by a concern for the rights, feelings and welfare of other people.

Anti-social behaviour is characterised by aggressive and sometimes violent behaviour.

Ways to prevent blind obedience to authority figures

Blind obedience is essentially doing something because you are told to; you follow the rules because they are the rules. There are a number of factors that can help individuals show less blind obedience to authority.

Proximity

Milgram wanted to see if having the experimenter in the room affected the level of obedience, so this was carried out with the experimenter in touch by phone. When the experimenter is not face-to-face with the participant, it is easier not to obey. Physical presence was an important force in maintaining levels of obedience, but when the distance between an individual and authority is greater, their authority is lessened.

Social support from others

If you are part of a group that has been commanded to carry out immoral actions, find an ally in the group who shares your perceptions and is willing to join you in opposing the objectionable commands. In one of Milgram's conditions, the naïve subject was one of a three-person teaching team. The other two were actually confederates who – one after another – refused to continue shocking the victim. Their defiance had a liberating influence on the subjects, so that only 10 per cent of them ended up giving the maximum shock.

Question the authority's legitimacy

We often give too wide a berth to people who project a commanding presence, either by their demeanour or by their mode of dress, and follow their orders even in contexts irrelevant to their authority. For example, one study found that wearing a fireman's uniform significantly increased a person's persuasive powers to get a passer-by to give change to another person, so he could feed a parking meter.

Independent thinking

When instructed to carry out an act you find objectionable, even by a legitimate authority, stop and ask yourself: 'Is this something I would do on my own initiative?' The answer may well be 'No', because, according to Milgram, moral considerations play a role in acts carried out under one's own steam, but not when they come from an authority's commands.

Do not even start what you cannot finish

In Milgram's experiments, the shock generator went up in 15-volt intervals and was the beginning of a step-by-step, escalating process of entrapment. The further you move along the continuum of increasingly destructive acts, the harder it is to remove yourself from the commanding authority's grip, because to do so is to admit the fact that the earlier acts of obedience were wrong.

Key term

Blind obedience is unquestionable or complete obedience without giving any thought, regardless of how devastating the consequences are.

Studies

Piliavin *et al.* (1969): good Samaritanism: an underground phenomenon?

Aim

The aim of this study was to conduct a field experiment to investigate the effect of several different variables on who responded to help, the speed of responding and the likelihood of responding. The main focus of the research was to investigate the effect of the type of victim (drunk or ill) and the ethnicity of victim (black or white) on the speed and frequency of the response and the ethnicity of the responder.

Importantly, the field experiment also investigated the impact of the presence of a model (someone who offers help first), as well as the relationship between the size of the group and frequency of helping.

Method

The participants were approximately 4,450 men and women travelling on a particular stretch of the New York underground system between 11 am and 3 pm on weekdays during the period of 15 April to 26 June 1968. Two particular trains were selected for the study. The trains were chosen because they did not make any stops between 59th Street and 125th Street. This means that for about 7.5 minutes the participants were a captive audience to the emergency. Therefore, a single trial was a non-stop, 7.5-minute journey in either direction.

There were four groups of confederates consisting of four students, two male and two females, who boarded the train. The procedure was always the same: the female confederates took seats and kept notes as unobtrusively as possible, while the male 'victim' and male model (potential 'helper') stood near a pole in the centre of the train and acted as the victim and model. The victims in all conditions were dressed identically. The 'drunk' victim carried a bottle of alcohol and smelled of alcohol; the 'ill' victim carried a cane. There was only one black confederate (reducing the number of black trials that were conducted).

As the train passed the first station (approximately 70 seconds after departing), the victim staggered forward and collapsed. Until receiving help, he remained motionless on the floor, looking at the ceiling. If he received no help by the time the train slowed to a stop, the model helped him to his feet. At the stop, the team got off and waited separately until other passengers had left the station before proceeding to another platform to board a train going in the opposite direction for the next trial.

There were four different helping conditions used in both 'drunk' and 'cane' situations:

1. Critical area – early. The model stood in the critical area and waited until after the train passed the fourth station, and then helped the victim (approx. 70 seconds after collapse).

2. Critical area – late. The model stood in the critical area and waited until after the train passed the sixth station before helping the victim (approx. 150 seconds after collapse).
3. Adjacent area – early. The model stood a little further away, next to the critical area, and waited until after the train passed the fourth station, and then helped the victim
4. Adjacent area – late. The model stood in the adjacent area and waited until after the sixth station before helping.

Results

The cane victim received spontaneous help on 62 out of the 65 trials, and the drunk victim received spontaneous help on 19 out of 38 trials.

On 60 per cent of the 81 trials where spontaneous help was given, more than one person offered help. Once one person had started to help, there were no differences for different victim conditions (black/white, cane/drunk) on the number of extra helpers that appeared. The race of the victims made no significant difference to helping behaviour, but there was a slight tendency for same-race helping in the drunken condition. It was found that 90 per cent of helpers were male.

It was also found that 64 per cent of the helpers were white; this was what would be expected based on the racial distribution of the carriage.

More comments were obtained on drunk than cane trials and most of these were obtained when no-one helped until after 70 seconds; this could be due to the discomfort passengers felt in sitting inactive in the presence of the victim, perhaps hoping that others would confirm that inaction was appropriate.

The following comments came from women passengers: 'It's for men to help him'; 'I wish I could help him – I'm not strong enough'; 'I never saw this kind of thing before – I don't know where to look'; 'You feel so bad that you don't know what to do.'

Conclusions

Where a model assists a victim early, it elicits further help from bystanders. Helping behaviour is not affected by proximity to the victim.

An individual who appears ill is more likely to receive help than someone who seems drunk.

With mixed groups of men and women, men are more likely than women to help a male victim.

People are more likely to help victims of the same race, especially if they are drunk.

People carry out a cost–reward analysis before deciding whether or not to help a victim. Men are more likely to help a male victim than women; the costs of not helping are lower for women (it is not a woman's role).

Strengths and weaknesses of Piliavin *et al.* (1969)

Participants were unaware that they were taking part in an experiment; therefore, they could not consent to take part and it was also not possible to withdraw from the study or be debriefed. Furthermore, seeing a victim collapse may have been stressful for the participants. They also may have felt guilty if they did not help, so leading to psychological harm.

Similarly, the participants are being deceived because they are unaware that it is not a genuine emergency. Participants were also not debriefed as this would have been almost impossible.

A problem with field experiments is that they are more difficult to control than laboratory experiments. For example, we could question whether travellers on the trains saw more than one trial. Field experiments are also more difficult to replicate and more time-consuming and expensive.

A main strength of the study has to be its high level of **ecological validity**. The study was done in a true-to-life environment and consisted of an incident which could, and does, happen. However, some of the participants were very close to the victim and were in a situation where they could not escape. This is often unlike many other emergency situations we come across and this may be one of the reasons why diffusion of responsibility did not occur.

The sample size was also very large, and we would assume a fairly representative sample of New Yorkers. The researchers should therefore be able to generalise their findings to the target population.

Key term

Ecological validity refers to whether the results can be applied to real-life situations.

Haney, Banks and Zimbardo (1973): a study of prisoners and guards in a simulated prison

Aim(s)

The aim of the study was to investigate the effects of being assigned to the role of either a prison guard or a prisoner. Haney, Banks and Zimbardo (1973) were interested in finding out whether the brutality reported among guards in American prisons was due to the personalities of the guards or had more to do with the prison environment.

Procedure

To study the roles people play in prison situations, Haney, Banks and Zimbardo converted a basement of the Stanford University psychology building into a mock prison.

The participants were respondents to a newspaper advertisement, which asked for male volunteers to participate in a psychological study of 'prison life' in return for payment of $15 per day. Twenty-four men were selected after being judged to be the most physically and mentally stable; they were predominantly middle class and white. The main data was qualitative and was obtained using video, audiotape and direct observation. Participants were told that they would be randomly assigned to the roles of prisoner or guard and they agreed to play these roles. They were also made aware that they would be under constant surveillance through observations, video and audio recordings.

The guards were to 'maintain the functioning' of the prison and believed that the purpose of the study was to observe the prisoners' behaviour. The only direct instruction was that physical punishments were not to be used on prisoners.

The guards' uniform consisted of a plain khaki shirt and trousers, a whistle, a police night stick and reflecting sunglasses, which made eye contact impossible.

The prisoners' uniform consisted of a loose-fitting muslin smock with an identification number, no underwear, rubber sandals and a hat made from a nylon stocking.

The prisoners' uniforms were designed to de-individuate the prisoners and to be humiliating. They also wore an ankle chain, which was a constant reminder of the oppressiveness of the environment. The stocking cap removed any distinctiveness associated with hair length, colour and style. The ill-fitting uniforms made the prisoners feel awkward in their movements; the prisoners were forced to assume unfamiliar postures, more like those of a woman than a man.

The prisoner participants were unexpectedly 'arrested' at their homes. A police officer then charged them with suspicion of burglary or armed robbery, advised them of their rights, handcuffed them, thoroughly searched them and drove them in the back of a police car to the police station. Here they had their fingerprints and photographs taken and were put in a detention cell. Each prisoner was then blindfolded and driven to the mock prison. Throughout this arrest procedure, the police officers involved maintained a formal, serious attitude, and did not tell the participants that this had anything to do with the mock prison study.

Each prisoner was stripped and made to stand alone and naked in the 'yard'. After being given their uniform, the prisoner was put in his cell and ordered to remain silent. The warden read them the rules of the institution (developed by the guards and the warden), which were to be memorised and had to be followed. Prisoners were to be referred to only by the number on their uniforms, also in an effort to depersonalise them.

Three times a day prisoners were lined up for a 'count' (one on each guard work-shift). The original purpose of the 'count' was to establish that all prisoners were present, and to test them on the knowledge of the rules and their ID numbers. The first 'counts' lasted only about ten minutes but as conditions in the prison deteriorated, they increased in length until some lasted for several hours.

Self-evaluations using questionnaires and tests were completed by prisoners and guards over the duration of the study in order to assess the individuals' moods and personalities.

The experiment was terminated on day six, eight days earlier than scheduled. The prisoners were extremely pleased at this, but the guards were not as happy.

Results

Within hours of beginning the experiment, some guards began to harass prisoners. They behaved in a brutal manner, apparently enjoying it. Other guards joined in, and other prisoners were also tormented. As the prisoners became more compliant, the guards became more aggressive and assertive. They demanded ever greater obedience from the prisoners. The prisoners were dependent on the guards for everything so tried to find ways to please the guards, such as telling tales on fellow prisoners.

The rules were modified or ignored by the guards. They also forgot about privileges, such as movies. None of the guards were ever late to work, and some remained on duty voluntarily after their shift had ended, receiving no pay for their time.

Five prisoners had to be released early due to extreme emotional reactions; for example, crying, extreme depression, anxiety or rage. For four of these prisoners, the symptoms began as early as day two and they were released. The fifth participant required treatment for a rash covering his body before he was released. Other prisoners requested a lawyer to get them out of the prison. After four days, prisoners attended a 'parole' meeting, where three out of five said they would give up their money (the incentive to take part) if it would get them out of the prison.

Some guards were fair, others became very cruel and some were quite passive and did not exercise power over the prisoners.

Conclusion

The findings support the situational explanation of behaviour rather than the personality one. The guards had shown no signs of being aggressive upon selection, but once in the prison, the environment was an important factor in creating the guards' aggressive behaviour.

Strengths and weaknesses of Haney, Banks and Zimbardo (1973)

A main strength of the study was the way it managed to maintain some degree of control and some ecological validity. The guards and prisoners were randomly allocated and were selected using strict criteria and so the situation was very tightly controlled. The researchers went to great extremes in making the study as true to life as possible – for example, in the way that they had the prisoners arrested from their homes, demonstrating ecological validity.

There are many ethical criticisms, including lack of fully informed consent by participants, as Haney, Banks and Zimbardo themselves did not know what would happen over the two weeks. The prisoners did not consent to being 'arrested' at home. Participants playing the role of prisoners were not protected from psychological harm, experiencing incidents of humiliation and distress. However, in the researchers' defence, extensive group and individual debriefing sessions were held, and all participants returned post-experimental questionnaires several weeks, then several months later, and then at yearly intervals.

As the sample comprised US male students, it lacks population validity and so findings cannot be applied to those from other countries. For example, America is an **individualist culture** (where people are generally less conforming) and the results may be different in **collectivist cultures** (such as Asian countries). Similarly, since the experiment was conducted using 24 normal, healthy, male college students who were predominantly middle class and white, we have to be careful generalising the results to other people.

Key terms

Individualistic cultures are characterised by individualism, which is the emphasis of the individual over the entire group.
Collectivist cultures emphasise family and work group goals above individual needs or desires.

Issues and debates

Social and cultural issues in psychology

One social issue in psychology is: what causes crowds to engage in anti-social behaviour, such as fighting and rioting? Hundreds of rioters descended on the centre of Manchester in 2011 and began looting shops. The riots were planned and organised via social media and said to be caused by anger and poverty. Eyewitnesses described that 'everyone' was doing it, men, women and children. As people rioted and looted, they covered their faces and wore masks. When the police intervened, the rioters clashed with them, fought them and flaunted their looted items.

Deindividuation can help explain the riots as a large number of participators used social media to arrange where to meet. When social media is employed, people often say/suggest things they would not in real life as it does not seem real, so they lose their sense of self and also, therefore, their sense of responsibility for their actions as they believe they are anonymous. By using social media, this also allows the strength of the message to be increased as it can be passed to many more people, who then joined in the riots.

Rioters were wearing masks and/or hoods in an attempt to hide their identity; they thought they could not be identified and so they were not accountable for their actions. The idea of deindividuation has also been supported by Haney, Banks and Zimbardo's research, which found that when participants were assigned a number rather than a name as prisoners, they adopted their role regardless of their personality.

Rioters can develop a sense of power over people normally considered to be in a position of authority, such as the police. This is because they can riot/loot and boast about it in front of the police (the people in a position of authority). This sense of power developed as the size of the group was too large for the police to handle, so they were no longer in control (and able to make people obedient), meaning that people can more easily disobey.

Crowds could engage in anti-social behaviour such as fighting and rioting due to the influence of other people, such as peers and parents. This could cause conformity, as we learn as children to imitate our peers and obey figures of authority, such as our parents. This was shown during the 2011 riots as children as young as nine were see rioting, suggesting they had been influenced by the situation they were in.

Culture

Milgram presumed at the start of his study that 'Germans were different', which would explain why the Nazi regime was successful in Germany in World War II. However, Milgram found such high levels of obedience in Americans that he came to believe that obedience was actually a culturally universal behaviour. In the 1990s, Blass reviewed replications of Milgram worldwide and found obedience rates of 60.94 per cent in the USA and 65.94 per cent elsewhere, which is not very different, supporting it as a universal aspect of behaviour. Individualistic cultures are those that stress the needs of the individual over the needs of the group as a whole. In this type of culture, people are seen as independent and autonomous. Collectivistic cultures, in contrast, emphasise the needs and goals of the group as a whole over the needs and wishes of each individual. In such cultures, relationships with other members of the group and the interconnectedness between people play a central role in each person's identity.

Smith and Bond (1998) found that people who belong to individualistic cultures, such as American and British cultures, are more likely to behave independently than those from collectivist cultures, such as China and Japan. In collectivist cultures, group decision making is highly valued, but in individualistic cultures people are more concerned with their independent success than the well-being of their community.

Although cultures have different views on obedience and how to react to requests and orders made by legitimate authorities, evidence is inconclusive that cross-cultural differences exist. The high obedience rates found by Milgram indicate that not all individualist cultures resist obedience due to their upbringing of uniqueness and independence. Obedience levels have not seemed to increase or decrease as a result of time and generation.

Exam questions

1. Megan is told by her boss to tidy the restaurant after closing. Megan had made plans to go out with her friends at the end of the day, but instead she tidies the restaurant. Why might Megan have tidied the restaurant instead of going out with her friends? (3)

2. Kristina had recently moved to a new school and noticed that students had a strong allegiance to the local football team, Cyprus City. Kristina purchased a replica team shirt and started to wear it daily to school. Almost immediately she was asked if she would like to attend games with fellow student supporters of the team. Kristina readily agreed, even though she actually had no interest or knowledge of football at all. Identify the type of social influence illustrated and refer to features of the situation to justify your answer. (3)

3. Will arrives at his new job to find his new colleagues drinking coffee in the rest room, even though the store is now open. Will knows he should not really join them but he does so anyway. Later he is asked to move from the tills to the shelf-stacking area. He has not been trained for this, so at first, he stays back and watches what the others do and then follows their lead.

   (a) From the description of Will's behaviour above, identify one example of normative social influence. Explain why you think this is an example of normative social influence. (3)

   (b) From the description of Will's behaviour above, identify one example of informational social influence. Explain why you think this is an example of informational social influence. (3)

4. Jemima and Millie are at a peace march in Wandsworth. Jemima has spent much of the day talking to other marchers about their views and beliefs and has agreed to march with them again the following week. Millie has enjoyed the company of other marchers and is beginning to feel as if she is part of the group. When they discuss marching the next week, Millie does not commit herself and sign up for the march until she sees that most of the others are going to march again, whereas Jemima is one of the first to sign up for the march next week. Explain how social influence research can help us to understand Jemima's and Millie's behaviour. (6)

5. Gemma passed her psychology exam and got one of the highest grades. What might she say if she has an internal locus of control? What might she say if she has an external locus of control? (4)

6. Using your knowledge of psychology, explain why some people might resist pressures to conform. (4)

7. There is the sound of an explosion outside a large school. The staff in the school all witness the scene but none of them go outside to help the injured. Why might the staff have remained inside? (3)

8. Zoe is out with four of her friends and they begin to shout at someone across the road. Zoe joins in with the shouting, but later she feels upset at her behaviour. Why might Zoe have joined in with the others and feel disappointed? (3)

9. Describe and evaluate Piliavin's study on good Samaritanism. (9)

End of chapter summary

You should now have an understanding of all the points below:

Know the terms:

- obedience
- conformity
- deindividuation
- bystander effect.

Understand factors affecting bystander intervention, including:

- personal factors
- situational factors.

Understand conformity to majority influence and factors affecting conformity to majority influence, including:

- personality
- the situation.

Understand obedience to authority and factors affecting obedience to authority figures, including:

- personality
- the situation.

Understand the behaviour of crowds and the individuals within them and the effect of collective behaviour, including:

- pro- and anti-social behaviour.

Understand possible ways to prevent blind obedience to authority figures. Understand the aims, procedures and findings (results and conclusions), and strengths and weaknesses of:

- Piliavin *et al.* (1969): good Samaritanism: an underground phenomenon?
- Haney, Banks and Zimbardo (1973): a study of prisoners and guards in a simulated prison.

Understand social and cultural issues in psychology, including:

- the terms 'society' and 'social issues'
- the term 'culture'
- the use of content, theories and research drawn from social influence to explain social and cultural issues in psychology.

Now test yourself answers

1. Obedience.
2. Informational social influence.
3. Normative social influence.
4. Competence.
5. Less likely.
6. 25 per cent.
7. Four.
8. 100 per cent.
9. As it was held at the prestigious Yale University, participants may have thought researchers were experts and trustworthy.
10. A 44.5 per cent drop.

Chapter 6
Criminal psychology – why do people become criminals?

This chapter deals with understanding what makes someone turn to crime and whether it is a learned behaviour or something that some of us are born to do. This in turn can help society deal with crime prevention and how prisoners can be rehabilitated or treated in prison.

Criminal psychology looks at the criminal justice processes, including the identification, judgement and development of treatment programmes for offenders. These are used in the community or in prisons to rehabilitate criminals and prevent **recidivism**.

Key term

Recidivism is when a criminal returns to crime after being punished so starts reoffending again.

Learning theories as an explanation of criminality

Learning theories of criminality assume that offending is a behaviour that is learned in the same way as other behaviours, usually through the environment.

Operant conditioning as an explanation of criminality

Operant conditioning uses reinforcements and punishments to explain how characteristics may be learned:

- Positive reinforcement involves receiving something good for an action, which 'reinforces' or encourages the behaviour to be repeated. For example, one might get material gain from criminal activity, such as robbery, and so be likely to repeat it for the same rewards.
- Negative reinforcement involves the removal of a burden or something bad when a certain behaviour is reproduced, which again reinforces that behaviour to be repeated. For example, a criminal who steals might have their financial hardship removed, and so will sustain this by stealing again.

Another method of changing behaviour is by using punishment. Punishment involves causing physical or mental distress by either giving some unpleasant stimulus or withdrawing a pleasant one. If we know that we will be punished severely for doing something, we are less likely to do it. Punishment is defined as the opposite of reinforcement since it is designed to weaken or eliminate a response rather than increase it.

Like reinforcement, punishment can work either positively or negatively.

Positive punishment involves directly applying an unpleasant stimulus like a shock after a response. In terms of criminality, going to jail for committing an offence would be positive punishment.

Negative punishment involves removing a potentially rewarding stimulus – for instance, deducting someone's pocket money to punish undesirable behaviour. Similarly, a criminal who is driving illegally may have their licence taken away, or a prisoner may lose their right to read books from the prison library due to poor behaviour. For this reason, negative punishment is often referred to as 'punishment by removal'.

One of the easiest ways to remember this concept is to note that, in behavioural terms, positive means adding something while negative means taking something away.

Key terms

Positive reinforcement is the addition of a reward following a desired behaviour.

Negative reinforcement is the removal of something negative following a desired behaviour.

Positive punishment is the addition of something unpleasant after a behaviour, so we are less likely to do it again.

Negative punishment is the removal of something pleasant after a behaviour, so we are less likely to do it again.

Active learning

The main purpose of reinforcement is to encourage the learning of a behaviour, so a reinforcer can be anything which leads to some behaviour being repeated. Reinforcers may be primary or secondary.

- A primary reinforcer is one which is necessary for survival.

Can you think of an example?

- Secondary reinforcers are those which provide the means to obtain a primary reinforcer.

Can you think of an example?

Strengths and weaknesses of operant conditioning

Operant conditioning can explain the acquisition of many aspects of criminal behaviour. For example, stealing can be explained using the concept of positive reinforcement. Getting away with stealing is a positive reinforcer which occurs unpredictably and so keeps the individual motivated to steal more.

It is difficult to show that a criminal behaviour was acquired through operant conditioning. This is because we haven't been able to study the person from birth and, therefore, it is impossible to identify the specific causes or consequences which may have led to that criminal behaviour.

Operant conditioning fails to offer an adequate explanation of individual differences in criminal behaviour. For example, different individuals may respond differently to the same stimulus. We don't all commit crime purely based on reinforcement or punishment. Therefore, other factors must be involved in criminality, such as our cognitive thought processes and genetic factors.

Operant conditioning has a range of practical applications in the real world. The principles of operant conditioning, such as positive and negative punishment, have been used in our criminal justice system to try and remove undesirable criminal behaviours. The principle of positive reinforcement has also been used to manage prisoners' behaviour by introducing tokens as a reward for good behaviour, which can then be exchanged for bigger rewards, such as longer visiting times for families or more time at the prison gym, etc.

Now test yourself

1. True or false? If a crime has been learned through the environment, it can also be unlearned.
2. A father cannot bear the pain of seeing his children go hungry so steals some bread to feed his family. Which type of reinforcement is being used here?
3. Losing access to a toy or being grounded are examples of which type of punishment?

Social learning theory as an explanation of criminality

Social learning theory believes we learn behaviours through others via reinforcement and through a process known as **modelling**. Modelling can only take place where someone identifies with another person in some way (this person will be their role model). Role models are likely to be of the same sex, roughly the same age and share similar interests as the person doing the learning and are likely to be in a position of power, success or fame.

Modelling is a key part of social learning theory as an explanation of crime; a person can directly or indirectly observe the criminal behaviour in real life or via the media so that it can be remembered or reproduced. Observation uses the principles of **vicarious reinforcement**, whereby behaviours are learned through reinforcement, but by observing others and seeing them be rewarded or punished appropriately (for example, if someone sees a criminal getting sentenced to imprisonment, they are less likely to commit the crime themselves, whereas if a criminal friend makes a lot of money from theft, they might learn to do the same so they can have the same rewards).

Key terms

Modelling is the learning of a new behaviour by imitating a role model.
Vicarious reinforcement is not direct punishment or reward, it is how an individual learns by watching others being rewarded or punished.

There are two types of motivation which determine whether we commit a crime or not:

1. External motivation happens if the behaviour (crime) is rewarded by external factors, such as the money received after a robbery.
2. Internal motivation happens if the behaviour (crime) is motivating and satisfies a need – for example, crimes such as joyriding may cause excitement to the criminal.

There are four stages to the process of modelling:

1. The learner needs to pay attention to the important parts of the behaviour being observed. For example, Adam notices everything Darren does because he admires him and spends time with him.
2. The important details about the observed behaviour will need to be stored in long-term memory, such as visually (images) or semantically (meaning). For example, Adam sees Darren stealing from a shop and continually thinks about it as it was too exciting to forget.
3. Once the modelled behaviour is in memory, it will be reproduced, provided the consequences of that behaviour are sufficiently reinforced. Adam imitates the behaviour of his role model, Darren, by stealing from the same shop.
4. The likelihood of a person repeating the behaviour is largely dependent on the reinforcements that follow – rewards will motivate people to behave in a certain way, whilst punishment is likely to demotivate them. For example, Darren heaps praise on Adam for being brave and cool, which motivates Adam to do it again.

Active learning

Use the four processes above to explain how someone may break traffic laws by driving through a red light.

Strengths and weaknesses of social learning theory

The theory has practical applications to real life as the principles can be used to rehabilitate offenders, using good role models to reinforce appropriate behaviours with appropriate reinforcements to change the ways of criminals. As the explanation is based on learning, people should be able to 'unlearn' anti-social behaviour using appropriate role models as 'mentors'.

Similarly, the theory has contributed significantly to the media violence debate and whether the media have any effect on criminal behaviour. There are some cases where a film, programme or video game is said to have been imitated, leading to 'killing sprees', such as the one at Columbine High School in the USA.

The theory does not look at individual differences, only at how an individual is affected by social factors. It assumes all behaviour is learned. The theory does not consider possible biologically determined personality traits. Research suggests that violent children come from violent homes, but this could be explained by either learning or genetics, or an interaction between the two.

The theory does not provide an explanation for opportunistic crime which has not been observed and learnt first. Although it can explain smaller crimes, such as theft and aggression, the theory cannot explain more serious crimes, such as murder and fraud, as these will not have been observed in the same way.

Now test yourself

4. Name three things which make us more likely to view someone as a role model.

Biological explanations of criminality

Cesare Lombroso (1890) wondered whether some people are just destined to be criminals. He was one of the founding fathers of the biological theory of criminology, which says that criminals are biologically different from non-criminals.

Genetic explanation for criminality

There are many ways to see if criminality has a biological basis. We can compare the family trees of criminals and non-criminals. If many criminals' relatives are also criminals, there might be a biological link, and conversely the fewer criminal relatives, the weaker the link.

Research into the similarity of twins, particularly their criminal similarity, to investigate genetic links use **monozygotic** (MZ) and **dizygotic** (DZ) twins. MZ twins share the same genes, whereas DZ twins do not.

Christiansen (1977) found that from 3,586 pairs of twins, if an identical twin was a criminal, 52.5 per cent of the time the other twin was also a criminal. In dizygotic twins, the rate was only 22 per cent. We can also look at adoption studies. Adopted children and their biological parents share genes but not environment, so in these cases we can be sure that genetics are the cause of criminality. There is evidence to suggest that individuals are more likely to be criminals if their parents are criminal. However, it could be that it is nothing to do with genetics at all; family members are raised together and treated similarly, so therefore social learning theory could explain their criminal behaviour.

Key terms

Monozygotic twins develop from one egg, which splits and forms two embryos; they are genetically identical.
Dizygotic twins develop from two different eggs, and are not genetically identical.

Eysenck's (1964) personality theory

One theory of crime states that whether we become criminal or not is hard-wired into us as part of our personality; essentially, we are born with a tendency to become criminal or not. Hans Eysenck (1964) put forward a 'type theory' of personality. He argues that a genetically inherited nervous system which is under- or over-aroused may cause criminality.

Our personality type responds to the environment differently, based on our biology. Eysenck developed a psychometric test for measuring personality – the EPQ (Eysenck Personality Questionnaire), which measured people on: **introversion–extraversion** (E), emotional **stability–neuroticism** (emotional instability) (N) and **psychoticism** (emotional independence) (P).

Extraverts are difficult to condition, which has been used to explain their lack of conscience – normally when we do something wrong, we feel bad about it because our conscience tells us it was wrong, and then we don't do it again, to avoid feeling bad. In those with high E scores, Eysenck believed that they don't easily learn to avoid the bad feelings. According to Eysenck, this dimension is controlled by the **ascending reticular activating system (ARAS)**, which is thought to be involved in alertness and arousal. Extraverts, being chronically under-aroused, are more likely to be risk-seeking and engage in anti-social activity, such as crime.

Neurotics may be more likely to become criminals as a reaction to an emotional event, or as a habit they find difficult to break. Neurotic individuals are unstable and find it hard to inhibit their behaviour, so often act impulsively and show violence more quickly.

Eysenck (1966) added the third trait/dimension later – psychoticism. High P scorers are often uncaring of others, insensitive and do not feel guilt, so committing crime may be easy as they will not worry about the effects on others. As they lack empathy, they can harm or distress others without feelings of shame of remorse.

It is thought that people who have high P, E and N scores may be more likely to commit violent crime.

Key terms

Introverts are typically reserved and reflective.
Extraverts are sociable and crave excitement and change, and thus can become bored easily. They tend to be carefree, optimistic and impulsive.
Stability refers to someone who is calm and unworried.
Neurotics tend to be anxious, worrying and moody. They are overly emotional and find it difficult to calm down once upset.
Psychoticism refers to lacking in empathy, being cruel, a loner, aggressive and troublesome.
Ascending reticular activating system (ARAS) is a system that triggers the release of hormones and neurotransmitters.

Strengths and weaknesses of Eysenck's (1964) personality theory

There is good evidence for the link between 'psychoticism' and violent crime. In a study by Berman and Paisey (1984) on American **juvenile delinquents**, there were significantly higher scores on the psychoticism scale in the violent offenders.

Personality theories have been regarded as outdated as an explanation of anti-social behaviour because findings of studies have been inconsistent – especially findings that high extraversion scores are linked to criminal behaviour, and the link between neuroticism and offender behaviour is even weaker. Lane (1987) found higher neuroticism scores in non-delinquents. Similarly, Silva *et al.* (1986) found delinquents scored higher on P and N but non-delinquents scored higher on E.

Hare (2001) developed a psychoticism personality test which is used in prisons to assess and diagnose anti-social personality disorder. A high score on this test can be used to keep potentially dangerous individuals detained in secure accommodation. Also, because this is a biological theory, there is not much use for rehabilitation as individuals can't change their behaviour. However, this means the EPQ can lead to labelling, which in turn can lead to the **self-fulfilling prophecy**, whereby someone who is labelled as high on P, E or N and told they will always be a criminal may take on this belief and act as one.

A common objection to Eysenck's theory is that it is based on research using questionnaires. The EPQ uses simple yes/no questions which offer a 'forced choice' between an answer which is high in the trait or an answer which is low. However, more recent versions of the questionnaire offer Likert-style questions, where participants tick a box saying whether they 'never' or 'frequently' feel a certain way, or something in between.

Key terms

Juvenile delinquents are teenagers between the ages of 15 and 17 who engage in anti-social behaviour.

The **self-fulfilling prophecy** is when an individual who has been labelled in a certain way takes on board that label and starts acting in the manner by which they have been labelled.

Now test yourself

5. Which type of twins share the same genes?
6. Eysenck believes we are born with a tendency to become criminals. Which side of the nature–nurture debate does this put him on?

The effects of punishment on recidivism

Around half of all crime is committed by people who have already been through the criminal justice system. The cost to the taxpayer of reoffending is estimated to be £9.5 to £13 billion per year. There has been little change in reconviction rates and almost half of those released from prison go on to reoffend within 12 months.

Prison

The use of prisons to control crime has increased in frequency in the last decade. The main reason for imprisonment is the belief that length of time in jail acts as a **deterrent** to future recidivism.

Three schools of thought dominate the area. The first is that prisons suppress criminal behaviour. Given the unpleasantness of prison life and the shame associated with imprisonment, these should serve as deterrents to later criminal behaviour.

The second, the 'schools of crime' viewpoint, proposes just the opposite, that is, that prisons increase criminality. By this account, the barren, inhumane and psychologically destructive nature of prison makes offenders more likely to recidivate upon release.

The third school of thought contends that the effect of prison on offenders is, for the most part, minimal. This view states that prisons are essentially 'psychological deep freezes', in that offenders enter prison with a set of anti-social attitudes and behaviours which are little changed during imprisonment.

Key term

A **deterrent** is about preventing or controlling actions or behaviour through fear of punishment.

Strengths and weaknesses of prison as a punishment

One obvious strength is that prison protects society from dangerous and violent criminals, such as murderers and rapists. This in turn is reassuring for the public and can put their minds at ease in terms of understanding that any crime will be punished in the correct manner. The existence of prisons helps to justify the authority of the law; it shows that crime and punishment is taken seriously and ensures that the law is respected and upheld.

Prison acts as **retribution** as the criminal suffers being separated from society and locked in a small room for up to 23 hours a day. It isolates those who deserve such a punishment from their family and friends and so also acts as a deterrent, making people afraid of committing crime.

It can offer a chance of reform as inmates can gain an education or new skills whilst they are in prison to help them when they are released. It gives offenders the chance to reflect on their actions and gives them time to reform their behaviours.

However, a major weakness is many prisoners learn criminal skills when they meet other criminals in prison. This can lead to higher rates of reoffending or more serious crimes being committed after release. This creates a school of crime, where prisoners educate each other in criminal matters. Inmates learn more effective crime strategies from each other, and time spent in prison may weaken the threat of future imprisonment.

Prisons are good for punishing criminals and keeping them off the street, but prison sentences (particularly long sentences) are unlikely to deter future crime. Prisons may have the opposite effect: research shows long prison sentences do little to deter people from committing future crimes. However, a consistent finding is that increases in already lengthy sentences produce at best a very modest deterrent effect.

British prisons are massively overcrowded. Many prisons have twice the number of occupants than they were built to hold. This creates an atmosphere in which criminals are resentful of society and may not wish to fit back in when they are released; most prisoners reoffend on release, so it doesn't bring about reform.

Key term

Retribution is the term for the punishment given in return for the crime that has been committed.

Community sentencing

Community sentences are given by courts where they believe that this will be more productive than a prison sentence. Community sentences can be given for crimes such as damaging property, benefit fraud or assault.

You may get a community sentence if:

- the court thinks you are more likely to stop committing crime than if you go to prison
- it is the first time you have committed a crime
- you have a mental health condition that affects your behaviour.

A community sentence combines punishment with activities carried out in the community. It can include one or more of 13 requirements on an offender. They can expect to complete anything from 40 to 300 hours of community payback, depending on how serious the crime was. This might include things like removing graffiti or clearing overgrown areas. It could also mean the offender is required to have alcohol or drug treatment; this aims to tackle the reasons why they have committed crimes. Offenders might also be required to keep to a curfew, which aims to keep them out of trouble. Offenders will usually work in their local area and be managed by a community payback supervisor. Offenders must wear a high visibility orange vest while they work.

The work will be arranged outside their working hours if they have a job, e.g. evenings or weekends. They have to work three or four days each week if they are unemployed.

Overall, the requirements aim to punish offenders, to change offenders' behaviour so they don't commit crime in the future and to make amends to the victim of the crime or the local community.

Now test yourself

7. What is meant by a curfew?

Strengths and weaknesses of community sentencing as a punishment

Sentencing can help improvements within the community without the cost. Many community service opportunities focus on offenders working within the community in which they caused harm. Programmes across the country create low-income housing, remove debris from parks and build community gardens. Often, these projects receive little or no funding, so the labour provided by offenders allows those projects to be completed.

Studies have shown that both victims and offenders view the use of community service as beneficial. Some communities even allow the victim to have input as to the type of community service to be performed by the offender. Community service has a positive reputation in the community because the work done by offenders benefits society as a whole.

Sentencing means offenders are held accountable, while reducing prison overcrowding. Non-violent offenders are given the opportunity to remain part of the community while still receiving consequences for their actions. Community service may be a part of probation or may be used as a sanction prior to revoking, or violating, his or her probation.

Some see it as less favourable compared to imprisonment as, although supervised, the criminal is still exposed to the public and therefore they can still be a danger. Research has shown that many offenders fail to turn up to their community sentence and avoid returning to court, claiming they overslept or producing their own sick note. There is also an issue of unpaid fines, which makes fines an ineffective punishment.

The dividing line between which crimes should come under community service and which come under prison is somewhat blurred. Community service is deemed appropriate for low-level, non-violent crimes, such as vandalism, minor driving offences, shoplifting or joyriding. All violent crimes such as rape, murder and gun crime are seen to come under prison, regardless of whether it is a first offence. However, research reveals the view that some non-violent crimes, such as burglary, can result in serious emotional consequences for the victim and therefore community service is too lenient an option.

Restorative justice

Restorative justice seeks to bring together the victim with the offender. It allows the victim to say how they feel and express their emotions face to face with their attacker, and often can cause the offender to face what they have done more openly. Coupled with facing up to what was done, offenders are more likely to receive treatments that will help them stay away from crime in the future. It is a form of 'community justice' in which offenders are offered forgiveness in exchange for full disclosure of their crimes, accountability for their actions, apologies and acts of restitution. It enables people to reflect on how they interact with each other and consider how best to prevent harm and conflict.

Restorative justice was first passed with children who have more of a chance of turning their lives and actions to a new path than someone who has only known the same thing for many more years. In addition, it is believed that younger offenders often feel more regret than older offenders because they haven't had time to harden their emotions.

Key term

Restorative justice is when those harmed by the crime and those responsible for the crime come together to make the offender understand the impact of their behaviour.

Strengths and weaknesses of restorative justice as a punishment

Those in support of restorative justice say that victims claim to receive significant benefit. Research from the University of Montreal (2005) reports that victims who participated in restorative justice programmes generally believed the process was fair, and their personal feelings of fear and anger declined after participating. In addition, they concluded restorative justice tends to reduce repeat offending, particularly with serious, violent crimes, and is as good as or better than short prison sentences for combating repeat offending. Also, they found that it reduces the stated victim's desire for violent revenge against offenders.

Restorative justice may also recognise the reality that there may be a continuing relationship of some kind between offender and victim. The offender and victim may be part of the same community or they may be members of the same family, and it may be impossible for them to avoid each other. It may create a genuine understanding of the harm which has been caused to the victim and an acknowledgement of it could create greater empathy.

However, restorative justice can prove problematic in several ways, particularly regarding victims' needs. Restorative justice is viewed by many as a way for offenders to avoid entering the formal criminal justice system and as a prevention method for overcrowded prisons.

Another weakness is that it offers offenders a chance to do their crime again with no severe or hard punishment having been given. It is felt that no lesson is learned and that changes in behaviour won't happen. Those who do not follow through with the programmes that restorative justice offers are using up valuable resources of the justice system that could otherwise have gone to those who really are looking for a change.

Token economy programmes

A **token economy** is a behavioural treatment based on the principles of operant conditioning. The essential idea is that criminal behaviour is learned in the same way as any other behaviour and therefore can be 'unlearned' and more acceptable behaviour learned in its place. You therefore need to reward offenders' appropriate behaviour and punish their inappropriate behaviour.

To give the offender something that gives them pleasure or happiness would be using positive reinforcement, whereas to take away something that is not pleasurable or is causing unhappiness would be an example of negative reinforcement.

Token economy programmes are a form of **behaviour modification** and use tokens as secondary reinforcers to reward desired behaviour – these are then exchanged for primary reinforcers that the prisoners want, such as cigarettes and family visits. The use of tokens allows behaviour to be rewarded immediately – it would not be possible to give primary reinforcers for every 'desired' behaviour.

Some token economies are more complex and use punishment and negative reinforcement as well, where behaviour has to be performed to avoid something the person dislikes. In many programmes, in the first few weeks the tokens must be 'spent' quickly or they go 'out of date'. This ensures that the real reward follows the behaviour fairly quickly to build up a strong association between behaviour and reward. They also assume the learning that goes on in the institution will generalise to behaviour in the outside world.

Key terms

Token economy programmes are used to obtain desirable behaviour in prisons and are used for adult and juvenile offenders.

Behaviour modification is a method of changing (or modifying) someone's behaviour using rewards.

Active learning

Put the following statements in the correct order, 1–8, to show how the token economy is used:

- Staff and inmate interaction becomes more positive.
- When an offender behaves as desired, they are given a token.
- Positive reinforcers encourage appropriate behaviours to be repeated.
- Token economy programmes are based on operant conditioning principles.
- Tokens may be exchanged subsequently for reinforcers, such as cigarettes, drinks and magazines.
- A list of desirable behaviours is drawn up by the management of the institution, e.g. complying with rules, completing chores and interacting in a positive way.
- Tokens are used to manage behaviour not rehabilitate.
- Tokens control behaviour in the short term, making prison life more harmonious.

Strengths and weaknesses of token economy programmes

Hobbs and Holt (1976) introduced the token economy to young delinquents. Tokens were given for behaviours such as obeying rules, doing chores properly and being cooperative. Extra positive reinforcers, such as home passes, sweets, cigarettes and leisure activities, were also given. Results showed that desired behaviours increased among the young delinquents.

The programme is cost effective as professionals are not needed to implement them, so they are relatively quick to start and can run as required. The therapy can be administered by anyone and tokens and rewards are relatively cheap so the programme is not expensive. This contrasts with other forms of rehabilitation which can take a long time and usually involve lots of other staff from outside the prison setting.

Critics have argued that the treatment leads to **learned helplessness**, where prisoners feel they have no choice but to comply, otherwise basic privileges are withheld. It can also be argued that the programme violates human rights. Staff have the power to reward or withhold rewards. Staff can use their position to coerce the prisoner to behave in a certain way and so the system is more open to abuse.

One major weakness is that it changes behaviour but not the underlying reasons for the behaviour. This is shown in the high levels of recidivism when prisoners go back into society. When rewards are no longer given for good behaviour, people will revert to old habits because they have not changed their thinking patterns. The techniques may change behaviour but another kind of problem behaviour may develop because the causes have not been addressed.

Key term

Learned helplessness is when people feel helpless to avoid negative situations because previous experience has shown them that they do not have control.

Now test yourself

8. Giving a criminal more time at the prison gym would be an example of which type of reinforcer?

Anger management programmes

Therapists from this approach believe that problems such as anger, anxiety or depression are caused by **faulty cognitions**, and so to change behaviour is not enough – people need to change their thinking first. Anger management is a cognitive behavioural technique (it seeks to change both behaviour and thinking, unlike the token economy, which only changes behaviour).

Key term

Faulty cognitions are a lack of planning or processing information inaccurately.

An anger management programme will be based around three key stages:

1. Cognitive preparation

This involves analysing past aggression and discovering patterns. For example, the trainer will look for recurring triggers or environmental situations that regularly precede a loss of temper in the offender. The offender must also examine the consequences of this aggression both in the long and short term and then must recognise that they need to change this behaviour.

2. Skills acquisition

Offenders are taught cognitive skills aimed at changing thoughts and perceptions of the situation to damp down the emotional response, e.g. counting to ten or self-instructional techniques like 'be calm, be calm'. They are also taught behavioural skills aimed at reducing the physiological fight or flight response and given options for dealing with the situation, e.g. relaxation training to try and damp down the release of hormones and assertiveness training to help the client maintain their view without resorting to violence.

3. Application practice

This allows the offender to test their skills in a range of situations. Often the programmes are run as group therapy and therefore the other group members can role-play situations that reflect the triggers of a member and allow them to practice dealing with it in a non-aggressive way. This is then reinforced by the group and the good behaviour will serve as a model for others in the group.

Strengths and weaknesses of anger management programmes

As offenders can take part voluntarily this increases the programme's effectiveness, as offenders who take part voluntarily are usually more committed to the programme's success. This contrasts with other treatments, such as token economy, which are often enforced over an entire prison system, meaning that it may not be successful in all cases.

The chances of recidivism occurring after the treatment are relatively low. This is because the techniques which are taught can be used outside of the prison system, and the treatment is gradually reduced over time. Again, this contrasts with the token economy, which is not effective outside of a prison system and which ends suddenly.

Ireland (2000) compared 50 young offenders on an anger management programme with 37 on the waiting list for anger management. Ninety-two per cent of the treatment group showed some drop in aggression.

Some people must take part in an anger management programme as part of their sentence, which provides an ulterior motive and, although the offender may appear to have made progress, this could be false, and the issue of anger may not actually have been addressed. This means that anger management may not be effective for everyone and does not consider individual differences.

The treatment does not include the giving or withholding of rewards so in that way is more ethical than token economy programmes. Some psychologists have suggested, however, that men convicted of domestic violence become less physically violent but more verbally and emotionally abusive after anger management. This suggests that the therapy is showing people new ways of hurting people, which is obviously an ethical problem.

Studies

Bandura, Ross and Ross (1961): transmission of aggression through imitation of aggressive models

Aim

To see whether observation of the same-sex role model would lead to copying the aggressive behaviour of the same-sex role model.

Procedure

Children aged three to six years (36 boys and 36 girls) were divided into three groups. There was a control group, who did not see a model. There were two groups who were exposed to adult models who behaved in either aggressive or non-aggressive ways. Half of each group saw a same-sex model; the others an opposite-sex model. The children were then tested in different situations to see how much they would imitate the aggressive acts of the model.

The experimenter took each child to a playroom where they met an adult (the model), who was invited to 'join in the game'. The child sat at a table offering potato printing and coloured stickers to play with. The model sat at another table with Tinker toys, a mallet and a five-foot-high inflated 'Bobo' doll.

In the non-aggressive condition, the model assembled the Tinker toys for ten minutes. In the aggressive condition, this lasted only one minute, after which the model attacked the Bobo doll. The sequence of behaviour was identical each time. Bobo was laid on its side. Then it was sat upon, punched on the nose, picked up and hit on the head with the mallet. It was then thrown up in the air and kicked about the room. The model also made aggressive comments such as 'kick him' and 'pow'.

After exposure to the model, all participants were put in a situation designed to frustrate them. This was to increase the likelihood of aggression being displayed. They were taken to a room containing attractive toys, such as a fire engine and a doll. After a short opportunity to play, the children were told these toys were for other children and were moved to another room.

In the final stage, the children were offered non-aggressive toys. These toys were crayons, dolls, a ball, cars, a tea set and plastic farm animals. They were also given aggressive toys, including a Bobo doll, a mallet and dart guns. The children could play here for 20 minutes. They were observed by the experimenters using a one-way mirror. Records were made of aggressive acts, which replicated the model's behaviour (both physical and verbal), other aggression with the mallet and non-aggressive behaviour.

Results

Children who observed violent models imitated their exact behaviours. They were much more aggressive than those children who did not see the aggressive model. This effect was the same for both physical and verbal aggression. The increase in aggression for boys was greater than for girls. Girls were more likely to imitate verbal aggression and boys were more likely to imitate physical aggression. Boys were also more likely to imitate a same-sex model. Girls were also more likely to imitate a same-sex model, but to a lesser extent.

Table 6.1 Mean number of aggressive acts

		Aggressive role model		Non-aggressive role model	
		Female	Male	Female	Male
Physical	Girls	5.5	7.2	2.5	0.0
	Boys	12.4	25.8	0.2	1.5
Verbal	Girls	13.7	2.0	0.3	0.0
	Boys	4.3	12.7	1.1	0.0

Conclusion

The results showed that observation and imitation can explain how specific acts are learnt. This learning occurred without reinforcements being given. A possible explanation for the results is that children think behaving aggressively is OK. This could then encourage children to behave aggressively, because they do not think they will be punished. Children may then carry on behaving aggressively.

Strengths and weaknesses of Bandura, Ross and Ross (1961)

Bandura used two observers behind the one-way mirror. This creates **inter-rater reliability** because a behaviour had to be noted by *both* observers, otherwise it didn't count. A **standardised** procedure was followed, including the set-up of each room and what children saw; this means it is replicable and can be tested for reliability.

The findings have a major application to real life in that Bandura has shown how we are likely to imitate role models, especially those of the same gender. This has implications for media violence and how children should not be exposed to aggressive images as they may imitate them, and how pro-social behaviour can be drawn from imitating positive role models.

The study was conducted in one nursery setting, and only on children. These findings may be different for children who do not regularly attend nursery, or to different age groups. Also, as this took place in the USA, it may be culturally biased and other cultures may be different. The samples were all taken from the same nursery, which was used by the students and staff at one of the world's top universities. These children might have unusual home lives and particularly educated parents, making them unrepresentative of normal children.

The situation was not natural, and it may be that children were simply doing what they thought adults expected of them: 'Look mummy, there's the doll we had to hit.' This suggests the children may have responded to demand characteristics. The children were put in a strange situation, exposed to some unusual adult behaviour and given toys to play with which encouraged them to act unnaturally. For example, a Bobo doll is *designed* to be hit and knocked over (it bounces back upright); children would suppose the experimenters *wanted* them to play with the Bobo doll in this way.

Key terms

Inter-rater reliability refers to the agreement between two or more observers about what they are watching.

In a **standardised** procedure, all the participants are treated in the same way and so all have the same experience.

Now test yourself

9. How were the children in Bandura's study put in a situation designed to frustrate them?

Studies

Charlton *et al.* (2000): children's playground behaviour across five years of broadcast television: a naturalistic study in a remote community

Aim

To investigate whether the introduction of satellite TV would increase aggressive behaviour in children.

Procedure

Charlton and his colleagues began their study of children's behaviour two years before TV was connected to an island. This is a natural experiment because the researchers didn't have to set up the experiment themselves – the introduction of television was happening naturally.

The independent variable was television – before and after its introduction.

The dependent variable was the children's behaviour on the island.

Children aged 3–8 years old from two schools on the island of St Helena took part. Until 1995, television was not transmitted to this part of the world. In 1994, experimenters observed aggressive behaviour prior to the introduction of transmitted television in 1995. This was done through filming 256 minutes' worth of free play in the school playground.

Five years later, in 2000, after satellite TV became available, the children's free play was observed and recorded again, filming free play totalling 344 minutes. Play was recorded for a two-week period and a schedule of 26 playground behaviours was used. The experimenters devised an 'observation schedule', which was used when analysing the results; this included behaviours such as pushing, hitting and kicking, as well as turn taking and affection. The analysis of results was based on four anti-social and four pro-social behaviours in addition to gender and number of children involved. The researchers collected information on the children, using questionnaires and asking parents and teachers about the behaviour of the children.

The researchers content-analysed what and how much the children watched on television. They were particularly interested in how much violence the children watched and for how long.

A pair of independent observers scored the videos; if they disagreed, the video was replayed until they reached a conclusion.

Results

Charlton found very little difference in the children's behaviour before and after the introduction of television. The island had a very low rate of behavioural problems with children before the study and this did not significantly increase after TV was introduced.

Only 9 of the 64 comparisons made between pre- and post-television showed significant differences:

- Two of these nine showed a significant decrease in anti-social behaviour in the post-television phase compared to the pre-television phase.
- Five of these nine showed a significant decrease in pro-social behaviour in the post-television phase compared to the pre-television phase.

Significant differences were found between girls' and boys' levels of anti-social behaviour, with boys committing nearly four times more anti-social acts.

Pro-social behaviour took place approximately twice as much as anti-social behaviour.

Because the population of St Helena was so small, with everyone knowing everyone else, and parents having a high level of control over their children's behaviour, the effect of television was reduced. TV did not have the impact it could have had in a less isolated environment.

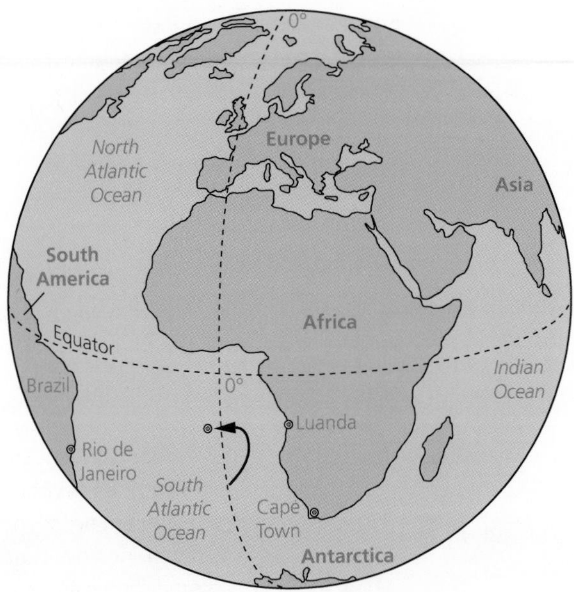

Figure 6.1 The location of the island of St Helena

Conclusion

This study shows that TV did not have a significant impact on children's behaviour. Even if violence was watched, it was not copied. This was due to high levels of community control and surveillance and parents' control over behaviour.

Now test yourself

10. What is meant by a natural experiment?

Strengths and weaknesses of Charlton *et al.* (2000)

The study has high ecological validity and was obviously not an artificial task. This study was a natural experiment, which means it has greater realism than a laboratory or field experiment. Discreet cameras were used so the children would have acted naturally because they did not know that they were being watched. Similarly, demand characteristics are low, considering that the participants were too young to realise that they were part of a study, all of which means it can be applied to real life.

There is high inter-rater reliability as the observations were made by more than one psychologist and everything was recorded so that any disagreements among the experimenters about the observational data collected could be resolved using the video footage. This in turn avoids any subjective interpretation or researcher bias, which adds **credibility** to the study.

It is difficult to compare results against any similar community as the experiment was completed on an isolated island, which lowers its cross-cultural validity. Thus, it is difficult to generalise the study for all cultures that have been influenced by urbanisation and modernisation.

The programmes available in St Helena were not the mainland programmes watched by children in places like Europe. So, the differences in the shows watched, since the mainland programmes may have been more violent than the ones available in St Helena, cause the study to have lower validity.

Key term

Credibility refers to whether something can be trusted or believed.

Exam questions

1. Explain how inter-rater reliability was used in the Charlton *et al.* (2000) study. (2)
2. Describe two features of operant conditioning. (4)
3. Describe two findings of the Bandura, Ross and Ross (1961) study. (4)
4. Describe two ways in which the Bandura, Ross and Ross (1961) study lacks validity and explain how the validity of this study could have been improved. (6)
5. Hussain is arguing with his sister about which TV programme to watch. They both start shouting and so are told to go to their bedroom. Explain which type of reinforcement is shown in this example. (1)
6. John has been given a sentence for burglary; he stole from his neighbour's home. Explain whether prison or restorative justice might be best for all concerned. (4)
7. Genevieve has always been calm and never been in trouble at school. Her best friend Kat, however, likes excitement and change and can become bored easily. With reference to Eysenck, explain which of the friends is more likely to turn to crime. (4)
8. A judge is deciding whether prison or community sentencing is best for a crime committed by Simon, who was a teacher and stole expensive IT equipment from his sixth form. Outline how these two forms of punishment would be used with Simon and give one evaluation point for each type of punishment. (9)

9. What advice would you give to communities such as St Helena about the possible introduction of television? (3)

10. Adam has been told to go on an anger management programme. Describe the process that Adam will go through as part of the programme. (5)

End of chapter summary

You should now have an understanding of all the points below:

Understand learning theories as an explanation of criminality, including strengths and weaknesses of each theory:

- operant conditioning (Skinner, 1948), to include:
  - positive reinforcement
  - negative reinforcement
  - positive punishment
  - negative punishment
  - primary reinforcers
  - secondary reinforcers
- social learning theory (Bandura, 1977), to include:
  - role models
  - modelling
  - identification
  - observational learning
  - vicarious reinforcement.

Understand biological explanations of criminality, including personality types (Eysenck, 1964), to include strengths and weaknesses of the theory:

- extraversion
- introversion
- neuroticism
- psychoticism.

Understand the effects of punishments on recidivism, including strengths and weaknesses of each punishment:

- prison
- community sentencing
- restorative justice.

Understand two treatments to rehabilitate and reduce criminal and anti-social behaviour and increase pro-social behaviour, including strengths and weaknesses of each treatment:

- token economy programmes
- anger-management programmes.

Understand the aims, procedures and findings (results and conclusions), and strengths and weaknesses of:

- Bandura, Ross and Ross (1961): transmission of aggression through imitation of aggressive models
- Charlton *et al.* (2000): children's playground behaviour across five years of broadcast television: a naturalistic study in a remote community.

Now test yourself answers

1. True.
2. Negative reinforcement.
3. Negative punishment.
4. Same sex, age and similar interests.
5. Monozygotic.
6. Nature.
7. A law requiring people to remain indoors between specified hours, typically at night.
8. Primary reinforcer.
9. They were told the toys were for other children and were moved to another room.
10. The researchers didn't have to set up the experiment themselves; it occurred naturally.

Chapter 7
The self – what makes you who you are?

This chapter deals with how our '**self**' develops and what makes us who we are and in turn how we see ourselves. Our **self-concept** is an important part of defining who we are and includes our happy and sad times, which impact upon our self-esteem, meaning how good or bad we feel about ourselves.

Concepts of the self and self-concept

The term self-concept is generally thought of as our individual perceptions of our behaviour, abilities and unique characteristics. For example, beliefs such as 'I am a good friend' or 'I am a kind person' are part of an overall self-concept.

Self-concept tends to be more flexible when people are younger and still going through the process of self-discovery and identity formation. As people age, self-perceptions become much more detailed and organised as people form a better idea of who they are and what is important to them.

Existential self

The **existential self** is the most basic part of the self-concept. The child realises that they exist as a separate entity from others and that they continue to exist over time and space.

According to Lewis (1990), infants as young as two to three months old begin to understand their relationship with the world. For example, the child smiles and someone smiles back, or the child touches a toy and sees it move.

Categorical self

The **categorical self** refers to how the child becomes aware that he or she is also an object in the world. Just as other objects, including people, have properties that can be experienced (big, small, red, smooth, etc.), so the child is becoming aware of themselves as an object which has properties. Two of the first categories to be applied are age ('I am three') and gender ('I am a girl'). In early childhood, the categories children apply to themselves are very concrete (e.g. hair colour, height and favourite things).

Key terms

Our **self** is who we believe we are.
Self-concept is a mental picture of who you are as a person.
The **existential self** is the sense of being separate and distinct from others.
The **categorical self** takes the form of placing oneself in many categories, such as size, age and gender.

Now test yourself

1. A child who understands he is smaller than his big brother is demonstrating which type of self: existential or categorical?

Carl Rogers (1959) and the self

Rogers views the individual as having the greatest knowledge about themselves and that the individual is the best person to judge their own feelings and problems. Rogers believes that the self-concept has three different components:

- the view you have of yourself (self-image)
- how much value you place on yourself (self-esteem or self-worth)
- what you wish you were really like (ideal self).

Self-image is about how you see yourself in the present moment. Given this, it is crucial to recognise that a self-image is only your own perception of yourself and has no real basis in reality. For example, a teenage boy might believe that he is clumsy and socially awkward when he is quite charming and likeable. A person's self-image is affected by many factors, such as parental influences, friends, the media, etc.

One way of investigating the self-image is to ask people to answer the question 'Who am I?' 20 times. This typically produces two main categories of answers: social roles and personality traits. Social roles are usually quite objective aspects of our self-image (e.g. student, son, daughter, sister). They are 'facts' and can be verified by others. Personality traits are more a matter of opinion as what we think we are like might be different from how others see us.

Active learning

Make a list of 20 answers to the question 'Who am I?'

Now categorise these into social roles, e.g. 'I am a brother', and personality traits, e.g. 'I am hard working'.

Check these answers with family and friends – do they agree with your personality traits?

Self-esteem involves a degree of evaluation and we may have either a positive or a negative view of ourselves. Those with high self-esteem will have a positive view of themselves. This can to lead to confidence in our own abilities, being optimistic and self-acceptance.

Those with low self-esteem will have a negative view of themselves. This can lead to lack of confidence, being pessimistic and wanting to be like someone else. Argyle (2008) believes there are four major factors that influence self-esteem:

1. The reaction of others – if people admire us, we tend to develop a positive self-image; if they avoid us, we develop a negative self-image.
2. Comparison with others – if the people we compare ourselves with appear to be more successful, we tend to develop a negative self-image but if they are less successful than us our image will be positive.
3. Social roles – some social roles, such as being a doctor, promote self-esteem, whereas other roles, such as being unemployed, can lower self-esteem.
4. Identification – we identify with the positions we occupy, the roles we play and the groups we belong to.

When people respond positively to our behaviour, we are more likely to develop positive self-esteem. When we compare ourselves to others and find ourselves lacking, it can have a negative impact on our self-esteem.

Ideal self is how we would like to be. Sometimes, the way we see ourselves and how we would like to see ourselves do not quite match up. If there is a mismatch between how you see yourself (self-image) and what you'd like to be (ideal self) then this is likely to affect how much you value yourself.

Now test yourself

2. A teenage girl believes she is overweight when she is actually quite thin. Is this an example of self-image or ideal self?
3. How might others influence our self-esteem?

Key terms

Self-image includes the labels you give yourself about your personality and the beliefs you have about how others see you.

Self-esteem refers to the extent to which we like, accept or approve of ourselves or how much we value ourselves.

Ideal self is how you wish you could be.

Now test yourself

4. A bus driver who always wanted to be an important politician may be in a state of what?

Congruence and incongruence

A person's ideal self may not be consistent with what happens in life and experiences of the person – this is known as **incongruence**. Rarely, if ever, does a total state of **congruence** exist; all people experience a certain amount of incongruence. Generally, the greater the gap between our self-image and our ideal self, the lower our self-esteem.

Rogers believed that incongruence has its earliest roots in childhood. When parents place conditions on their affection for their children (only expressing love if children 'earn it' through certain behaviours and living up to the parents' expectations), children begin to distort the memories of experiences that leave them feeling unworthy of their parents' love.

Unconditional love, on the other hand, helps to increase congruence. Children who experience such love feel no need to continually distort their memories to believe that other people will love and accept them as they are.

When you were a little boy or girl, did you want to grow up to be a firefighter, a movie star or a ballet dancer? At some point, you probably gave up that dream in favour of something more attainable. Many people wind up abandoning their dreams, believing they are impossible to achieve, so they have learned the pain of incongruence.

Key terms

Incongruence is when there is a difference between a person's ideal self and actual experience.
Congruence is where a person's ideal self and their actual experience are consistent or very similar.

Active learning

Briefly describe your *real self* in the space below. How you are as a person. You may want to consider what you have achieved so far – for example, how *you* see yourself, what characteristics you have (good and bad!).

____

____

Now write a statement describing your ideal self. Don't be too realistic. Include what you would like it to be.

____

____

What do you think might happen if there is any incongruence between your answers?

Self-actualisation

Rogers believed we are born with a **self-actualising** tendency, a motive which drives us to grow and develop into mature, healthy individuals.

> **Key term**
>
> **Self-actualisation** is the process of reaching our potential in life, becoming all that we can be.

The role of identity and free will in the development of self

Free will is the idea that we are able to have some choice in how we act and assumes that we are free to choose our behaviour.

Erikson (1959) and the eight stages of identity development

Erikson's theory of **psychosocial** development is an eight-stage theory that describes how personality develops and changes throughout the course of the entire lifespan.

During each stage, the person experiences a psychosocial crisis which could have a positive or negative outcome for personality development.

According to the theory, successful completion of each stage results in a healthy personality. Failure to successfully complete a stage can result in a reduced ability to complete further stages and therefore an unhealthier personality and sense of self. These stages, however, can be resolved successfully later. While each stage builds on the experiences of earlier stages, Erikson did not believe that mastering each stage was necessary to move on to the next.

> **Key term**
>
> **Psychosocial** involves psychological needs of the individual (i.e. psycho) conflicting with the needs of society (i.e. social).

> **Now test yourself**
>
> 5. According to Erikson, a child who always feels they are to blame for not being able to try new things may not have fully completed which psychosocial stage?
> 6. Someone who has faith in their own ability and has a superior belief in themselves may have successfully completed which psychosocial stage?

Table 7.1 Erikson's eight stages of identity development

Stage	Age in years	Major question	Virtue	Successful outcome	Unsuccessful outcome
Trust vs mistrust	0–2	'Can I trust the world?'	Hope	Children develop a sense of trust in the world and the people who are supposed to care for them.	Failure at this stage leads to a sense of distrust in the world and not believing that others are dependable.
Autonomy vs shame and doubt	2–4	'Can I do things myself or must I rely on others?'	Will	Children develop a sense of independence and personal control.	Children may be left with feelings of doubt and shame over their own abilities.
Initiative vs guilt	4–5	'Is it OK for me to do things?'	Purpose	Kids develop a sense of purpose and the motivation to try new things.	Children are left with feelings of guilt and a lack of initiative.
Industry vs inferiority	5–12	'How can I be good?'	Competence	Success leads to feelings of competence.	Failure leads to feelings of inferiority.
Identity vs role confusion	12–19	'Who am I?'	Fidelity	Teens develop a strong sense of self.	Teens may emerge from this stage not sure of who they are.
Intimacy vs isolation	20–40	'Can I love and be loved?'	Love	Adults can form loving and lasting relationships with others.	Failure at this stage can lead to feelings of loneliness and isolation.
Generativity vs stagnation	40–65	'What can I contribute to the world?'	Care	Contributing to the world helps adults feel a sense of accomplishment.	Failure at this stage may lead people to feel uninvolved in the world.
Integrity vs despair	65–Death	'Was my life a good one?'	Wisdom	Older adults look back on their lives with a sense of satisfaction.	Failure at this stage may lead people to look back at their lives with regret, sorrow and bitterness.

Strengths and weaknesses of Erikson (1959)

One of the strengths of Erikson's theory is its ability to tie together important psychosocial development across the entire lifespan. Erikson was one of the first psychologists to attempt the difficult task of providing a stage account of the whole of human development, and so he helped to open up the psychology of adulthood as an area of study. It is now generally accepted that people do develop and show significant psychological changes throughout their lives rather than simply during childhood.

Some common criticisms of Erikson's theory are that it doesn't say much about the underlying causes of each development crisis. It also tends to be somewhat vague about the experiences and events that mark the difference between success and failure at each stage. Also, the theory lacks any objective way to determine if a person has 'passed' or 'failed' a particular stage of development.

Another problem is that the stages imply that most people change and develop in the same ways, which is not always the case. Neugarten (1975) found that working-class men tend to get married, have children and have a full-time job during their early 20s, whereas middle-class men often delay settling down and getting married until their 30s.

Baumeister (2008) and the consequences of belief in free will

At the core of the question of free will is a debate about the psychological causes of action.

The **deterministic** position leaves no room for free human choice. The universe resembles a giant machine, grinding along exactly as it must; everything that happens is inevitable.

On the other side, Sartre argued passionately in favour of human freedom. He contended that people are always, inevitably, free. Life is a series of choice points, and at each choice point, you could have chosen differently than you did. When people say they could not help acting as they did, they are deceiving themselves, because they could have acted otherwise and other outcomes really were possible.

In between those extremes, many thinkers have proposed limited or partial freedom. Kant proposed that people have a capacity for free action but only use it sometimes. Free will should be understood not as the starter or motor of action but rather as a passenger who occasionally grabs the steering wheel, or even as just a navigator who says to turn left up ahead.

Baumeister believes psychologists should focus on what we do best: collecting evidence about behaviour, and we should explain what happens differently between free and unfree actions. Thus, we need to find out what people mean when they use freedom, choice and responsibility in their daily lives. Baumeister claims a belief in free will can help with an individual's self-control, and that self-control itself has multiple benefits. People who are high in self-control (and so act freely) end up more successful in work and school, are more popular and better liked, have healthier and more stable relationships and commit fewer crimes.

Those with self-control and willpower use inner strength to fend off strong temptations and cope with crises.

Self-control has been especially successful at predicting performance at school and work. Some people use their willpower to study all night before the exam, but others use it more effectively by keeping up with their work, so they don't have to stay up all night at the last minute. In both cases, self-control is a weapon of our free will.

Belief in free will is highly relevant to our justice system. For example, if all actions are fully caused and therefore inevitable, why does the legal system spend so much time trying to establish whether an individual was acting freely?

Key term

Deterministic is the opposite of free will. Everything that happens is the unavoidable product of prior causes.

Strengths and weaknesses of Baumeister (2008)

Vohs and Schooler (2008) found that participants who had been led to disbelieve in free will were subsequently more likely than a control group to cheat on a test. Similarly, Baumeister *et al.* (2006) found that causing participants to disbelieve in free will made them more aggressive and less helpful towards others. It therefore seems reasonable to suggest that belief in free will is conducive to better, more harmonious social behaviour.

To expect moral responsibility, one must accept the concept of free will. If an individual's behaviour is determined by forces beyond an individual's control, then the individual cannot be held responsible for their actions. However, our laws insist that adults do have individual responsibility for their actions and so implicitly society supports free will.

Skinner argued that free will is an illusion and that our behaviour is in fact environmentally determined. Libet *et al.* (1983) found that the motor regions of the brain become active before a person registers conscious awareness of a decision, i.e. the decision to move the finger was a pre-determined action of the brain. This strongly suggests that many responses are biologically determined and that, although we may believe that we have free will, Skinner's claim that free will is an illusion may be correct.

Many psychologists do not favour a deterministic point of view. If behaviour is determined by outside forces, that provides a potential excuse for criminal acts. For example, in 1981 Stephen Mobley argued that he was 'born to kill', after killing a pizza shop manager, because his family had a disposition towards violence and aggressive behaviour.

Now test yourself

7. What is the opposite of having free will?
8. Did Kant believe in free will or determinism, or both?

The humanistic theory of self

In the humanistic view, people are responsible for their lives and actions and have the freedom and will to change their attitudes and behaviour.

Humanistic explanations of the development of self-esteem and personality

Humanistic psychology begins with the assumption that people have free will. Our self-esteem and personality are consequences of the free choices made by us.

Rogers (1951): humanistic theory

Carl Rogers was a therapist who had a respect for the dignity of people as subjects rather than objects. His theory of personality started from the premise that people are basically good.

Rogers (1951) viewed the child as having two basic needs: positive regard from other people and **self-worth**.

A person who has high self-worth – that is, has confidence and positive feelings about him or herself – faces challenges in life, accepts failure and unhappiness at times, and is open with people. A person with low self-worth may avoid challenges in life, not accept that life can be painful and unhappy at times and will be defensive and guarded with other people.

Rogers believed feelings of self-worth developed in early childhood and were formed from the interaction of the child with the mother and father. As a child grows older, interactions with significant others will affect feelings of self-worth.

Key term

Self-worth refers to how we think about ourselves and the likelihood that we can achieve goals and ambitions in life and achieve self-actualisation.

Rogers believed that we need to be regarded positively by others; we need to feel valued, respected, treated with affection and loved. Positive regard is to do with how other people evaluate and judge us in social interactions. Rogers made a distinction between **unconditional positive regard** and **conditional positive regard**.

Key term

Unconditional positive regard is where parents and significant others accept and love the person for what he or she is. Positive regard is not withdrawn if the person does something wrong or makes a mistake.

The consequences of unconditional positive regard are that the person feels free to try things out and make mistakes, even though this may lead to getting it wrong at times. People who can self-actualise are more likely to have received unconditional positive regard from others, especially their parents, in childhood.

Key term

Conditional positive regard is where positive regard, praise and approval depend upon the child – for example, behaving in ways that the parents think are correct. Hence the child is not loved for the person he or she is, but on condition that he or she behaves only in ways approved by the parents.

The development of congruence is dependent on unconditional positive regard. Carl Rogers believed that for a person to achieve self-actualisation they must be in a state of congruence.

According to Rogers, we want to feel, experience and behave in ways which are consistent with our self-image and which reflect what we would like to be like, our ideal self.

As we prefer to see ourselves in ways that are consistent with our self-image, we may use defence mechanisms like denial or repression to feel less threatened by some of what we consider to be our undesirable feelings. A person whose self-concept is incongruent with her or his real feelings and experiences will defend because the truth hurts.

Strengths and weaknesses of Rogers (1951)

Rogers gave us a better insight into an individual's behaviour and helped to provide a more holistic view of human behaviour, in contrast to the reductionist position of science. Rogers shifted the focus of behaviour to the whole person rather than the unconscious mind, genes, observable behaviour, etc.

His theory has real-life applications, such as cognitive behavioural therapy, which tries to incorporate humanistic ideals of unconditional positive regard and empathy to help the individual. The therapist has a very positive and optimistic view of human nature.

The main problems with this theory are related to the lack of precision and unscientific approach regarding some of the terms and concepts which are too subjective. Krebs and Blackman (1988) also suggest that some connections between concepts such as the self and empathy are not completely clear.

Some human conditions, such as psychopathy, do not make much sense according to this theory. The psychopath apparently feels no guilt, discomfort or remorse for their actions; there is no anxiety. Incongruence is not apparent, although the theory suggests it would be quite large.

Now test yourself

9. Conditional positive regard can lead to incongruence. True or false?

Maslow (1943): hierarchy of needs

Maslow stated that people are motivated to achieve certain needs and that some needs take precedence over others. Maslow's hierarchy of needs is made up of five levels of human needs.

1. Biological and physiological needs – air, food, drink, shelter, warmth and sleep.
2. Safety needs – protection from elements, security, order, law and stability.
3. Love and belongingness needs – friendship, intimacy, trust and acceptance.
4. Esteem needs – for oneself (dignity, achievement and independence) and the desire for reputation or respect from others.
5. Self-actualisation needs – realising personal potential, self-fulfilment, seeking personal growth and peak experiences, a desire 'to become everything one is capable of becoming'.

Instead of focusing on what goes wrong with people, Maslow formulated a more positive account of human behaviour which focused on what goes right. He was interested in human potential, and how we fulfil that potential.

Maslow specified that human motivation is based on personal growth that is present throughout a person's life. Self-actualised people are those who are fulfilled and doing all they are capable of.

As we are all unique, the motivation for self-actualisation leads people in different directions. For some, it can be achieved through art or literature; for others, through sport, in education or within a company. Maslow believed self-actualisation could be measured through peak experiences of joy and wonder.

Maslow believed that only 2 per cent of people would reach the state of self-actualisation. He was especially interested in the characteristics of people whom he considered to have achieved their potential, including Abraham Lincoln and Albert Einstein.

Strengths and weaknesses of Maslow (1943)

The biggest strength of Maslow's theory is the focus on awareness of emotions. Each person has an individual motivational framework with which they work and which drives their behaviour; this framework differs from person to person and even for a single individual from day to day. So, Maslow can explain individual differences amongst us and his theory can be applied universally.

Maslow's theory has applications in many fields, such as helping managers in understanding how to motivate employees, sports coaches motivating their students and of course in education with teachers and pupils.

Maslow's theory is based on the biographies of 18 people he identified as being self-actualised. It could be argued this is extremely subjective as it is based entirely on the opinion of the researcher, which reduces the validity of any data obtained. Therefore, Maslow's definition of self-actualisation is not scientific fact but instead subjective opinion.

Maslow states that the lower needs must be satisfied before a person can achieve their potential and self-actualise. This is not always the case. Those that live in poverty are still capable of higher order needs such as love and belongingness. However, according to the theory, people who have difficulty achieving very basic physiological needs are not capable of meeting higher growth needs.

Internal and external influences on the self and self-esteem

Our behaviour can be influenced by internal factors that come from within us or from external factors that come from outside us, such as the environment.

Internal factors which can influence our self and our self-esteem

In psychology, **temperament** refers to those aspects of an individual's personality that are often regarded as biologically based rather than learned. Our temperament can influence our emotion, activity and attention.

An important dimension of temperament is **effortful control**, which is about adapting to the situation even if you may not want to. For example, the abilities to focus attention when there are distractions, to not interrupt others, to sit still in church or class and to force oneself to do an unpleasant task are aspects of effortful control. These abilities underlie the emergence of self-regulation, a major milestone in children's development.

Robins *et al.* (2010) examined the relation between self-esteem and temperament in a sample of 646 Mexican-American early adolescents. Findings showed that adolescents with high self-esteem showed higher levels of effortful control. The study contributed to an emerging understanding of the link between self-esteem and temperament, and provided data on the nature of self-esteem in ethnic minority populations

Key terms

Temperament refers to the personality differences in infants and young children that are present prior to the development of higher cognitive thinking.

Effortful control is the ability to voluntarily manage attention and inhibit behaviour when required, especially when we may not particularly want to do so.

Now test yourself

10. Sakina finds it difficult to sit still at the local mosque and concentrate on what she is learning as she keeps being distracted by the girl sitting next to her. What may Sakina be lacking?

External factors which can influence our self and our self-esteem

Low self-esteem can be deeply rooted in traumatic childhood experiences, such as prolonged separation from parent figures, neglect, or emotional, physical or sexual abuse. In later life, self-esteem can be undermined by ill health, negative life events, such as losing a job or getting divorced, and a general sense of lack of control. This sense of lack of control may be especially found in victims of discrimination on the grounds of religion, culture, race, sex or sexual orientation.

The relationship between low self-esteem and mental disorder and mental distress is very complex. Low self-esteem predisposes to mental disorder, which in turn knocks self-esteem. In some cases, low self-esteem is in itself a feature of mental disorder, as, for example, in depression.

Low self-esteem in children tends to be related to physical punishment and withholding of love and affection by parents. Carl Rogers would describe this as conditional positive regard, whereby individuals only receive positive attention from parents when they act in a certain way. This reinforces to the child that they are only a person of value when they act a certain way, e.g. achieving an A grade on a test.

Self-esteem continues to decline during adolescence (particularly for girls). Researchers have attributed this decline to body image and other problems associated with puberty.

Although boys and girls report similar levels of self-esteem during childhood, a gender gap emerges by adolescence, in that adolescent boys have higher self-esteem than adolescent girls (Robins *et al.*, 2002). Girls with low self-esteem appear to be more vulnerable to perceptions of the ideal body image shown in the media than boys.

How personality can be measured

Psychologists seek to measure personality through many methods, the most common of which are scales that determine someone's personality traits.

Personality scales

The **rating scale** is one of the oldest and most versatile of assessment techniques. Rating scales are used by observers and by individuals for self-reporting. A teacher, for example, might be asked to rate students on the degree to which the behaviour of each reflects leadership capacity, shyness or creativity. Peers might rate each other along dimensions such as friendliness, trustworthiness and social skills. Several standardised, printed rating scales are available for describing the behaviour of psychiatric hospital patients. Relatively objective rating scales have also been devised for use with other groups.

Various kinds of rating scales have been developed to measure attitudes directly (i.e. the person knows their attitude is being studied). The most widely used is the Likert scale.

A Likert-type scale usually runs from strongly agree to strongly disagree and assumes that attitudes can be measured. Respondents may be offered a choice of five to seven or even nine pre-coded responses with the neutral point being neither agree nor disagree.

I would rather play a sport than sit and watch TV

Strongly agree – Agree – Don't know – Disagree – Strongly disagree

Key term

Rating scales present users with an item and ask them to select from many choices, like a multiple-choice test, but its options represent degrees of a characteristic.

Personality types

There are many ways to measure personality; most psychologists focus on personality traits.

The most widely accepted of these traits are the Big Five:

- Openness – being honest, as in you do not try to hide anything
- Conscientiousness – being careful, such as wanting to do well on a task
- Extraversion – someone who is sociable likes talking and being with others
- Agreeableness – being warm, friendly and getting along well with others
- Neuroticism – having anxiety, fear, anger, frustration and loneliness.

You can remember these traits with the handy OCEAN or CANOE mnemonic. The Big Five are the ingredients that make up everyone's personality. A person might have a dash of openness, a lot of conscientiousness, an average amount of extraversion, plenty of agreeableness and almost no neuroticism at all.

Personality types are still used by career counsellors and in the corporate world to help people's understanding of themselves. Perhaps the most famous of these is the Myers-Briggs Type Indicator.

A questionnaire sorts people into categories based on six areas: sensation (S), intuition (N), feeling (F) and thinking (T), as well as extraversion (E) and **introversion** (I).

Sensing and intuition refer to how people prefer to gather information about the world, whether through concrete information (sensing) or emotions (intuition). Thinking and feeling refer to how people make decisions. Thinking types go with logic, while feeling types follow their hearts.

The use of trait theory as a measure of personality

This approach assumes behaviour is determined by **traits**, which are the fundamental units of one's personality. Traits remain consistent across situations and over time but may vary between individuals. It is presumed that individuals differ in their traits due to genetic differences.

Allport (1936): cardinal, central and secondary personality traits

In 1936, psychologist Gordon Allport found that one English language dictionary alone contained more than 4,000 words describing different personality traits. He categorised these traits into three levels:

People with **cardinal traits** can become so well-known for these traits that their names are often associated with these qualities. For example, the word Freudian, an adjective that is related to deeply hidden desires or feelings, is linked to Sigmund Freud. Allport suggested that cardinal traits are rare and tend to develop later in life.

While not as dominating as cardinal traits, **central traits** are the major characteristics you might use to describe another person. Terms such as 'intelligent', 'honest', 'shy' and 'anxious' are considered central traits. According to Allport, every person has around 5–10 central traits, and they are present in varying degrees in every person. They are responsible for shaping most of our behaviour.

Finally, **secondary traits** often appear only in certain situations or under specific circumstances. For example, a person whose cardinal trait is assertiveness may display signs of obedience when the police stop him for speeding.

Key terms

Introversion refers to being focused more on internal thoughts, feelings and moods rather than seeking out external stimulation (opposite of extraversion).

Traits are a distinguishing quality or characteristic, typically one belonging to a person.

Cardinal traits are traits that dominate an individual's whole life, often to the point that the person becomes known specifically for these traits.

Central traits are the general characteristics that form the basic foundations of personality.

Secondary traits are the traits that are sometimes related to attitudes or preferences.

Cattell (1946): 16PF personality factor assessment

While a graduate student at London University, Raymond B. Cattell was hired as a research assistant to Charles Spearman, a well-known name in the field of intellectual assessment, who developed a mathematical formula known as **factor analysis.** Imagine the power of this technique for lesser understood concepts such as intelligence and personality.

In 1946, Cattell used factor analysis to publish his findings in an assessment known as the 16PF. According to Cattell's research, human personality traits could be summarised using 16 personality factors (PF) or main traits. Everybody has some degree of every trait, according to Cattell. The 16 traits are shown in Table 7.2.

Table 7.2 Cattell's 16 personality traits

Factor	**Low score**	**High score**
Warmth	Cold, selfish	Supportive, comforting
Intellect	Instinctive, unstable	Cerebral, analytical
Emotional stability	Irritable, moody	Level-headed, calm
Aggressiveness	Modest, docile	Controlling, tough
Liveliness	Sombre, restrained	Wild, fun-loving
Dutifulness	Untraditional, rebellious	Conformity, traditional
Social assertiveness	Shy, withdrawn	Uninhibited, bold
Sensitivity	Coarse, tough	Touchy, soft
Paranoia	Trusting, easy-going	Wary, suspicious
Abstractness	Practical, regular	Strange, imaginative
Introversion	Open, friendly	Private, quiet
Anxiety	Confident, self-assured	Fearful, self-doubting
Open-mindedness	Close-minded, set-in-ways	Curious, self-exploratory
Independence	Outgoing, social	Loner, craves solitude
Perfectionism	Disorganised, messy	Orderly, thorough
Tension	Relaxed, cool	Stressed, unsatisfied

Key term

Factor analysis is a statistical technique which allows you to take raw data and determine patterns of data. In other words, if you and many others took a general test that had both maths and English questions, a factor analysis would likely determine that there were two factors or patterns on this test.

Strengths and weaknesses of trait theory as a measure of personality

The biggest strength of trait theory is its reliance on statistical or objective data. Unlike other theories, the subjectivity or personal experience of the theorists play no role in trait theory. Traits are observable and can be measured, which means there is no need for interpretation from anyone, making it more valid.

Trait theory provides an easy-to-understand continuum that provides a good deal of information regarding a person's personality, interaction and beliefs about the self and the world. Understanding traits allows us to compare people, to determine which traits allow a person to do better in college, in relationships or in a specific career. We can help guide people towards a more agreeable future by knowing how they interact with the world.

Some of the most common criticisms of trait theory centre on the fact that traits are often poor predictors of behaviour. While an individual may score high on assessments of a specific trait, they may not always behave that way in every situation. Another problem is those trait theories do not address how or why individual differences in personality develop or emerge.

Because it is based on statistics rather than theory, it provides no explanation of personality development, which means it provides little or no guidance in the changing of negative aspects of a trait. Without understanding how a trait develops, how do we then change that trait? Many argue that the application of trait theory is significantly reduced because it lacks a means for change. What good is to measure something or to know something if we can do nothing about it?

Studies

Vohs and Schooler (2008): the value of believing in free will: encouraging a belief in determinism increases cheating

Aim

To see whether participants who believed that behaviour is under the control of **pre-determined** forces would cheat more than would participants who believed more in free will.

Procedure

Thirty university students (13 female and 17 male) took part and were first asked to read one of two passages from a book written by Francis Crick.

In the anti-free will condition (experimental condition), participants read statements claiming that most scientists today recognise that actual free will is an illusion. Another group of participants read portions from the same book taken from a chapter on consciousness, which did not discuss free will (control condition). All participants completed a separate Free Will and Determinism (FWD) scale to assess changes in their beliefs and mood.

Participants were then given a computer-based mental arithmetic task in which they were asked to mentally calculate equations (e.g. 1+8+18–12+19–7+17–2+8–4= ?). Participants were told, however, that the computer had a programming glitch and that the correct answer would appear on screen while they were attempting to solve the problem. They were then told that there was a method of stopping the answer from appearing, however, which was to press the space bar after the maths problem appeared on screen. Furthermore, participants were told that the experimenter could not know whether they hit the space bar, but that they should honestly solve the problems on their own. The computer had been rigged not only to show the answer but also to record the number of space bar presses. A total of 20 problems were presented individually and the number of times participants stopped the answer from appearing was the dependent measure of cheating. Afterwards, participants were debriefed and thanked.

Results

Scores on the Free Will and Determinism (FWD) scale showed that participants in the anti-free will condition reported weaker free will beliefs (M=13.6) than participants in the control condition (M=16.8).

Whether participants would allow the answers to the arithmetic questions to be revealed was the dependent measure of cheating. As predicted, participants cheated more after reading the anti-free will essay (M=14.00) than after reading the control essay (M=9.67).

Conclusion

Participants cheated more on a simple arithmetic task after reading an essay that refuted the notion of free will as causing human behaviour than after reading a neutral essay. This is like accidentally receiving an extra £5 from the shop owner but not returning the additional money.

These conclusions were supported by a follow-up experiment where participants in the anti-free will condition paid themselves more money for a task than other groups, thereby showing active cheating.

Key term

Pre-determined is when something is decided by previous events or by people rather than by chance.

Strengths and weaknesses of Vohs and Schooler (2008)

One strength is how the results can be applied to support the determinism side of the free will versus determinism debate. Reading the anti-free will essay reduced participants' belief in free will, a change that accounted for the impact of the essay on cheating behaviour. The results therefore support the idea that human cheating behaviour is more linked to a belief in determinism than free will.

Supporting evidence for the study and its conclusions comes from Schab (1991), who found that between 1969 and 1989, student responses reflected increasingly pessimistic opinions about dishonesty in school and society. Fear of failure remained the most common reason for cheating, and more students admitted to cheating on tests and homework. This was due to having a belief that their results in tests were already determined and had little to do with any free will or control on their part.

One weakness is how cheating was measured (by not pressing the space bar). This method of assessing cheating also means that simply doing nothing is coded as cheating. So, the anti-free will essay may have caused non-participation generally, rather than cheating behaviour specifically. Although participants were instructed to press the space bar to avoid receiving the answers, their failure to do so does not guarantee they were cheating.

The method was laboratory based, which means both the setting and the task were artificial and cannot be applied to real life. Demand characteristics are a common part of experiments like this and the participants may have felt they had to act in a certain way due to all the instructions given from the researchers regarding pressing the space bar. What the participants were asked to do also lacks task validity as it is not a normal, everyday procedure to do what they did.

Van Houtte and Jarvis (1995): the role of pets in preadolescent psychosocial development

Aim

Van Houtte and Jarvis wanted to investigate the impact of pet ownership on teenage personality. They hypothesised that pet-owning adolescents would report higher levels of autonomy and self-esteem than non-pet owners.

Procedure

A sample of 130 white students (71 boys and 59 girls, aged between 8 and 13) from Illinois, USA was selected for research based on pet ownership. Participants were divided into two groups: pet owners and non-pet owners. They were also matched on three aspects; marital status of their parents, socio-economic status of the parents and number of siblings they had.

Questions were also asked about details of their pet: age of pet, type of pet, duties they had in looking after it, etc. They were given questionnaires and asked to rate statements about autonomy, self-concept, self-esteem and attachment to animals.

- Autonomy was measured on a four-point scale response to such sentences as 'My parents and I agree on everything'.
- Self-concept was measured on a five-point scale response to adjectives, such as 'I am happy'.
- Self-esteem was measured on a four-point scale response to items such as 'On the whole I am satisfied with myself'.
- Attachment to pets was measured on a seven-point scale response to a series of statements such as 'I consider my pet a friend'.

Permission was gained from the participants and they were given the right to withdraw from the study at any time.

Results
- In general, higher self-esteem was reported in pet owners than in non-pet owners.
- For 11-year olds, pets were found to positively influence self-concept.
- Higher autonomy was reported by all pet owners across the age groups tested.
- 13-year olds with pets had a more positive self-concept.
- Attachment to animals is not reliant on pet ownership. There was no relationship between the perceived benefits of owning a pet and actual ownership of a pet. The benefits of having a pet could therefore be the presence of the pet, not attachment to the pet.

Conclusion
Pets may have the greatest impact on children's lives as they move into adolescence.

Pets can offer unconditional positive regard and increase well-being and self-esteem.

Strengths and weaknesses of Van Houtte and Jarvis (1995)

One strength is that the results can be applied to real life in that pets can be used to help people suffering from low self-esteem, as a support for others in times of stress and to enhance feelings of responsibility for elderly people.

A weakness of the study is that it over-simplifies difficult concepts such as self-esteem and self-concept on a scale, in turn ignoring the depth of these important aspects of the self. Therefore, the study uses a lot of quantitative data that may not be appropriate when dealing with complex emotional views. This suggests that the way the researchers chose to measure the dependent variable may not be valid to draw conclusions from.

Another limitation is that the research lacks population validity. Although the sample size was large, we cannot generalise the findings to the wider population. This is an issue because it might be that younger children have different ideas of concepts such as self-esteem and autonomy. For example, the questionnaire was only given to pupils between the ages of 8 and 13. Therefore, this weakens the credibility of this research to support the notion of pets influencing the development of our self-esteem.

The study may lack internal validity as researchers used a self-report questionnaire to investigate self-esteem. Consequently, it may be difficult for children to have accurate insight into aspects such as their self-esteem and self-concept and therefore the questionnaire might not measure what it set out to measure.

Exam questions

1. Explain the difference between the existential and categorical self. (2)
2. Catherine got a dog for Christmas, whom she adores and spends all her time with. Using your knowledge of Van Houtte and Jarvis (1995), discuss how the puppy will benefit Catherine. (4)
3. James did not want to lie to the teacher but felt like he had to as all his friends were encouraging him to do so. James looked embarrassed as he lied about why his homework was late and the teacher could tell he wasn't telling the truth. James was given a detention as punishment. Using Baumeister (2008), explain the issues around James detention. (4)
4. Tom hates doing rugby at school and wishes he was bigger and stronger like the other kids. Tom is struggling to persuade himself to go to rugby as he feels nervous when his teacher asks him. How would Rogers (1959) explain why Tom feels nervous? (3)
5. Kyle has recently changed careers as he needed a new challenge after 30 years in the same job. He feels he has a lot more to offer and is proud of his achievements but is now ready to move on to the next stage of his life. Using Erikson (1959), explain which psychosocial stage Kyle is in and whether he has successfully resolved this stage. (4)

6. Describe and evaluate Maslow's hierarchy of needs. (9)
7. Compare Cattell's (1946) trait theory of personality with Allport's (1936) trait theory, giving two similarities and two differences. (4)
8. Jack finds it difficult to concentrate at school and control his emotions. His teachers describe him as having no self-regulation. Jack is also aware of what his classmates think of him and does not have a happy time at home with his parents. With reference to Jack, explain internal and external factors that may influence our self-esteem. (6)
9. With reference to the conclusions drawn by Vohs and Schooler (2008), what advice would you give to others about moral behaviour, free will and cheating? (2)
10. Zia has a lack of confidence, is pessimistic and wants to be like someone else. Use Argyle's (2008) four major factors to describe why Zia has a lack of self-esteem. (4)

End of chapter summary

You should now have an understanding of all the points below:

Understand the concepts of the self and self-concept, including:

Lewis (1990):

- existential self
- categorical self.

Rogers (1959):

- self-image
- self-esteem
- ideal self
- self-actualisation
- congruence
- incongruence.

Understand the role of identity and free will in the development of self, including strengths and weaknesses of each theory:

- Erikson (1959): the eight stages of identity development
- Baumeister (2008): the consequence of belief in free will.

Understand the humanistic theory of self, including strengths and weaknesses of each theory:

- humanistic explanations of the development of self-esteem
- humanistic explanations of the development of personality.

Rogers (1951):

- conditional positive regard
- unconditional positive regard
- conditions of worth
- congruence
- incongruence.

Maslow (1943):

- hierarchy of needs.

Understand the role of internal and external influences on the self and self-esteem, including:

- temperament
- experience.

Understand how personality can be measured, including:

- personality scales
- personality types.

Understand the use of trait theory as a measure of personality, including strengths and weaknesses of trait theory:

- Allport (1936): cardinal, central and secondary personality traits
- Cattell (1946): 16PF personality factor assessment.

Understand the aims, procedures and findings (results and conclusions), and strengths and weaknesses of:

- Vohs and Schooler (2008): the value of believing in free will: encouraging a belief in determinism increases cheating
- Van Houtte and Jarvis (1995): the role of pets in preadolescent psychosocial development.

Now test yourself answers

1. Categorical.
2. Self-image.
3. By responding positively to our behaviour.
4. Incongruence.
5. Autonomy vs shame and doubt.
6. Industry vs inferiority.
7. Determinism.
8. Both.
9. True.
10. Effortful control.

Chapter 8
Perception – how do you interpret the world around you?

This chapter deals with our **perception** of the world around us and how this differs from just seeing what's around us. We are all guilty of making the wrong interpretation of something and perceiving things in the wrong way. The job of our brains is to perceive information around us, so we can make sense of our world.

Monocular and binocular depth cues

We receive information from the environment through our sense organs, e.g. eyes, ears and nose. Each sense organ receives sensory inputs and transmits sensory information to the brain in a process known as **sensation**. This information is sent to our brains, where perception comes into play. Perception is the way we interpret these sensations and therefore make sense of everything around us.

Visual cues

We can judge depth in the real world (in 3D) and we can understand depth in pictures (2D) using **depth cues**, which are pieces of visual information that trigger or 'cue' our understanding of distance. **Monocular depth cues** use one eye, while **binocular depth cues** require the use of both eyes.

Key terms

Perception involves interpreting what we see so we can form an understanding of an object.

Sensation refers to the process of sensing our environment through touch, taste, sight, sound and smell.

Depth cues are the visual 'clues' that we use to understand depth or distance.

Monocular depth cues give us information about distance that comes from one eye.

Binocular depth cues relate to information about distance that needs two eyes, such as **stereopsis**.

Stereopsis allows us to see one image when we are presented with two images side by side (one image from the right eye and one image from the left eye).

Figure 8.1 An example of a texture gradient

Examples of monocular depth cues include:

Superimposition – tells us that objects in front of (or partly covering) other objects are closer to us. A partly hidden object like a bus must be further away than the other traffic covering it.

Relative size – we perceive bigger objects as being closer than smaller objects, which we perceive as further away.

Texture gradient – an area with a detailed pattern is perceived to be nearer than one with less detail. So, when looking at cobblestones or a sandy beach, we see that close up the surface is very detailed, while further away the texture is less clear.

Height in the plane – when we look at pictures that include the horizon, objects lower in the scene appear closer than those objects higher up, which appear further away.

Linear perspective – parallel lines appear to converge (meet) in the distance. Very long, straight roads and railway lines appear to converge in the distance (even though we know they don't).

The greater the difference between the view seen by the left eye and the right eye, the closer the viewer is looking.

When we look at an object with both eyes open, our brain forms one perception from the two images. The image on the right retina and the image on the left retina are combined. When we are looking at something far away, the two images are very similar, but when we are looking at something closer, the two images are very different – this helps us to judge depth.

Figure 8.2 An example of linear perspective

Now test yourself

1. True or false? Objects lower in the scene appear further away than those objects higher up, which appear closer.
2. Outline the difference between monocular and binocular depth cues.

Visual illusions

Visual illusions occur when our perception conflicts or disagrees with reality; we are not seeing the world as it really is. We see an illusion when we misinterpret the stimulus, so the physical reality and our perception disagree.

Key term

A **visual illusion** is a conflict between reality and what we perceive.

There are several instances where our brains struggle to make sense of objects, such as:

- fiction – an illusion caused when a figure is perceived even though it is not present in the stimulus
- illusory contour – a boundary (edge) that is perceived in a figure but is not present in the stimulus
- motion after-effect – an illusion caused by paying more attention to movement in one direction and perceiving movement in the opposite direction immediately afterwards

- colour after-effects – an illusion caused by focusing on a coloured stimulus and perceiving opposite colours immediately afterwards
- ambiguous figure – a stimulus with two possible interpretations, in which it is possible to perceive only one of the alternatives at a time; swapping between the two interpretations is quite difficult
- distortion illusion – where our perception is deceived by some aspect of the stimulus; this can affect the shape or size of an object.

Some common geometrical illusions only work when seen on paper. If you see the object in real life and walk around it, the illusion goes away.

In the Ponzo illusion (Figure 8.3a), people tend to see the top horizontal line as longer than the one below, whereas they are both the same length. In the Ebbinghaus illusion (Figure 8.3b), people tend to see one of the central circles as larger than the other, although they are both the same size. In the cafe wall illusion (Figure 8.3c), the horizontal lines between the bricks are all parallel but are perceived not to be.

Visual constancies

There are different types of **visual constancy** – for example, colour, shape and size constancy.

As regards **colour constancy**, imagine you are looking at a bowl of fruit, which has in it a bright red apple, bananas, grapes and some mangos. If you saw only a small portion of the apple, but did not know that it was an apple, the colour would appear to change a little as the light changed. However, once you know it is an apple, you will still perceive the colour as bright red even when the light changes a little (really).

Figure 8.3a The Ponzo illusion

Source: www.illusionsindex.org/i/ponzo-illusion.

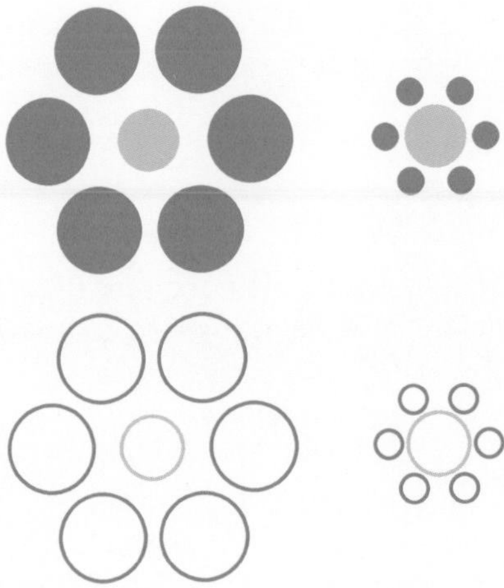

Figure 8.3b The Ebbinghaus illusion

Source: www.illusionsindex.org/ir/ebbinghaus-illusion.

Figure 8.3c The cafe wall illlusion

Source: www.illusionsindex.org/i/cafe-wall-illusion.

Key terms

Visual constancy is our ability to perceive that an object remains the same, even when the object projects different images onto our retinas in our eyes.

Colour constancy is the ability to hold the image of an object's colour even though it appears to alter on our eye.

Now test yourself

3. In which illusion do you tend to see the top horizontal line as longer than the one below?

Figure 8.4 Shape constancy – despite viewing the door at different angles, we know that the door remains rectangular

The phenomenon of your perceiving the 'real' shapes of objects regardless of their retinal projections is called **shape constancy**. For example, when we look head-on at a rectangular picture frame hanging on the wall, it appears as a rectangle. If we walk off of to the side and look at the frame from an angle, we still recognise that it is in the shape of a rectangle, but really, from that angle, the image processed by our retina is that of a trapezoid. Our brain compensates for the distortion of the shape by considering visual cues about distance and depth to keep our perception of the frame constant. Have you ever noticed, for example, when you approach the dinner table that the shapes of the plates do not change? When you look at them from some distance away from the table, the shapes of the round plates are elliptical on your retina. The only time that the image of a round plate is approximately round on your retina is when you look at it straight on.

Size constancy allows us to understand that a person walking into the distance stays the same height and doesn't 'shrink' within our view frame. We perceive an object as the same size even when its distance from us changes. When we look at an object that is close, our brain scales it down so that it looks normal sized and when an object is further away we scale it up, so it looks normal rather than tiny. This reminds us that the size of the object remains constant but helps us to make sense of our world.

Key terms

Shape constancy is the tendency to perceive an object as having the same shape regardless of its orientation or the angle from which we view it.
Size constancy is the ability to perceive objects as the same size although the images projected to us differ in size.

Now test yourself

4. The ability to understand that the properties of an object stay the same even when its size, shape and colour change is known as?

Direct theory of perception (Gibson, 1966)

The main theme of Gibson's theory is that the sensations received by the visual system are so highly organised and rich in information that we do not need to interpret them to make them meaningful; we can perceive them directly. Sensation is perception; what you see is what you get. There is no need for interpretation as the information we receive about size, shape and distance, etc. is sufficiently detailed for us to interact directly with the environment

The optic array

The most important source of information is the **optic array**. Gibson argued that, as we move around the environment, we effortlessly detect information from the whole of the optic array. Since this optic array provides a great deal of unambiguous information, little or no information processing is required.

The optic flow

Gibson was particularly interested in the problems pilots experience when landing. Imagine you are a pilot coming in to land. The point you focus on, called the 'pole', is stationary, while the remainder of your field of vision is moving. The further from the pole an object or scene is, the quicker it appears to move. All this information is known as the **optic flow pattern.** Changes in the flow of the optic array contain important information about what type of movement is taking place. The flow of the optic array will either move from or towards a particular point. If the flow appears to be coming from the point, it means you are moving towards it. If the optic array is moving towards the point, you are moving away from it.

In the normal course of our daily lives, we may not be flying aeroplanes, but we are moving around our environment. Gibson consistently argued that there are very close links between perception and action. We do not perceive our world from a static viewpoint but by moving around and interacting in it, and this supports the idea that perception is entirely dependent on action.

Invariants

As we move around our environment, we identify those aspects of it that remain the same – that are **invariant**. This makes the layout of objects in space unambiguous, so they can be picked up directly by the perceiver. For a pilot, the 'pole' is an invariant.

Affordances

We attach meaning to the type of visual information we receive; all the potential uses of an object, called **affordances**, are perceived directly. We would, for example, 'afford' a ladder the properties of being able to assist ascent or descent, by considering the gaps between successive rungs in relation to the length of our legs.

Key terms

The **optic array** contains all the visual information available at the retina.
The **optic flow pattern** provides unmistakable information on direction, speed and altitude.
Invariants provide essential information about the layout of the environment.
Affordances are visual clues of the possibilities for action offered by objects in the environment.

Strengths and weaknesses of the direct theory of perception (Gibson, 1966)

Gibson's theory is a highly ecologically valid theory as it puts perception back into the real world. Many applications can be applied in terms of his theory, e.g. training pilots, runway markings and road markings. It is an excellent explanation for perception when viewing conditions are clear.

It draws attention to the rich source of information available to the perceiver. Gibson pointed to the amazingly rich source of stimulation that is available to a moving perceiver and to the fact that the light reflected from objects must be organised in some way. Previously, theorists had concentrated only on the image on the retina, not the way in which this changed as the observer moved. Gibson pointed out that we have far more information than that at our disposal.

His theory is reductionist as it seeks to explain perception solely in terms of the environment. There is strong evidence to show that the brain and long-term memory can influence perception. In this case, it could be said that Gregory's theory is far more plausible.

However, Gibson's approach is threatened by the existence of many visual illusions which can't be explained by his theory. In the Müller-Lyer (see below), Ebbinghaus and Ponzo illusions, our perception becomes very inaccurate. These illusions would not occur if perception was directly from the environment, as Gibson suggests.

Now test yourself

5. Explain how Gibson's theory is seen as reductionist.

Constructivist theory of perception (Gregory, 1970)

Stimulus information from our environment is frequently ambiguous so to interpret it, we require information either from past experiences or stored knowledge in order to makes **inferences** about what we perceive. A lot of information reaches the eye, but much is lost by the time it reaches the brain; therefore, the brain has to guess what a person sees based on past experiences. We actively construct our perception of reality.

Gregory argues that perception is an active and **constructive** process. **Schemas** based on expectations are amongst the most important of these. Constructivists like Gregory suggest that our perception of the world is strongly affected by our existing schemas. One example of a schema in the world of visual perception is that of faces. Our 'face' schema tells us that however different one face is from another, they have certain common features, such as a nose that protrudes, two eyes, a mouth and so on.

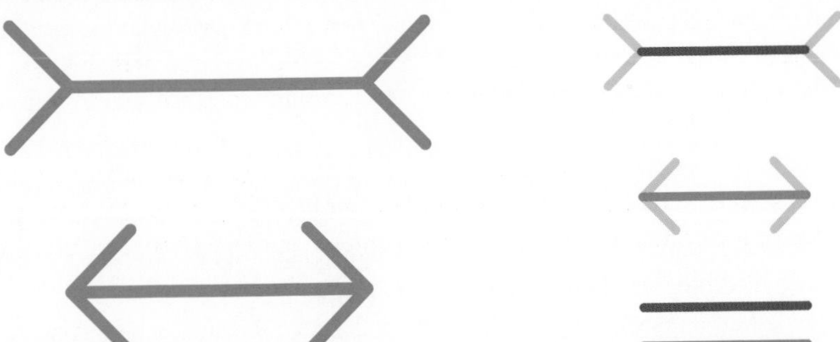

Figure 8.5 The Müller-Lyer illusion

One of Gregory's favourite demonstrations of the role of schemas based on expectation is the 'hollow face illusion', in which people view a hollowed mask of a face. Although there is sufficient information to see the mask as hollow, we still perceive a normal face. Our schema of a face overrides the evidence of our own eyes and we accept an incorrect hypothesis.

According to Gregory, perception is a series of hypothesis-testing exercises. As we encounter certain life experiences, we 'call up' the most appropriate, the most relevant or the most recent schemas and use these to provide the context in which to interpret our present experience. Most of the time these hypotheses are accurate – they fit our expectations. Sometimes, however, the schema does not fit the occasion and perception is made difficult or inaccurate.

Key terms

Inferences are best guesses about what we perceive.
Constructive refers to using past information to help us construct what we perceive.
Schemas are categories into which we incorporate the information from our experiences.

Gregory argued that we treat two-dimensional illusions as if they were three-dimensional, even though we know they are only two-dimensional. Gregory suggests the misapplied size constancy theory explains several illusions. Gregory suggests that when we look at the Müller-Lyer illusion (Figure 8.5) and the 'fins' out of context, there are no cues to help us perceive their length, so we draw on existing hypotheses and expectations. These tell us that the figure with the fins diverging represents an inside corner and the one with the fins converging represents an outside corner. Since it is part of our expectation that outside corners are usually further away than inside ones, when the vertical line is the same length, the 'outside' corner one is perceived as longer since it is perceived as further away.

Strengths and weaknesses of the constructivist theory of perception (Gregory, 1970)

Evidence that expectations influence our everyday perception comes from situations in which expectations produce errors in perception. For example, proofreading often involves numerous mistakes. Daneman and Stainton (1993) found that errors were more common when readers were proofreading an essay handwritten by them rather than an essay written by someone else. Their extreme familiarity with their own writing meant that they focused less on possible errors in their own essay.

Similarly, Bruner and Goodman (1947) asked rich and poor children to estimate the size of coins. The poor children over-estimated the size of every coin more than did the rich children, which may reflect the greater value placed on money by the poor children.

The most obvious problem with the theory is that there are numerous variations on the Müller-Lyer illusion that produce just as strong an illusion, if not stronger, and yet cannot be explained in terms of misapplying the rules of size constancy. The illusion still works if the lines are horizontal, if they are absent or if the fins are replaced by squares, circles or other shapes. None of these figures could be said to represent the corner of a building.

The research involves the very rapid presentation of visual stimuli. This reduces the impact of bottom-up processes, thus allowing more scope for top-down processes to operate. This is very artificial because in real life we have longer than a fraction of a second to look at an object.

Now test yourself

6. Why is Gregory's theory seen as constructivist?
7. According to perceptual set, are you more likely to draw bigger pictures of Santa Claus just before or just after Christmas?

Perceptual set

Perceptual sets can impact how we interpret and respond to the world around us and can be influenced by several different factors.

Motivation can play an important role in perceptual sets and how we interpret the world around us. If we are cheering for our favourite sports team, we might be motivated to view members of the opposing team as overly aggressive, weak or incompetent. In one classic experiment, researchers deprived participants of food for several hours. When they were later shown a set of ambiguous images, those who had been food-deprived were far more likely to interpret the images as food-related objects. Because they were hungry, they were more motivated to see the images in a certain way.

As mentioned above, Bruner and Goodman (1947) aimed to show how motivation may influence perception. They asked rich and poor children to estimate the sizes of coins and the poor children over-estimated the size of every coin more than the rich children.

Expectations also play an important role. One of the classic experiments by Bruner and Minturn (1955) involved showing participants either a series of numbers or a series of letters. Then, the participants were shown an ambiguous

Key term

Perceptual set refers to a predisposition to perceive things in a certain way. In other words, we often tend to notice only certain aspects of an object or situation while ignoring other details.

image that could either be interpreted as the number 13 or the letter B. Those who had viewed the numbers were more likely to see it as a 13, while those who had viewed the letters were more likely to see it as the letter B.

Expectation affects other aspects of perception – for example, we may fail to notice printing errors or writing errors because we are expecting to see particular words or letters. For example, 'The cat sat on the map and licked its whiskers' – could you spot the deliberate mistake?

Active learning

Can you spot the mistakes below, which are made because of your expectations?

- *Paris in the the spring*
- *Once in a a lifetime*
- *A bird in the the hand*

Culture also influences how we perceive people, objects and situations. Surprisingly, researchers have found that people from different cultures even tend to perceive perspective and depth cues differently.

Segall *et al.* (1963) compared Africans, Filipinos, South Africans and Americans on various illusions. They found that with the Müller-Lyer illusion the Africans and Filipinos were much less susceptible than the other two groups. To explain such findings, Segall suggested the 'carpentered world' hypothesis. In the Western world, rooms are nearly always rectangular and many objects in our environment have right-angled corners and sharp edges. Such things as roads and railways in our world are common, presenting long parallel lines which seem to converge because of perspective. In the Western world, we have a visual environment rich in perspective cues to distance. In other words, we tend to interpret illusion figures such as the Müller-Lyer in terms of our past experiences – this means that in the Western world we add a third dimension (depth), which is not actually present in the drawing.

Studies of people who live in dense forests have been carried out because such people do not experience distant objects as they live in small clearings and do not get the chance to see wide open spaces. Turnbull (1961) studied the Bambuti pygmies, who live in the rainforests of the Congo. They have a closed-in world without open spaces. Turnbull brought a pygmy out to a vast plain where a herd of buffalo was grazing in the distance. The pygmy said that he had never seen one of those insects before! When he was told that they were buffalo, he was very offended – so Turnbull drove his jeep towards the herd and the pygmy was amazed when they began to 'grow' into buffalo in front of him. This is a good example of a lack of size constancy.

Emotions can have a dramatic impact on how we perceive the world around us. Many researchers suggest that our emotional state will affect the way that we perceive. McGinnies (1949) came up with the term 'perceptual defence', which refers to words which evoke unpleasant emotions taking longer to perceive at a conscious level than neutral words. It is almost as if our perceptual system is defending us against being upset or offended and it does this by not perceiving something as quickly as it should. McGinnies (1949) investigated perceptual defence by presenting subjects with 11 emotionally neutral words (such as 'apple' and 'glass') and seven emotionally arousing, taboo words (such as 'whore' and 'rape'). Each word was presented for increasingly long durations until it was named. There was a significantly higher recognition threshold for taboo words – i.e. it took longer for subjects to name taboo words. This suggested that perceptual defence was in operation and that it was causing alterations in perception.

Now test yourself

8. What is meant by the 'carpentered world' hypothesis?

Active learning

Try the following examples out to demonstrate perceptual set:

- Tell your friend to spell the word 'fork' and then say it five times. Then ask them the question, 'What do you eat soup with?' and they will probably answer 'fork' instead of spoon. They answer incorrectly because you have just put the idea of a fork in their mind and they expect the next word they say to be fork.
- Say the words 'silk', 'dilk', 'rilk', 'tilk' and then ask a friend what cows drink. Their perceptual set will cause them to say 'milk', even though cows really drink water.
- You see your friend in the hall who is expecting you to say, 'How's it going?', but instead you say, 'What's up?' and your friend says, 'Good'.

Studies

Haber and Levin (2001): the independence of size perception and distance perception

Experiment 1

Aims(s)

To investigate estimations in size of familiar objects that show either very little variation in size (token invariant) or a lot of variation in size (token variable).

Procedure

Experimental psychologists were asked to rate a list of common objects for likely familiarity to be used with a sample of 109 male undergraduate students from a psychology course at the University of Illinois, Chicago. A total of 50 items were selected for the final list, with the psychologists agreeing on these objects having high familiarity. Researchers then measured as many of these objects as possible to get an accurate rating of their size. To ensure reliability and accuracy, they did this by visiting several local shops to measure at least ten of each object; for example, measuring ten bowling balls. The participants were given a questionnaire and asked to estimate the height of all 50 objects in feet and inches. This was distributed after a lesson and returned within 48 hours. Size estimates were all obtained without the object being present.

Results

Depending on whether items were token invariant or token variable, the size estimates varied in accuracy. Accuracy decreased as token variance increased; so, size estimate accuracy was more accurate for items with less token variance, i.e. for familiar objects such as a basketball and bowling ball.

Conclusions

Prior knowledge of the object was used to estimate size, and participants who were familiar with objects which were token invariant were accurate in size estimation. This suggests past experience is important in estimating size.

Experiment 2

Aim

Haber and Levin wanted to see if they could apply results from Experiment 1 to a follow-up study and see whether participants could estimate the distance of objects which were either token invariant, token variable or unfamiliar.

Procedure

Nine male college students, who had been tested for good eyesight, were driven out to a large grassy field surrounded on three sides by trees. The field had been divided and prepared into four separate sections. The first section was the arrival area and was empty.

In the second section, the experimenters had placed, at random distances, 15 real-world objects which have a known size (e.g. a milk bottle, a door).

In the third section, they placed 15 real-world objects which could be different sizes (e.g. a Christmas tree, a teddy bear).

In the fourth section, they had placed upright 15 cardboard cut-outs of three geometric figures (i.e. circles, rectangles, triangles).

Haber and Levin used a repeated measures design. The students were taken in line to the centre of the field through the empty section and asked to face one or other section of the field, in groups of three. They had been given clipboards to record their estimates about how far away the objects were. When they had all made their estimates the groups turned in a new direction and repeated the task until they had looked at all 45 objects in all three directions.

Results

They found the participants' estimates of distance were most accurate for the real-world objects that were a standard size. Their estimates were good for both near and far objects. However, their estimates for the other real-world objects and for the cut-out shapes were not so accurate.

Conclusion

Haber and Levin concluded that it was easier to estimate the distance of familiar objects because the participants were relying on their past experiences. They expected objects such as milk bottles and doors to be certain sizes, and so could work out how far away they were based on their relative size. However, with the other objects they could not use their prior knowledge in the same way. They could not be sure of their size and so could not be sure of their distance.

Now test yourself

9. Why were experimental psychologists asked to rate a list of common objects for likely familiarity?

Strengths and weaknesses of Haber and Levin (2001)

A strength is the fact psychologists were independently brought in prior to the investigation to judge what were seen as familiar objects; it was they who decided, not the researchers, which helps rule out any researcher bias. This also gives the study more validity as they can confirm they were actually testing the impact of familiarity on size.

As the nine participants all had an eyesight check, it means they all had a similar level of vision, which rules out any individual differences between the participants based on vision. This prior screening test also gives the study more credibility and demonstrates a more rigorous approach to the investigation.

It is difficult to draw conclusions from a sample that is not representative. The sample of nine is very small so cannot be generalised; also the sample was biased as the participants were all male and all college students.

Also, the task and setting lacked ecological validity as it was artificial and unfamiliar, and judging the distance of randomly placed items does not reflect or relate to real-life situations. Also, testing city dwellers in a field may have distorted the findings.

Carmichael, Hogan and Walter (1932): an experimental study on the effect of language on the reproduction of visually perceived form

Aim(s)

Carmichael, Hogan and Walter (1932) wanted to find out whether words shown with pictures would affect the way the pictures were remembered.

Procedure

A laboratory experiment with an independent groups design was employed with a sample of 95 subjects (60 female, 35 male) who were all college students or teachers.

A set of 12 ambiguous figures was designed, and two names were given to each figure.

One name was used in List 1 and one name was used in List 2. Participants in the two experimental groups were then presented with the figures and associated 'name'.

Reproduced figure →	Word list 1 →	Stimulus figure →	Word list 2 →	Reproduced figure
	Curtains in a window		Diamond in a rectangle	
	Bottle		Stirrup	
	Crescent moon		Letter C	
	Bee hive		Hat	
	Eye glasses		Dumbbells	
7	Seven	7	Four	4
	Ship's wheel		Sun	
	Hour glass		Table	
	Kidney bean		Canoe	
	Pine tree		Trowel	
	Gun		Broom	
2	Two	2	Eight	8

Figure 8.6 Word lists and stimuli from Carmichael, Hogan and Walter (1932)

The participants were put into three groups with an equal representation of males and females, as follows:

- List 1 had 48 participants.
- List 2 had 38 participants.
- The control group had 9 participants.

The independent variable was which word they heard in List 1 or List 2. The participants were then asked to draw the pictures they had seen, and their drawings were compared to the original – this was the dependent variable. The control group saw the pictures but did not hear any words. Where they could not reproduce the figure, the list was shown again, replicating the instructions and naming of the figure as per the initial presentation. This required between two and eight trials to achieve reproduction of all 12 figures.

These reproduced figures were scored by independent raters for quality of reproduction using a five-degree scale, with 1 being almost perfectly reproduced and 5 being almost completely changed from the original.

Results

- The drawings by people who heard List 1 were very different from the drawings by people who heard List 2.
- In each case the drawings looked like the words the participants had heard.
- There were over 3,000 reproductions, with 905 of those reproductions put into the category 'almost completely changed'.
- In the List 1 group, 73 per cent of the drawings resembled the word given.
- In the List 2 group, 74 per cent resembled the word given.
- In the control group, which had not heard any words, only 45 per cent resembled either one of the words.

Conclusion

Memory for pictures is reconstructed. The verbal labels given to the image affect the recall because the memory of the word alters the way the picture is represented.

Now test yourself

10. Carmichael, Hogan and Walter used a control group in this study. What is the purpose of a control group?

Strengths and weaknesses of Carmichael, Hogan and Walter (1932)

The researchers ensured they had a control group which did not hear any words at all, so they could be sure that there was actually a difference when the participants heard the words. By using two different lists, they showed clearly that the verbal labels affected people's drawings.

In real life, things are not generally as ambiguous as the stimulus figures were. When we see an object, we can generally tell what it is, and any verbal cues tend to match the stimulus, not contradict it. Prentice (1954) tested the effect of verbal labels on recognition rather than recall. The results showed that verbal labels didn't affect recognition. This would mean that Carmichael, Hogan and Walter's findings cannot be widely applied.

Exam questions

1. Imagine you are standing on the top of a building looking out across a city. Give examples of visual depth cues you might see. (4)
2. Hassan is driving down a road and passes a petrol station he needed to go to. He looks in his mirror and sees the petrol station in the distance. According to Gibson (1966), how does Hassan know the petrol station is getting further away from him? (2)
3. Hannah and Zoe are shown an ambiguous picture in psychology. Hannah says that the picture is of a rabbit, but Zoe says it is of a duck. How can Gregory's (1970) theory of perception help explain why they see two different images? (2)
4. Amelia is told to read the following sentence: 'Thanks God it's it's Friday', but she makes an error. Using perceptual set, explain why Amelia would make an error. (2)
5. Compare Gregory's (1970) and Gibson's (1966) theories of perception, giving at least one similarity and one difference. (4)
6. Irfan kept getting confused when looking at the Necker cube illusion as he kept seeing two cubes at different times. Using Gregory's theory of perception, explain why Irfan kept seeing two separate cubes. (2)
7. Outline the findings from one piece of research evidence that supports the existence of perceptual set. (2)
8. Explain how culture may explain differences in what you see and perceive. (3)
9. With reference to the conclusions drawn by Haber and Levin (2001), what advice would you give to someone who is waiting to see whether their train will be made up of small or large carriages? (2)
10. With reference to the conclusions drawn by Carmichael, Hogan and Walter (1932), what advice would you give to a teacher of art who is trying to get her students to draw objects? (4)

End of chapter summary

You should now have an understanding of all the points below:

Understand examples of, and the reasons for, monocular and binocular depth cues:

Visual cues, to include:

- superimposition
- relative size
- linear perspective
- stereopsis
- texture gradient
- height in the plane.

Visual illusions, to include:

- fictions
- ambiguous figures
- distortions.

Visual constancies, to include:

- shape
- colour.

Understand the direct theory of perception (Gibson, 1996) as an explanation of sensation and perception, including strengths and weaknesses of the theory:

- sensory input
- optic flow
- invariants
- affordances.

Understand the constructivist theory of perception (Gregory, 1970) as an explanation of sensation and perception, including strengths and weaknesses of the theory:

- sensory input
- perceptual hypothesis
- inferences
- prior knowledge.

Understand the effects of the following on perceptual set:

- motivation
- expectation
- emotion
- culture.

Understand the aims, procedures and findings (results and conclusions), and strengths and weaknesses of:

- Haber and Levin (2001): the independence of size perception and distance perception
- Carmichael, Hogan and Walter (1932): an experimental study on the effect of language on the reproduction of visually perceived form.

Now test yourself answers

1. False.
2. Monocular depth cues use one eye, while binocular depth cues require the use of both eyes.
3. The Ponzo illusion.
4. Visual constancies.
5. It seeks to explain perception solely in terms of the environment.
6. It explains how we construct our world through experience.
7. Just before Christmas, as you are more likely to be looking forward to it.
8. Living in an environment with more flat surfaces and 90-degree angles.
9. To help rule out any possible researcher bias.
10. A control group acts as a comparison group to measure the effect of any independent variable.

Chapter 9

Sleep and dreaming – why do you need to sleep and dream?

This chapter deals with something we spend nearly one third of our lives doing, sleeping and dreaming. Most of psychology looks at our waking behaviour but we all know that humans and animals need to sleep, and part of this period involves dreaming. Understanding the features, functions and benefits of sleep can help society explore what happens when you are deprived of sleep and the link to mental health issues.

Features, functions and benefits of sleep

Non-REM (nREM) sleep consists of four stages. When we are awake and alert, the **electroencephalogram** (EEG) shows beta waves; these are replaced by alpha waves when we are in bed and relaxed. As we begin to fall asleep, we enter a state of sleep and wakefulness; it is here that you may experience the sudden falling then jerking sensation in your body.

Stage 1 nREM: when we are relaxed, the brain displays slow, regular alpha waves. As we begin to fall asleep, these become theta waves, which are irregular and slower. Breathing and heart rate slows down, temperature drops and muscles relax. We may experience dream-like images (but they are not true dreams) and our bodies may suddenly jerk. Stage 1 is the lightest stage of sleep and we can easily be woken.

Stage 2 nREM: after about a minute of stage 1, brain activity slows down except for sudden spurts of activity known as 'sleep spindles'. No-one knows why we have these. We spend about 20 minutes in stage 2.

Stage 3 nREM: here, the brain shows slower delta waves. There are virtually no eye movements, and our bodies are totally relaxed. We are harder to wake up, as noise and lights do not disturb us.

Stage 4 nREM: heart rate, temperature and blood pressure are at their lowest. Our first episode of stage 4 sleep lasts for about 40 minutes.

Key terms

Non-REM refers to non-rapid eye movement sleep where the person is not dreaming.

An **electroencephalogram** is a machine which records the patterns of electrical activity in the brain.

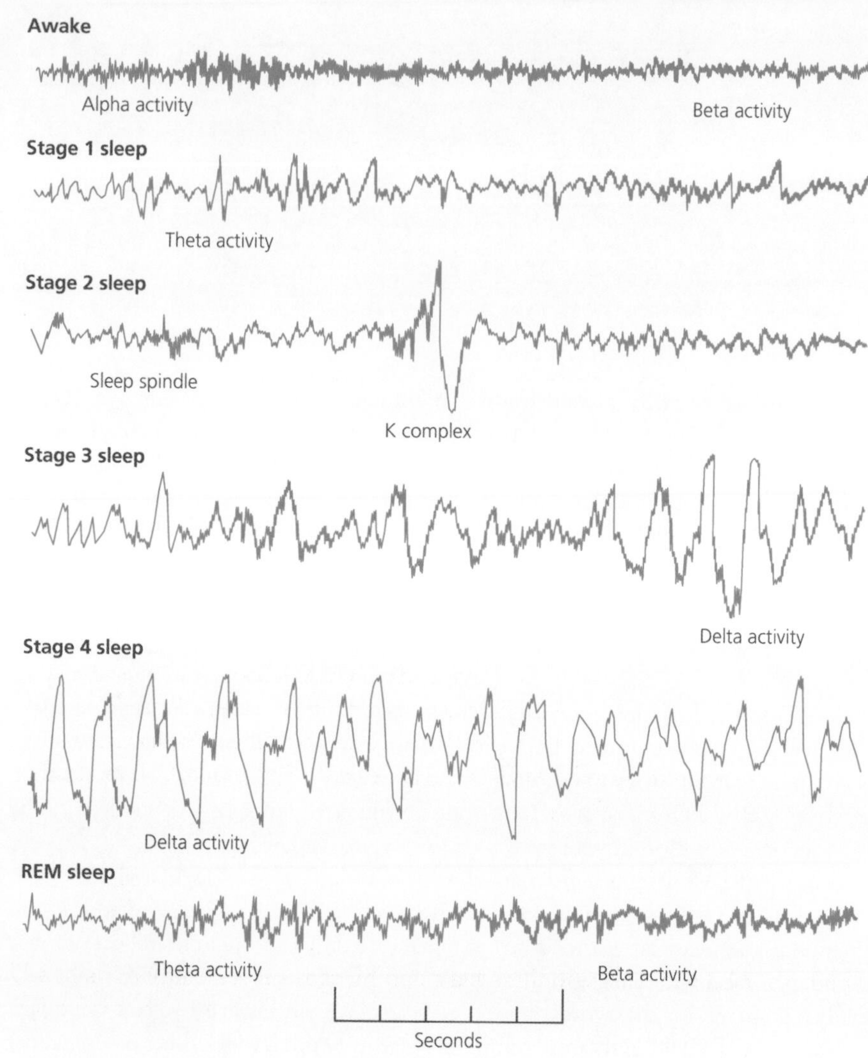

Figure 9.1 An EEG recording of the stages of sleep

Source: J.A. Horne, *Why We Sleep: The Functions of Sleep in Humans and Other Mammals* (England, Oxford University Press, 1988).

REM

After stage 4, we re-enter stage 3, then stage 2 but we never go back to stage 1. Instead, after stage 2 we enter **REM** sleep. The brain is very active; this is where we dream.

Key term

> **REM** is rapid eye movement sleep and involves fast and irregular eye movements, but virtual paralysis in the body.

Table 9.1 The four stages of sleep – summary

Stage	EEG	EOG	EMG
1 – lightest sleep; easily awakened; sometimes accompanied by a hallucinatory state	Theta waves	Slow, rolling eye movements	Relaxed but active muscles
2 – light sleep; fairly easy to awaken; k-complex activity (responding to external stimuli)	Theta waves, sleep spindles, k-complexes	Slight eye movement	Little control of muscles
3 – deep sleep; very difficult to awaken	Delta waves 20–50 per cent of the time	Virtually no eye movement	Virtually no muscle movement
4 – very deep sleep; very difficult to awaken	Delta waves for more than 50 per cent of the time	Virtually no eye movement	Virtually no muscle movement
REM – difficult to awaken; associated with vivid dreams	High levels of mixed wave activity	REM reflecting dream content	Muscles are virtually paralysed

Now test yourself

1. In which state does the brain seem most active?
2. When are we in our deepest sleep?
3. What other measure besides the EEG shows a person is in REM sleep?
4. What seems to be happening during REM?

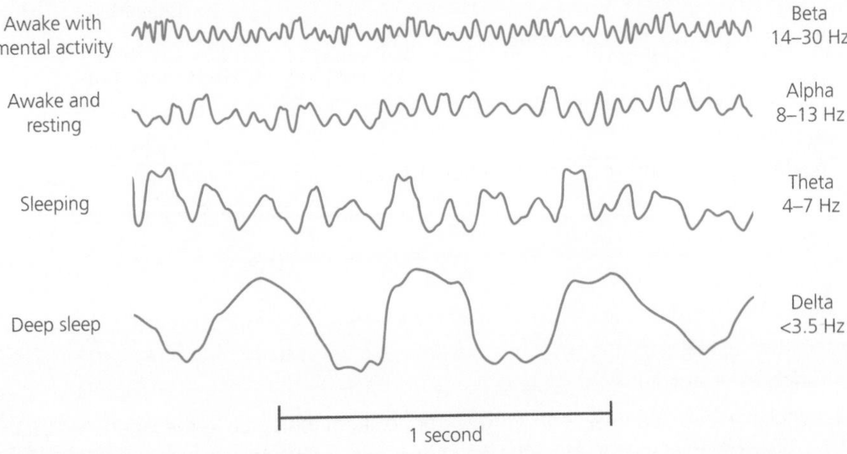

Figure 9.2 Normal adult brain waves

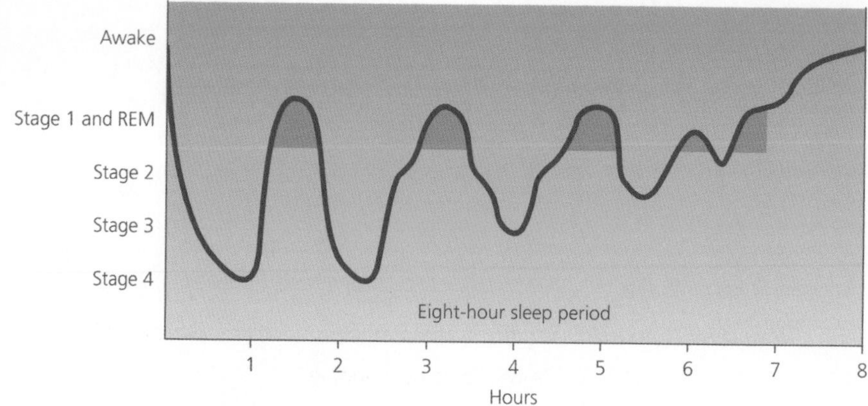

Figure 9.3 The sleep cycle

Most of the night is spent in nREM sleep. We move from relaxed wakefulness into sleep and then through deeper sleep stages before returning through shallower nREM to reach our first REM phase. We then alternate between REM and nREM during the night.

The deepest sleep occurs early in the night.
REM phases increase in length during the night.
Natural waking tends to occur during REM.
Each 'cycle' from stage 1 back to stage 1 or REM takes 90 minutes.

Internal and external influences on sleep

Ultradian rhythms

Ultradian rhythms last less than 24 hours but are longer than one hour, e.g. blinking, pulse and heart rate.

Circadian rhythms

Circadian rhythms are physiological and behavioural characteristics that follow a daily, or circadian, pattern.

Key term

The word **circadian** comes from a Latin phrase meaning 'about a day'.

Our bodies display hundreds of these circadian rhythms – a few of the most important are sleep and wakefulness, body temperature, blood pressure and the production of hormones and digestive secretions.

Circadian rhythms are controlled by a 'biological clock' in the brain known as the **suprachiasmatic nucleus (SCN)**. The SCN is strongly influenced by the daily change between sunlight and darkness, with morning sunlight promoting early wakefulness and darkness setting the stage for sleep. At what time people choose to sleep, how well they control bedroom darkness and workplace lighting also affect circadian rhythms.

How do you know when to get up and when to go to sleep?

Evidence suggests that we have several **endogenous** internal clocks, e.g. for mood, activity levels and temperature. The biological clock for our sleep–wake cycle can be controlled by external cues such as light. External cues in our environment that control our biological clocks are called **exogenous zeitgebers**. Morning sunlight automatically shifts the clock ahead, putting the rhythm in step with the world outside. This process of resetting the biological clock with exogenous zeitgebers is known as **entrainment**. The opposite of entrainment is a 'free running' cycle. Here biological clocks operate in the absence of any external cues.

Therefore, our biological clocks can run freely by themselves to control our bodily functions but are influenced by environmental cues like natural daylight to help keep our bodies synchronised with the world around us.

Key terms

The **suprachiasmatic nucleus (SCN)** is a tiny clump of cells which control our circadian rhythms and are set by external cues such as sunlight.

Endogenous refers to our internal cues that affect our biological clock.

Exogenous refers to external environmental cues that affect our biological clock.

Zeitgebers is German for 'time giver' and refers to the syncing of our biological clocks to external cues such as light and dark.

Entrainment refers to an individual's physical relationship with their environment. Specifically, to an individual's physical and mental adaptation to the time zone in which they live.

Active learning

Which of the following are examples of circadian and which are ultradian rhythms?

Eating and drinking; alertness; weight change; sleep–wake; heart rate; toilet habits

Type of rhythm	Description	Example
Circadian rhythm	A cycle which happens approximately every 24 hours	
Ultradian rhythm	A cycle which lasts less than one day	

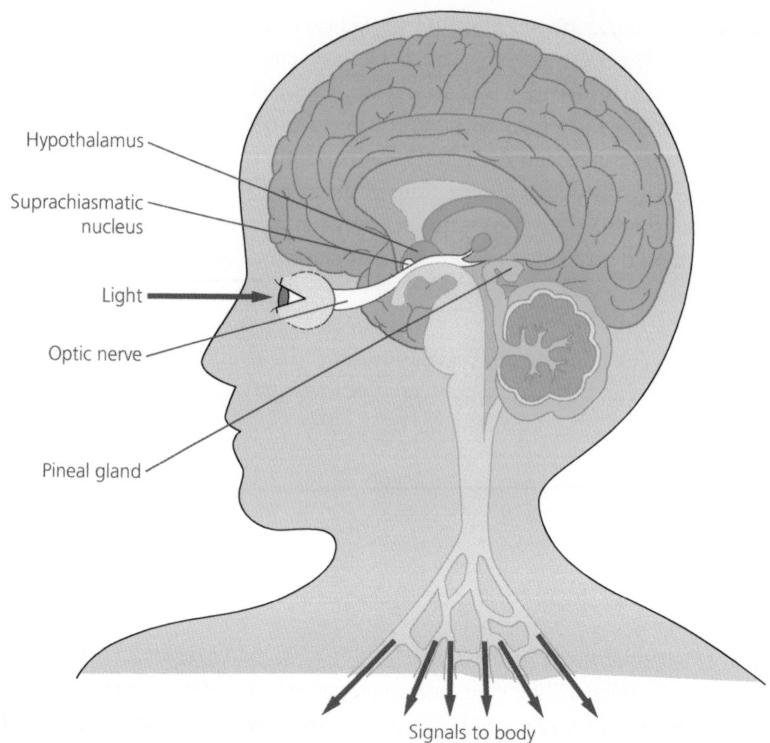

Figure 9.4 The brain showing where light enters and the location of the SCN, hypothalamus and pineal gland

Hormones

Endogenous pacemakers, or biological clocks, represent an inherited genetic control over our bodily rhythms. The most important pacemaker in the brains of reptiles and birds is the pineal gland. This regulates the release of **melatonin**, which causes sleep. As the amount of light increases on the **pineal gland** through our eyes, levels of melatonin fall and vice versa. Blinkley (1979) found that children wake and become more active as dawn breaks and melatonin secretion falls. The study also shows the importance of the environment on our sleep–waking cycle, as sunrise varies throughout the year and around the world.

Some hormones, such as adrenaline, make us feel more alert and prepared for action. This then makes it hard for us to go to sleep. To prevent this effect, it is best to do relaxing activities before bedtime, rather than stressful work tasks or intense exercise.

Key terms

Melatonin is a hormone involved in controlling energy levels and mood, which causes sleep.

The **pineal gland** is responsible for producing melatonin.

Strengths and weaknesses of internal and external influences on sleep

The findings from this research can be applied to medicine and has led to an improved use of drug therapy. As circadian rhythms affect digestion and hormone secretion, medications that act on certain hormones are administered when these hormones are at their peak level of production to increase the drug's effectiveness. For example, aspirin is used to help treat heart attacks. The best time to take aspirin is at 11 pm as this allows the aspirin time to dissolve and be at its peak in the bloodstream in the early morning hours (when most heart attacks happen).

The 90-minute sleep cycle is itself located within a 24-hour circadian cycle, so it would make sense to find that this 90-minute 'clock' was also ticking throughout the day. It is called the *basic rest–activity cycle* (BRAC). Friedman and Fisher (1967) observed eating and drinking behaviour in a group of psychiatric patients over periods of six hours. They detected a clear 90-minute cycle in eating and drinking behaviour. Therefore, supporting the existence of the 90-minute clock.

A weakness of the research is that it is typical of the biological approach for being deterministic. The circadian rhythm of the sleep–wake cycle is being explained solely in terms of endogenous pacemakers, e.g. brain function. However, there are often many factors that influence human behaviour. It concludes that the sleep–wake cycle is determined by the SCN, which is an endogenous pacemaker. The freedom of choice and free will to choose to sleep whenever is not accounted for.

This research has made a great contribution to the understanding of the human brain and behaviour. Knowing about the role of the SCN can improve understanding of sleep disorders and circadian rhythms, as very little is known. Therefore, the results of the study have real-life applications. For example, helping shift workers go to sleep by using blackout blinds to reduce sunlight in their bedrooms and so promote melatonin to help them sleep.

Research by Boivin *et al.* (1996) provides support for the role of exogenous zeitgebers in circadian rhythms. They found that after three days participants exposed to very bright light had an advancement in circadian rhythms by five hours; those exposed to bright light had advanced three hours; those exposed to ordinary room light had advanced by one hour; and those that remained in dim light had circadian rhythms that had drifted one hour later than normal.

This suggests that the exogenous zeitgebers of light are key in resetting the circadian clock.

Symptoms and explanations of sleep disorders

Insomnia

Insomnia can't be defined in terms of the number of hours slept, as there are large individual differences. Insomnia can be transient (short-term), intermittent (occasional) or chronic (lasting at least one month).

Primary insomnia describes cases where insomnia simply occurs on its own for more than one month. The individual may be feeling stressed or depressed, but the insomnia is the main problem. The individual may have developed bad sleep habits (e.g. staying up late or sleeping in a room that is too light) which have created the insomnia. Sometimes insomnia may have had an identifiable cause which has now disappeared, but the insomnia persists because of an expectation of sleep difficulty.

Secondary insomnia is where there is an underlying medical, psychiatric or environmental cause. Insomnia is a characteristic symptom of illnesses such as depression or heart disease. It is also typical of people who do shift work or who have circadian rhythm disorders, such as phase delay syndrome. Insomnia may also be the result of environmental factors, such as too much caffeine (coffee, tea or even chocolate) or alcohol.

People with anxious personalities may be more likely to suffer insomnia (this would be secondary insomnia). When we are anxious, we are physiologically aroused (increased heart rate, adrenaline), which prevents sleep. Life events can cause anxiety, which can then lead to insomnia.

Risk factors include age (old people are more likely to have insomnia due to physical conditions such as arthritis, which can disrupt sleep), gender (women are more likely to suffer due to hormonal changes, especially around menopause) and sleep apnoea (when the person stops breathing during sleep, which disrupts the sleep). Other parasomnias such as sleepwalking are also linked to insomnia.

Narcolepsy

Most of us sleep normally. Those with **narcolepsy** have frequent moments where they simply fall asleep. This can be at any time but is often after meals and in the afternoon. Some people find it worse if they are on shift work. There seem to be no other problems, but this condition can be very disabling, and dangerous – for example, if driving. Those who suffer are often aged 15–25, and more men are affected than women. The condition seems to come from dysfunction of the sleep–wake regulating mechanism that is in the hypothalamus.

The symptoms are that people fall asleep very unexpectedly. They then wake up very refreshed. The periods of sleep can vary from minutes to a few hours but are often very short. When asleep, the person can be woken up again quite easily, so you can distinguish narcolepsy from fainting. Many people with narcolepsy hallucinate and two-thirds have **cataplexy** too. Also, those with narcolepsy might suffer paralysis on waking, but just touching them can bring them out of it.

The exact cause of all forms of narcolepsy remains unknown, but research in 2010 found that the reduction of a substance called **hypocretin** is a major cause of narcolepsy. In 2010, the University of Lucerne and Geneva found what was causing the reduction in hypocretin: an antibody (called trib 2) was found to kill areas of the brain that produce hypocretin, which regulates sleep; this in turn triggers narcolepsy.

The researchers then tested people and found that those with narcolepsy, but not other people, had a lot of trib 2 antibodies.

The results indicate that trib 2 antibodies target the neurons which produce hypocretin in the hypothalamus and kill them. If it runs its full course, the trib 2 antibodies kill all the neurons and this leads to hypocretin deficiency.

Lin *et al.* (1999) found that mice lacking hypocretin receptors show behaviour similar to symptoms of narcolepsy and cataplexy. This was replicated by Dement (1999), who also found that mice that could not produce hypocretin developed symptoms of narcolepsy. Research into narcoleptic dogs has also supported the theory of hypocretins, and humans with narcolepsy have also been shown to have lower levels of hypocretin in their cerebrospinal fluid (Nishino *et al.*, 2000).

Key terms

Insomnia generally involves problems in falling asleep (initial insomnia), maintaining sleep (middle insomnia) and waking too early (terminal insomnia).

Narcolepsy is a sleep disorder that disrupts the normal sleep–wake cycle, in which a person experiences uncontrollable sleepiness, falling asleep or napping throughout most days.

Cataplexy is when the head suddenly slumps and knees buckle. Emotions like anger and extreme laughing can bring on an attack of cataplexy.

Hypocretin, is an antibody that regulates arousal, wakefulness and appetite.

Freud's (1900) theory of dreaming

Freud argued that dreams are a 'window on the **unconscious**', which, with skilful interpretation, can be understood as signs from the unconscious. He therefore described dream analysis as 'the royal road' to the unconscious and concluded that dreams are the disguised fulfilment of suppressed wishes. According to Freud, there are two types of dream content: the part of the dream that we remember when we wake is the **manifest content**, and this is the bit that we actually experience in the dream, while the underlying meaning of the dream, or the wish being fulfilled, is called the **latent content**. The manifest content often links together fragments of that day's events, with the repressed/forbidden wish. Dream analysis is often used in **psychoanalysis** as a way of accessing the unconscious desires of a patient.

Dreams are created through the process of dream work, which converts the underlying wish (latent content) into the actual dream (manifest content).

Dream work involves three processes: displacement, condensation, and concrete representation.

Displacement

This refers to the substitution of the real target of the dreamer's feelings, with another person or object that is symbolic of the true target, which then becomes the target of those feelings. This disguises the true meaning of the dream from the dreamer, so it protects them from any negative feelings that may come from the content of the dream by turning the underlying wish into an unthreatening form. It also protects the sleep of the dreamer by not waking them up due to anxiety resulting from knowing the true meaning of the dream.

Condensation

This involves the same symbolisation of the manifest content representing more than one aspect of the latent content or underlying wish. So one symbol may mean more than one thing in terms of the underlying meaning, so one dream idea may be 'condensed' into one manifest image.

Concrete representation

This refers to the expression of an abstract idea in a concrete way. For example, a king may represent authority, power or wealth. This stage is where the 'storyline' of the dream is developed.

Key terms

The **unconscious** consists of feelings, thoughts, urges and memories outside of our conscious awareness. Most of the contents of the unconscious are unacceptable or unpleasant, such as feelings of pain, anxiety or conflict.

The **manifest content** of a dream is the actual literal content and storyline of the dream.

The **latent content** of a dream is the hidden psychological meaning of the dream.

Psychoanalysis is a therapy which aims to treat mental disorders by investigating the interaction of conscious and unconscious elements in the mind.

Active learning

The manifest content of a dream is described below, and you are to interpret the *latent content*.

A man was suffering from depression, which he said was because he was bored at work. During psychoanalysis, he said that he had dreamed about running through a vast desert on his own. In his dreams, he felt very happy, although he knew he had a long way to go. He was looking forward to the journey and waved and shouted greetings to groups of people as he passed them. In his dream the people looked like animals – some were tied to stakes, others were in cages. In a previous session, he had stumbled over his wife's name. Her name was Lesley, but he had distinctly said 'Left me'. They had been unhappily married for 20 years and had only stayed together because of their children.

1. What might a psychoanalyst think the man meant when he said he was enjoying running through a desert on his own?
2. What might a psychoanalyst make of the people looking like animals who were either tied up or in cages?
3. How might this dream confirm the man's previous slip of the tongue?

Strengths and weaknesses of Freud's theory of dreaming

Analysis of dreams relies on the subjective interpretation of symbols by the analyst, so the meaning that they put on it may not be an accurate reflection of the dreamer's mind. This is clearly subjective and therefore argued to be unscientific. Any interpretation is possible, making the theory **unfalsifiable**. Therefore, it is not possible to validate the interpretation of dream symbols.

There are other reasons for the content of dreams other than wish fulfilment. For example, Hobson and McCarley (1977) from the physiological approach see dreaming as the result of random activity within the brain during sleep. Evans (1984) believes that dreams are the brain's way of organising and making sense of the events of the day.

Analysis of symbols provides a useful tool in psychotherapy. It appears to provide access to the unconscious, allowing subsequent interpretation. For example, phobias are often seen as symbols for underlying unconscious conflicts. Dreams are thought to provide a 'window' into the unconscious mind, which could be useful in psychoanalysis as it could help to reveal underlying wishes and fantasies that the client may be struggling with, and through analysis of the dream, the wish can be revealed and dealt with.

Key term

Unfalsifiable refers to being unable to be shown as false, although possibly not true either.

Hobson and McCarley's (1977) activation synthesis theory of dreaming

Hobson and McCarley (1977) proposed that, from a physiological perspective, what we experience as dreams are the result of the brain's attempts to interpret random nerve impulses. In the brain stem there is an area that, when we are awake, is involved in relaying information from the senses of the brain. As well as letting us know about what is happening around us, this region is responsible for feeding back to us what we ourselves are doing. The idea behind activation synthesis theory is that, when most of the brain is inactive, this region is prone to periodic bursts of random nervous activity occurring in 90-minute cycles. These are picked up and interpreted by other parts of the brain, with the result that we have sensory experiences of being in places and doing things.

There are two distinct stages to the process outlined by Hobson and McCarley:

- Activation stage – in this stage, the brain stem generates random nerve impulses. The brain stem is a primitive part of the brain unconcerned with thought or emotion, so it appears that the reasons for its activation are physiological rather than psychological. The activation begun in the brain stem spreads to other parts of the brain until it reaches areas of the cortex responsible for higher mental functions. These begin to interpret the information from the brain stem as they would if the dreamer was awake.
- Synthesis stage – in the second stage, the brain (cerebral cortex) produces the dream. It does this by interpreting the random nerve impulses sent by the brain stem. It puts together a story using any available information (e.g. from memory, the unconscious or the environment). According to Hobson and McCarley, dreams often contain bizarre and disjointed images because the brain has difficulty in synthesising a coherent story from a random series of nerve impulses.

Key term

Synthesising refers to joining or sticking together.

Now test yourself

5. What does the brain stem do when we are awake?
6. What happens to the brain stem when we are asleep or inactive?

Strengths and weaknesses of Hobson and McCarley's (1977) activation synthesis theory of dreaming

The activation synthesis theory of dreaming could be compatible with the psychodynamic theory of dreaming. Whereas a physiological approach aims to see what causes dreaming in general, the psychodynamic approach is more concerned with the meaning of individual dreams and their psychological functions. Hobson has fully supported the central psychodynamic assumption that dreams can reveal much about the conscious and unconscious mind of the dreamer. The synthesis process triggers the memories and emotions of the individual; hence the content of the dream will be highly personal and may reveal a lot about the dreamer's anxieties and wishes. The activation synthesis model is thus quite compatible with the psychodynamic idea of dream interpretation.

There is support for the idea that we synthesise dreams using whatever information is available to us at the time. Evidence comes from the fact that we tend to incorporate external events into our dreams if we can perceive them while dreaming. For example, Dement and Wolpert (1958) sprinkled water on the faces of sleepers in REM sleep and then woke them. The majority of dreamers had incorporated water into their dream.

There are, however, difficulties with the theory as a complete explanation of dreaming. For example, it cannot easily explain why we need REM sleep, nor why people deprived of REM sleep have a 'rebound effect' – i.e. when allowed to sleep normally they have longer periods of REM to make up for that they have missed.

Studies

Freud (1909): Little Hans, analysis of a phobia in a five-year-old boy

Aim

Little Hans, a five-year-old boy, was taken to Freud suffering from a phobia of horses. As in all clinical case studies, Freud's most important aim was to treat the phobia. However, Freud's therapeutic input in this case was extremely minimal, and a secondary aim of the study was to explore what factors might have led to the phobia in the first place, and what factors led to its remission. By 1909, Freud's ideas about the **Oedipus complex** were well-established and Freud interpreted this case in line with his theory.

Case history

Freud's information about the course of Hans' condition was derived partially from observation of Hans himself, but mostly from Hans' father, who was familiar with Freud's work, and who gave him weekly reports. Hans' father reported that from the age of three, Hans had developed considerable interest in his own 'widdler' and at the age of five his mother had threatened to cut it off if he didn't stop playing with it. At about the same time, Hans saw a horse die in pain and was frightened by it. Hans then developed a fear of white horses, believing they would bite him. Hans' father reported that his fear seemed to be related to the horse's large penis. At the time Hans' phobia developed, his father began to object to Hans' habit of getting into bed with his parents in the morning. Over a period of weeks, Hans' phobia got worse and he feared going out of the house in case he encountered a horse. He also suffered attacks of more generalised anxiety.

Key term

The **Oedipus complex** refers to a desire for the parent of the opposite sex and a sense of rivalry with the parent of the same sex.

Results

Over the next few weeks, Hans' phobia gradually began to improve. His fear became limited to horses with black harnesses over their noses. Hans' father interpreted this as related to his own black moustache. The end of Hans' phobia of horses was accompanied by two significant fantasies, which he told to his father. In the first, Hans had several imaginary children. When asked who their mother was, Hans replied 'Why, Mummy, and you're their Granddaddy'. In the second fantasy, which occurred the next day, Hans imagined the plumber had come and fitted him with a bigger widdler. These fantasies marked the end of Hans' phobia.

Freud saw Hans' phobia as an expression of the Oedipus complex. Horses, particularly horses with black harnesses, symbolised his father. Horses were particularly appropriate father symbols because of their large penises. The fear began as an Oedipal conflict was developing around Hans being allowed in the parents' bed. Freud saw the Oedipus complex happily resolved as Hans had fantasised himself with a big widdler like his father's and married to his mother with his father present in the role of grandfather.

Conclusion

Freud believed Hans' phobia was an expression of the Oedipus complex. The horse was interpreted as symbolising Hans' father due to the specific fear of horses with harnesses across their noses, and because they have big penises. The fear of being bitten by a horse was thought to symbolise castration anxiety. The fear, according to Freud, developed from Hans' willingness to share his parent's bed, which his father did not like, which would resemble the Oedipus conflict. The end of Hans' phobia was marked by the fantasies and dreams about being married to his mother, and having a larger penis, which Freud saw as resolution of Hans' Oedipus complex.

Now test yourself

7. How did Freud collect his information about Little Hans?
8. Explain the problem of gathering data in this way.

Strengths and weaknesses of Little Hans

The case of Little Hans does appear to provide support for Freud's theory of the Oedipus complex. Through analysis, Freud and Hans' father were able to use the idea of the Oedipus complex to explain the boy's phobia. For example, by recognising that horses symbolised the father and that Hans had displaced his fear of his father onto horses. By resolving this conflict, Hans was cured of his phobia. This shows that Freud's explanation worked because Hans got better.

Studying Hans in this way provided Freud with a greater amount of detail than other research methods. It was conducted over a long period of time. This meant a large amount of information and detail was gathered.

However, there are difficulties with this study. Freud only actually met Hans twice and instead received most of his information from Hans' father. He was already familiar with the Oedipus complex and interpreted the case in light of this. It is also possible therefore that he supplied Hans with clues that led to his fantasies of marriage to his mother and his new, larger widdler.

There are perhaps other more realistic explanations for Hans' fear of horses. It has been reported that he saw a horse die in pain and was frightened by it. This might have been sufficient to trigger a fear of horses (classical conditioning). The Little Albert study by Watson and Raynor (1920) suggests that phobias can be learned responses developed through the process of classical conditioning.

Siffre (1975): six months alone in a cave

Aim

To investigate what would happen to our natural sleep–wake cycle if we had no external cues from the environment such as daylight telling us what time it was. Siffre spent long periods of time living underground to study his own biological rhythms.

Procedure

Siffre was a speleologist (cave expert) who investigated the natural duration of his own sleep–wake cycle. Siffre spent six months in a cave with only weak artificial light starting on 14 February 1972. There was no natural light, so he didn't know what time it was, and he had no external cues to guide his rhythms – no daylight, no clocks, no radio. He had contact with researchers via a telephone, and his physiological functions were measured, and behaviour observed throughout.

Siffre had no clock or any reference to time; however, he did have verbal contact with the outside world. He would phone his team of researchers above ground to let them know he was awake and when he thought the day had begun. He simply woke, ate and slept when he felt like it. The only influence on his behaviour was his internal 'clock' or 'free running rhythm'.

His new temporary home was a large chamber in which there was a bed table and chair. He took frozen food and 780 gallons of water to sustain him whilst he carried out several experiments during his time underground. These included taking his blood pressure and various memory and physical tests, such as riding his exercise bicycle to monitor his progress.

Results

The findings were that his sleep–wake cycle settled naturally at around 25 hours, although sometimes it would range up to 48 hours. Siffre organised his day into a fairly normal pattern of alternating periods of sleep and activity, and his day was separated by his eating behaviours. However, his biological clock shifted to 25-hour days.

The effects on Siffre himself were quite severe. He became depressed and longed for company to break the monotony and his loneliness. He thought about abandoning the project many times and even had suicidal thoughts.

Conclusion

Siffre concluded that the absence of natural daylight allowed his biological clock to run at its natural rate, and that normally daylight acted as an exogenous zeitgeber to resynchronise the cycle. Siffre (1975) found that the absence of external cues significantly altered his circadian rhythm: when he returned from an underground stay with no clocks or light, he believed the date to be a month earlier than it was. This suggests that his 24-hour sleep–wake cycle was increased by the lack of external cues, making him believe one day was longer than it was, and leading to his thinking that fewer days had passed. There is internal control of the circadian rhythm, since even in the absence of external cues we are able to maintain a regular daily cycle.

Strengths and weaknesses of Siffre (1975)

Some have criticised this research since it is so artificial. In particular, they object to the use of artificial light by Siffre. On waking, Siffre switched on lights, which are likely to artificially re-set the body clock. Czeisler *et al.* (1999) has argued this is the equivalent of providing powerful drugs.

However, there is an issue of validity relating to the study. It may be described as a case study as it is the study of one individual and therefore has unique features. His body's behaviour may not be typical of all people and, in addition, living in a cave may have particular effects due to, for example, the fact that it is cold. Also, there is a question of internal validity as Siffre was not isolated from all exogenous zeitgebers as he had contact with the outside world, and the effect on his sleep–wake cycle of even dim artificial light was not fully understood.

However, subsequent studies above ground have confirmed the findings of research in cave environments. Siffre's study was also an experiment. He controlled key variables (exogenous zeitgebers) to observe their effects on the sleep–wake cycle. The experiment approach is important because it allows us to demonstrate casual relationships.

As he was underground for such a long time, he was able to gather vast amounts of qualitative and quantitative data, which produced a detailed record of his time. Siffre documented everything and logged all his results, which meant researchers got a wealth of information about how the absence of light can affect our sleep–wake cycle.

Now test yourself

9. How did Siffre stay in contact with the outside world?
10. Even though Siffre came out of the cave in August 1972, he believed the month was actually ________?

Exam questions

1. Morgan removed the brains from a mutant strain of hamsters that had a shorter sleep–waking cycle and inserted them into normal hamsters. The normal hamsters adopted the same mutant sleep–waking cycles.

   Does this suggest a genetic or environmental basis to our sleep–waking cycle? (1)

2. Miles *et al.* (1977) cite the study of a young blind man who obviously had no external light cues to time, and as a result lived a 25-hour day. Aschoff (1965) found that students living in a well-heated cave, with no external cues for several weeks, also lengthened their daily cycle to approximately 24.5 hours.

   What do these studies suggest about our genetic sleep–waking cycle? (2)

3. What role do environmental factors seem to play in our sleep–waking cycle? (1)

4. Eve is being monitored by an EEG machine. The machine is recording high levels of mixed wave activity. What stage of sleep is Eve in? (1)

5. It is winter in Norway and the days are quite short. Explain what might be happening to levels of melatonin in those that live in Norway. (1)

6. Compare the symptoms of narcolepsy and insomnia. (4)

7. Adam works the night shift at the local factory and cannot get to sleep during the day. Using your knowledge of both the sleep–wake cycle and circadian rhythms, explain why Adam may be finding it difficult to sleep. (4)

8. What two significant fantasies marked the end of Little Hans' phobia? (2)

9. Will and Jemima are arguing about the exact cause of Little Hans' phobia. Will believes Freud is correct and the phobia stems from fear of his father, whereas Jemima believes it is more to do with the association with seeing the horse die in the street, so Hans has been conditioned to fear them.

   Describe and evaluate the case of Little Hans (1909). In your evaluation, you must make reference to both arguments above. (9)

10. Tim decides to try and replicate Siffre's (1975) cave study. Describe the procedure that Tim would have to go through in order to match what Siffre did. (5)

End of chapter summary

You should now have an understanding of all the points below:

Understand the functions, features and benefits of sleep, including:

- the four sleep stages
- REM
- the sleep cycle.

Understand the internal and external influences on sleep, including strengths and weaknesses of each explanation:

- bodily rhythms, to include:
  - circadian rhythms
  - ultradian rhythms
- hormones, to include:
  - pineal gland
  - melatonin
- zeitgebers, to include:
  - light.

Understand symptoms and explanations of sleep disorders, including:

- insomnia
- narcolepsy.

Understand Freudian theory of dreaming (Freud, 1900), including strengths and weaknesses of the theory:

- manifest content
- latent content
- dream work.

Understand activation synthesis theory (Hobson and McCarley, 1977), including strengths and weaknesses of the theory:

- random activation
- sensory blockade
- movement inhibition.

Understand the aims, procedures and findings (results and conclusions), and strengths and weaknesses of:

- Freud (1909): Little Hans, analysis of a phobia in a five-year-old boy
- Siffre (1975): six months alone in a cave.

Now test yourself answers

1. REM.
2. Stage 4.
3. Rapid eye movement.
4. Dreaming.
5. Relays information from the senses of the brain.
6. Prone to periodic bursts of random nervous activity.
7. Mostly from Hans' father.
8. It is secondary data, so it is not gathered first hand, which makes it less valid.
9. Telephone.
10. July.

Chapter 10

Language, thought and communication – how do you communicate with others?

This chapter deals with understanding the possible relationship between language and thought, including spoken and body language, and how we use these as forms of communication. Are language and thought independent of each other or does one develop before the other? Does animal communication mirror that of humans or is it different? Body language is also a method of communication and our facial expressions and eye contact can relay different meanings to others.

The possible relationship between language and thought

According to Piaget, language depends on thought for its development (i.e. thought comes before language). For Vygotsky, thought and language are initially separate systems from the beginning of life, merging at around three years of age, producing verbal thought.

Piaget's (1950) explanation that representational thinking precedes language

Piaget's theory suggests that children's language reflects the development of their logical thinking and reasoning skills in 'periods' or stages, with each period having a specific name and age reference. According to Piaget, children are born with basic actions, such as sucking and grasping.

During the sensory motor period, children's language is **egocentric**: they talk either for themselves or for the pleasure of associating anyone who happens to be there with the activity of the moment. Piaget observed that during this period (between the ages of two and seven years), children's language makes rapid progress. The development of their mental schemas lets them quickly 'accommodate' new words and situations. From using single words (for example, 'milk'), they begin to construct simple sentences (for example, 'mummy go out').

Piaget's theory describes children's language as **symbolic**, allowing them to venture beyond the 'here and now' and to talk about such things as the past, the future, people, feelings and events. According to Piaget, children's language development at this stage reveals the movement of their thinking from immature to mature and from illogical to logical. Children's language also reflects their ability to **de-centre**, or view things from a perspective other than their own. It is at this point that children's language starts to become 'socialised', showing characteristics such as questions, answers, criticisms and commands.

Key terms

Egocentric refers to not being able to see from others' points of view.
Symbolic refers to children using one thing to represent another.
De-centre refers to being able to see things from others' points of view.

Strengths and weaknesses of Piaget's explanation

Piaget's theories focused on language development in stages. These stages help to explain a child's thought processes and how they see the world. This allows teachers and parents to have a greater understanding of a child's developmental level. Therefore, in an educational setting, children will benefit by working and learning at their own level.

Some experts, such as Margaret Donaldson, have argued that the clear-cut ages and stages forming the basis of Piaget's theory are actually quite blurred and blend into each other. Donaldson suggests that Piaget may have underestimated children's language and thinking abilities by not giving enough consideration to the contexts he provided for children when conducting his research.

According to Vygotsky, Piaget fails to see the transition from egocentric speech (when a child talks aloud to him/herself while alone) to **inner speech**. Piaget believes that egocentric speech simply fades away as the child becomes less egocentric and more socialised. Vygotsky, on the other hand, hypothesises that egocentric speech turns into inner speech; that it does not fade away but goes underground.

Key term

Inner speech is when a child stops thinking aloud and thinks internally instead.

Vygotsky's (1981) explanation that language and thinking are separate

Vygotsky (1981) differentiates between three forms of language: social speech, which is external communication used to talk to others (typical from the age of two); private speech (typical from the age of three), which is directed to the self and serves an intellectual function; and finally, silent inner speech (typical from the age of seven).

For Vygotsky, thought and language are initially separate systems from the beginning of life, merging at around three years of age. At this point, speech and thought become co-dependent: thought becomes verbal, speech becomes **representational**.

Vygotsky placed more emphasis on the importance of language in cognitive development than did Piaget. According to Vygotsky, language is critical to thought and also regulates behaviour. Language makes thought possible.

Key term

Representational speech is when a child starts using language to represent objects in the world.

Now test yourself

1. Outline one difference between Piaget and Vygotsky's views on language and thought.
2. Outline one similarity between Piaget and Vygotsky's views on language and thought.

Developmental stages

Table 10.1 Vygotsky's developmental stages of speech

Speech stage	Age	Function
Social/external speech	0–3	A child expresses simple thoughts and emotions to try and engage/copy others.
Egocentric speech	3–7	Words are spoken out aloud to help with thinking, the stage between social and inner speech.
Inner speech	7+	During the inner stage of speech this talking aloud disappears, and thinking is done internally.

Language develops from social interactions with others. At first, the sole function of language is communication, and language and thought develop separately. Later, the child **internalises** language and learns to use it as a tool of thinking. In the egocentric stage, as children learn to use language to solve problems, they speak aloud whilst solving these problems (you can often hear children doing this).

Key term

A child **internalises** when they adopt and use language as the main source of communication.

As the child's egocentric speech turns inward, he enters the final stage. He uses the skills he has acquired to perform logical tasks internally. Rather than counting aloud, he will count 'in his head' using part of his short-term memory. This is much faster than verbalising each thought and just as his initial speech developed with practice, the more internalised thought and logic is used, the better the child can perform.

Now test yourself

3. A child who is able to keep thoughts to themselves is demonstrating inner speech – true or false?

Pre-linguistic thought

As soon as a child is born, they are learning and developing pre-language or non-verbal skills, which will support later language learning. **Pre-linguistic thought** is the way in which we communicate without using words and includes things such as gestures, facial expressions, imitation, joint attention and eye contact. These are the skills that set children up to be ready to talk and communicate. Children who have difficulty in the development of pre-linguistic thought may go on to have verbal language and interaction difficulties.

Pre-intellectual language

From the age of two onwards, pre-linguistic thought begins to interact with **pre-intellectual language.** These first words, which might be jargon, also lead to copying others, such as playful sounds, but with little or no thinking involved. By developing copying skills, a child is more likely to have success at imitating words and sentences as their language develops. As the child begins to speak, he learns how to say words far before he learns their meaning and function.

So according to Vygotsky, language is, therefore, an accelerator for thinking and understanding. So, children who engage in large amounts of private speech are actually much more socially competent than children who do not use it that much. So, he believed that language develops from social interactions for communication purposes. And later language ability becomes internalised as thought. So, as we grow older, it becomes more internalised, which is called our inner speech, so basically, thought is a result of language.

Key terms

Pre-linguistic thought is thinking without language.
Pre-intellectual language is thinking with the use of language but without any real understanding of what is being said.

Strengths and weaknesses of Vygotsky's (1981) explanation

Vygotsky (1981) was the first psychologist to document the importance of private speech. He considered private speech as the transition point between social and inner speech, the moment in development where language and thought unite to constitute verbal thinking.

Vygotsky may have over-estimated the importance of culture on language development. If language is cultural in origin, we would expect different cultures to vary far more than they do in their language development. This is not the case as there are similarities between children from different cultures.

Vygotsky's work has not received the same level of intense scrutiny that Piaget's has, partly due to the time-consuming process of translating Vygotsky's work from Russian. Also, Vygotsky's sociocultural perspective does not provide as many specific hypotheses to test as did Piaget's theory, making refutation difficult, if not impossible.

How thought and language structures affect views of the world

Linguistic relativism and linguistic determinism are both concepts associated with the **Sapir–Whorf hypothesis**, which believes that the structure of a language affects its speakers' world view.

Key term

The **Sapir–Whorf hypothesis** states that our view of the world is affected by the structure of our language.

Linguistic relativism

Linguistic relativity argues that people who speak different languages perceive and think about the world quite differently from one another. The most fascinating example for this concerns the Aboriginal people who do not have the relative directions we have, such as left, right, forward, backward, up and down. Instead, they use the points on a compass to indicate the location of things. Therefore, instead of saying 'Can you pass the salt on your right', they will say 'Can you pass the salt on the north'. Unlike us, they always know which side which point is: east, north, west or south. Some use this example to support linguistic relativity and to show how language interacts with our mind.

Linguistic determinism

Linguistic determinism is based on the argument that language limits the speakers' way of thinking and how they conceptualise the world. A well-known example of this is the people of Pirahã, who have only three numbers in their language: one, two and many. They had great difficulty in comprehending the difference between, say, four and five, which was considered to be a sign that because their language does not include the numbers for four and five, their mind was not able to make that difference.

Key terms

Linguistic relativity suggests language affects our view of the world.
Linguistic determinism suggests language limits our view of the world.

Now test yourself

4. Both sides of the Sapir–Whorf hypothesis have either been described as 'weak Whorf' and 'strong Whorf' – which is which?

Strengths and weaknesses of linguistic relativism and determinism

Language does have a great influence on our thinking and culture. A language helps to reinforce certain ideas and beliefs, making them noticeable and pushing them into the foreground of attention, and it helps us to express our emotions. Linguistic relativism is supported by the findings that there are cultural differences in language.

Many of the experiments that support how language affects thinking are based on sound experimental conclusions held in controlled settings, which mean they can be tested for reliability. Evidence such as Boroditsky (2001) or Frank *et al.*'s (2008) study of the Pirahã people of Brazil can be used to highlight how language can shape views of the world.

The problem of **translatability**: if each language had a completely distinct reality encoded within it, how could a work be translated from one language to another? Yet, literary works, instruction manuals and so forth are regularly translated and communication in this regard is not only possible but happens every day.

On the one hand, people speaking the same language may have different world views; on the other hand, people speaking different languages may have similar political, religious and philosophical views. Even one language can describe many different world views. Therefore, we can't fail to notice that it's not really true to say that language determines our thought.

Key term

Translatability refers to how the meaning of something in one language is conveyed in another.

Active learning

Find someone who has the same hobbies and interests as you and then get them to write down as many words as they can about one particular area. For example, if you both share the same interest in the card game *Magic: The Gathering*, see how many words they can think of for one of the characters. Now compare that list with that of someone who has never played the game and see whether linguistic determinism or linguistic relativity is being demonstrated.

How communication is different in humans to animals

If someone asked you what separates humans from other animals, one of the first things that would probably come to mind is language.

Aitchison (1983): criteria of language features

Aitchison (1983) believed that there are four language features that are considered specific to the human species:

- Displacement – that humans can communicate real or hypothetical ideas. One of the key linguistic universals, language allows us to live with a past, present and future. Displacement is a key feature for evaluating whether animal communication systems represent a use of language.
- Semanticity – that human language conveys a range of meanings. Linguistic utterances, whether simple phrases or complete sentences, convey meaning by means of the symbols we use to form the utterances. All language conveys some meaning.
- Structure dependence – that humans have grammatical rules in languages. The linguistic principle that grammatical processes function primarily on structures in sentences, not on single words or sequences of words, is termed structure dependency.
- Creativity/productivity – that human language has a potentially infinite number of words. We can use language to say things no-one has ever said before, or state previous ideas in a new form. The fact that we can generate novel thoughts and ideas shows the great utility of language. Language evolves to fit the needs of the culture within a specific era.

Now test yourself

5. Being able to discuss things that took place days, weeks or years ago best describes which of Aitchison's (1983) criteria of language features?

Similarities and differences between human and animal communication

Displacement is evident in humans but not in animals. In human language, we can talk about the colour red when we are not actually seeing it, or we can talk about a friend who lives in another state when he is not with us. We can talk about a class we had last year, or the class we will take next year. No animal communication system appears to display this feature.

Productivity is also more evident in humans than in animals. Human language is an 'open-ended' system. However, in all animal communication systems, the number of signals is fixed. Even if some of the signals are complex, there is no mechanism for systematically combining discrete units to create new signals. These animal systems are thus called closed communication systems.

Animals communicate when prompted to by stimuli like hunger, danger and other immediate circumstances, but they do not have communicative choices, like people do. When we experience an environmental stimulus, like someone accidentally running into us, we may shriek in pain inadvertently, but we have speaking options too, such as 'Look where you're going!', or 'It's OK – my fault', or 'Fancy running into you here!'

Table 10.2 Features of human and animal language

Humans	**Animals**
Change rapidly as a cultural phenomenon.	Change extremely slowly, with the speed of genetic evolution.
Open ended. Grammar allows a virtually unlimited number of messages to be constructed.	Closed inventory of signs; only a set number of different messages can be sent.
Creative, can be adapted to new situations.	Not naturally used in novel way.
Signs often have multiple functions; one meaning can be expressed in many ways.	Each sign has one and only one function; each meaning can be expressed only in one way.
The capacity to be creative with signs is inborn, but the signs (words) themselves are acquired culturally.	The signs of animal systems are inborn.

Examples of non-verbal communication

Non-verbal communication has been defined as communication without words. It includes apparent behaviours such as facial expressions, eye contact, touching and tone of voice, as well as less obvious messages such as dress, posture and spatial distance between two or more people.

Facial expressions

Facial expression covers a considerable amount of non-verbal communication. With 80 facial muscles, one can create more than 7,000 facial expressions. Humans can adopt a facial expression as a voluntary or involuntary action. It can be nearly impossible to avoid expressions from certain emotions even if one is trying to conceal them. The face is highly developed as an organ of expression and some expressions can become quite habitual and almost fixed into the chronic muscular structure of the face. The overall appearance of the face offers information about age, sex, race, ethnicity and status.

Happiness: round eyes, smile, raised cheeks
Sadness: raised inner eyebrows, pulling down of outer lips
Surprise: eyebrows raised, wide open eyes, open mouth
Anger: lower eyebrow, intense stare
Fear: raised eyebrows and eyelids, slightly opened mouth, lip edges stretched back horizontally
Contempt: naturally occurs on one side of the face, pulling upper lip up and away
Disgust: wrinkled nose, lowered eyelids and eyebrows, raised upper lip

Now test yourself

6. What does the term *contempt* in the box above mean?

Eye contact

When it comes to body language, people often ask, 'Does good eye contact mean I have to look the other person directly in the eye all the time?' If you stare directly into one eye of a person, or switch back and forth between her/his eyes, it quickly becomes too psychologically intense. It is almost always interpreted (depending on the other signals and the context) as predatory behaviour, anger, attraction or deception.

When a person looks directly into your eyes while having a conversation, it indicates that they are interested and paying attention. However, prolonged eye contact can feel threatening. On the other hand, breaking eye contact and frequently looking away might indicate that the person is distracted, uncomfortable or trying to conceal his or her real feelings.

When a person tells a lie, their eye contact will often increase to what most people consider 'staring'. This is a great example of an **overcompensating** behaviour. It is also true that the opposite may occur – a dramatic drop-off of eye contact during lying.

Key term

Overcompensating is about how we try and overcorrect our behaviour.

Body language

It has been suggested that body language may account for between 50 and 70 per cent of all communication. Understanding body language is important, but it is also essential to pay attention to other cues, such as context.

Postures

How we hold our bodies can also serve as an important part of body language. Posture can convey a wealth of information about how a person is feeling as well as hints about personality characteristics, such as whether a person is confident, open or obedient.

Sitting up straight, for example, may indicate that a person is focused and paying attention to what's going on. Sitting with the body hunched forward, on the other hand, can imply that the person is bored or indifferent.

- Open posture involves keeping the trunk of the body open and exposed. This type of posture indicates friendliness, openness and willingness.
- Closed posture involves hiding the trunk of the body often by hunching forward and keeping the arms and legs crossed. This type of posture can be an indicator of hostility, unfriendliness and anxiety.

Now test yourself

7. What is meant by the term *posture*?

Gestures

Gestures can be some of the most direct and obvious body language signals. Waving, pointing and using the fingers to indicate numerical amounts are all very common and easy-to-understand gestures. Some gestures may be cultural, however, so giving a thumbs-up or a peace sign in one country might have a completely different meaning than it does in the United States.

The following examples are just a few common gestures and their possible meanings:

- A clenched fist can indicate anger in some situations or unity in others.

- A thumbs-up and thumbs-down are often used as gestures of approval and disapproval.
- The 'okay' gesture made by touching together the thumb and index finger in a circle while extending the other three fingers can be used to mean 'okay' or 'all right'. In some parts of Europe, however, the same signal is used to imply you are nothing. In some South American countries, the symbol is actually a rude gesture.
- The V sign, created by lifting the index and middle finger and separating them to create a V-shape, means peace or victory in some countries. In the United Kingdom and Australia, the symbol takes on an offensive meaning when the back of the hand is facing outward.

Personal space

Proxemics

- Intimate distance – 6 to 18 inches: this level of physical distance often indicates a closer relationship or greater comfort between individuals. It usually occurs during intimate contact, such as hugging, whispering or touching.
- Personal distance – 1.5 to 4 feet: physical distance at this level usually occurs between people who are family members or close friends. The closer the people can comfortably stand while interacting can be an indicator of the level of intimacy in their relationship.
- Social distance – 4 to 12 feet: this level of physical distance is often used with individuals who are acquaintances. With someone you know fairly well, such as a co-worker you see several times a week, you might feel more comfortable interacting at a closer distance. In cases where you do not know the other person well, such as a postal delivery driver you only see once a month, a distance of 10–12 feet may feel more comfortable.
- Public distance – 12 to 25 feet: physical distance at this level is often used in public speaking situations. Talking in front of a class full of students or giving a presentation at work are good examples of such situations.

Active learning

1. Students are separated into groups of two.
2. One student in each group is assigned as student A, and one as student B.
3. Each student receives a copy of a prewritten script.
4. Student A reads his/her lines out loud, but student B communicates his/her lines in a non-verbal way.
5. Student B is provided with a secret emotional distraction that is written on a piece of paper. For example, student B may be in a rush, may be really bored or may be feeling guilty.
6. After the dialogue, each student A should guess what emotion was affecting the student's partner B.

Now test yourself

8. What is meant by the term *proxemics*?

Cultural differences in non-verbal communication

It is also important to note that the level of personal distance that individuals need to feel comfortable can vary from culture to culture. One oft-cited example is the difference between people from Latin cultures and those from North America. People from Latin countries tend to feel more comfortable standing closer to one another as they interact, while those from North America need more personal distance.

A great number of cultural expressions are achieved through touch. In America, for example, using a firm handshake is considered appropriate to greet a stranger or another business professional. In France, however, it is common to kiss someone you greet on both cheeks. Touching children on the head is fine in North America. Yet in Asia, this is considered highly inappropriate, as the head is considered a sacred part of the body. In the Middle East, the left hand is customarily used to handle bodily hygiene. Therefore, using that hand to accept a gift or shake hands is considered extremely rude. There are also a wide range of cultural viewpoints on the appropriate rules regarding physical contact between both similar and opposite genders.

Countries that are densely populated generally have much less need for personal space than those that are not. The Japanese, for example, are less likely to react strongly to an accidental touch by a stranger than Americans. Less personal space is also needed in areas such as Latin America, and, in the context of one-on-one conversations, the Middle East.

Winking is a facial expression particularly varied in meaning. In Latin America, for example, the gesture is often considered a romantic invitation. The Yoruba people in Nigeria wink at their children if they want them to leave the room, and the Chinese consider the gesture rude.

Now test yourself

9. Why would someone in Japan be less offended if their personal space was invaded than someone in America?

Explanations of non-verbal communication

There is an argument that some non-verbal communication may have been as a result of evolution through survival of the fittest, which is based on the work by Darwin (1872).

Darwin's (1872) theory of evolution

Scientific research on non-verbal communication and behaviour was started in 1872 with the publication of Charles Darwin's book *The Expression of the Emotions in Man and Animals*. Darwin argued that all mammals, both humans and animals, showed emotion through facial expressions. He posed questions such as: 'Why do our facial expressions of emotions take the particular forms they do?' and 'Why do we wrinkle our nose when we are disgusted and bare our teeth when we are enraged?'

Darwin attributed these facial expressions to habits – behaviours that earlier in our evolutionary history had specific and direct functions. For example, for a species that attacked by biting, baring the teeth was a necessary act before an assault and wrinkling the nose reduced the inhalation of foul odours.

Critics ask why facial expressions persist even when they no longer serve their original purposes. According to Darwin, humans continue to make facial expressions because they have acquired communicative value throughout evolutionary history. In other words, humans utilise facial expressions as external evidence of their internal state. Although *The Expression of the Emotions in Man and Animals* was not one of Darwin's most successful books in terms of its quality and overall impact in the field, his initial ideas started the abundance of research on the types, effects and expressions of non-verbal communication and behaviour.

Now test yourself

10. Why do we still make facial expressions in today's society?

Studies

Yuki *et al.* (2007): are the windows to the soul the same in the East and West? Cultural differences in using the eyes and mouth as cues to recognise emotions in Japan and the United States

Aim(s)

Yuki *et al.* wanted to show that how we interpret facial expressions is a product of our culture and socialisation. They predicted that Japanese people would read the emotions of faces by using the eyes, whereas American people would read the emotions of faces by using the mouth.

Background

Emoticons are facial expressions created by computer symbols. American emoticons focus on the mouth and the Japanese emoticons focus on the eyes.

Procedure

A cross-cultural study was conducted using a volunteer sample of students from Japan and from the USA. The participants consisted of 118 American students (33 male and 85 female) and 95 Japanese students (72 male and 21 female; 2 students did not wish to give their gender). The participants were shown a set of six emoticons and were instructed to complete a questionnaire to rate the emotional expressions on a scale from 1 (extremely sad) to

9 (extremely happy). The researchers then worked out the average rating for each face within each culture.

Figure 10.1 Emoticons used in Yuki *et al*. (2007)

Results

Japanese participants gave higher ratings to faces with happy eyes than American participants did. This was especially true when the mouth was sad.

American participants gave their highest ratings when the mouths were happy (even when the eyes were sad). This was not true of Japanese participants.

Japanese participants gave their lowest ratings when eyes were sad (and the mouth neutral), whereas American participants gave their lowest ratings when mouths were sad (even though eyes were neutral or even happy).

Conclusions

Japanese and American people do interpret facial expressions differently. Japanese people pay more attention to the eyes and American people pay more attention to the mouth.

Yuki *et al.* suggested that this was a result of socialisation. They argued that Japanese people are brought up to hide their emotions more so have to use the eyes as an indicator of feelings.

Strengths and weaknesses of Yuki *et al.* (2007)

The study was highly controlled, and Yuki *et al.* had a high degree of control by eliminating extraneous variables and used a standardised procedure for participants to view the same emoticons and give their responses. Furthermore, using standardised equipment helped to enable the research to be checked for reliability.

The study has low levels of ecological validity as Yuki *et al.* used computer-generated faces to test participants' interpretations and not real faces, which would have been truer to life and involved more realistic emotions. This means the artificial nature of the experiment weakens its conclusions and means we cannot say Yuki *et al.* were really testing emotional responses from cues given.

Emotional expression and interpretation are complex ideas and the researchers may have over-simplified them by just scoring them on a simple rating scale. This makes the study reductionist as it reduces emotions such as happiness to one simple cue from the eyes or mouth of the emoticon, which is far too simplistic. Furthermore, the researchers only tested one dimension of emotion (happy/sad), so their findings may not generalise to other emotions, e.g. anger, surprise, disgust.

Boroditsky (2001): does language shape thought? Mandarin and English speakers' conceptions of time

In English, we predominantly use front/back terms to talk about time. We can talk about the good times ahead of us or the hardships behind us. In Mandarin, however, the terms up and down are frequently used to talk about the order of events, weeks and months.

Aim

To investigate whether language affects our understanding of time in Mandarin and English speakers.

Procedure

The sample consisted of 26 native English speakers and 20 native Mandarin speakers, who were all students at Stanford University.

The participants were **primed** to think in a certain way, either vertically or horizontally, by being shown images of an object with another object in front of it (horizontal priming) or above it (vertical priming). Half of the horizontal primes used the 'X is ahead of Y' phrasing and half used the 'X is behind Y' phrasing. Likewise, half of the vertical primes used the 'X is above Y' phrasing and half used the 'X is below Y' phrasing. Primes were equally often TRUE and FALSE.

After solving a set of two primes, participants answered a TRUE/FALSE target question about time. Half of the target questions were designed to test the immediate effect of metaphors on processing and so used a horizontal metaphor, such as March comes before April. If horizontal metaphors are processed by activating horizontal knowledge, then people should be faster to understand such a metaphor if they have just been primed horizontally than if they have just seen a vertical prime.

The other half of the target questions were designed to test the long-term effects and so did not use a metaphor, but instead used the terms earlier and later. e.g. March comes earlier than April.

Each participant completed a set of six practice questions and 64 experimental trials. Each experimental trial consisted of two spatial prime questions (both horizontal or both vertical) followed by one target question about time.

If one's native language does have a long-term effect on how one thinks about time, then Mandarin speakers should be faster to answer purely temporal target questions (e.g. 'March comes earlier than April') after solving the vertical spatial primes than after the horizontal spatial primes. English speakers, on the other hand, should be faster after horizontal primes because horizontal metaphors are predominantly used in English.

Results

Both groups responded to horizontal before/after target questions quicker following horizontal primes compared to vertical primes.

English speakers answered questions more quickly (2,128 milliseconds) following horizontal primes than they did following vertical primes (2,300 milliseconds).

Mandarin speakers answered questions more quickly (2,347 milliseconds) following vertical primes than they did following horizontal primes (2,503 milliseconds).

There was an overall effect on English speakers of the prime, but this did not have an effect on Mandarin speakers.

Conclusion

English speakers were faster after horizontal primes, indicating a habit of thinking about time in a horizontal manner. The opposite effect was found for Mandarin speakers, suggesting a habit of thinking about time in a vertical manner. This was apparent in Mandarin speakers even though they were being tested using the English language, so native language had an effect on how they thought about time.

Key term

Priming is about setting up the situation to make someone think in a certain way.

Strengths and weaknesses of Boroditsky (2001)

The study was highly controlled and took place in a laboratory of Stanford University. As a result, Boroditsky had a high degree of control by eliminating extraneous variables and using fixed timings and a standardised procedure for participants to view the slides and give their responses. Furthermore, using standardised equipment helped to enable the research to be checked for reliability.

The findings of the study are correlational and cannot demonstrate a causal relation between language and thought. This means we cannot say for definite that language *causes* thought; it is only a link or relationship between the two variables.

The study has low levels of ecological validity as participants were asked to carry out a priming task, which is unlike anything people would do in their everyday lives. As a result, we are unable to apply these results to everyday examples of language and are unable to conclude if the language shapes thought.

Exam questions

1. Outline the difference between pre-linguistic thought and pre-intellectual language. (2)

2. Compare Piaget's and Vygotsky's theories of language and thought in terms of two strengths and two weaknesses. (4)

3. Li speaks Mandarin and is planning to visit his friend Joe, who lives in Sheffield, next week. Li explains the visit as being 'earlier than Monday' and Joe says it will be 'before Monday'. Using your knowledge of Boroditsky (2001), explain the differences in these dates. (4)

4. Gill will count 'in her head' when at school, whereas Simon will count the numbers out loud. Using Vygotsky's developmental stages, explain the difference between Gill and Simon's counting. (4)

5. Tom believes Eskimos really do have lots of words for snow, whereas Ben thinks it is all nonsense and they have just the same words as we do. With reference to Tom and Ben, assess how thought and language structures affect our view of the world. (9)

6. Describe Aitchison's (1983) criteria of language features. (4)

7. Compare human and animal communication in terms of two similarities and two differences. (4)

8. Ali and Jamie have been friends since childhood. They often stand close to each other when they are talking. They have both known Mr Wickham, their old science teacher, for ten years, and are now good friends; however, they do not stand as close to Mr Wickham as they do to each other. Brendan is an old school associate whom they see every now and then, but they do not stand as close to him as they do to Mr Wickham when having conversations. How could the idea of proxemics explain these differences in personal space? (6)

9. Donald arrives in Egypt to visit Ahmed and greets him with his left hand, which offends Ahmed. Later, Donald feels uncomfortable when walking through the crowded marketplace. With reference to Donald and Ahmed, explain cultural differences in personal space. (6)

10. Describe and evaluate the study by Yuki *et al.* (2007). (9)

End of chapter summary

You should now have an understanding of all the points below:

Understand the possible relationship between language and thought, including strengths and weaknesses of each theory:

- Piaget's (1950) explanation that representational thinking precedes language
- Vygotsky's (1981) explanation that language and thinking are separate, to include:
  - pre-linguistic thought
  - pre-intellectual language.

Understand how thought and language structures affect views of the world, including strengths and weaknesses of each theory:

- linguistic relativism
- linguistic determinism.

Understand how communication is different in humans to animals, including:

- Aitchison's (1983) criteria of language features
- similarities and differences between human and animal communication.

Understand examples of non-verbal communication, including:

- facial expressions
- eye contact
- body language, to include:
  - postures
  - gestures
- personal space, to include:
  - proxemics
  - cultural differences in non-verbal communication.

Understand explanations of non-verbal communication, including Darwin's (1872) theory of evolution.

Understand the aims, procedures and findings (results and conclusions), and strengths and weaknesses of:

- Yuki *et al.* (2007): are the windows to the soul the same in the East and West? Cultural differences in using the eyes and mouth as cues to recognise emotions in Japan and the United States
- Boroditsky (2001): does language shape thought? Mandarin and English speakers' conceptions of time.

Now test yourself answers

1. According to Piaget, language depends on thought for its development (i.e. thought comes before language). For Vygotsky, thought and language are initially separate systems from the beginning of life, merging at around three years of age, producing verbal thought.
2. They are both age and stage theories in that, at various stages, language will develop in different ways.
3. True.
4. Linguistic relativism is weak Whorf and linguistic determinism is strong Whorf.
5. Displacement.
6. Dislike.
7. The term *posture* refers to how we hold our bodies as well as the overall physical form of an individual.
8. The term *proxemics* refers to the distance between people as they interact.
9. Countries that are densely populated, such as Japan, generally have much less need for personal space than those that are not, such as America.
10. Because facial expressions still convey our mood and thoughts to others.

Chapter 11

Research methods – how do you carry out psychological research?

This chapter deals with something which is central to psychology, and that's research methodology. Theories and ideas can only be tested using research, which in turn gives psychology scientific credibility.

Designing psychological research

Independent and dependent variables

The **independent variable (IV)** is the variable that the researcher manipulates. This is because the experimental conditions to test this variable are set up independently before the experiment even begins. In other words, independent variables are the potential cause of the behaviour under investigation.

The **dependent variable (DV)** refers to a behaviour that is dependent on the way the experimenter manipulates the independent variable. In other words, the dependent variable can be seen as an effect and what is being measured.

When carrying out research, you want to find out whether the IV affects the DV. To do this, the variables we are testing need to be **operationalised**, which means defining in very specific terms the variables (behaviour) being tested. It is very important that you state *how* the IV is being manipulated and *how* the dependent variable is being measured. This is the first step in ensuring that the data collected from your research will be both valid (i.e. measuring what it is supposed to be measuring) and reliable (i.e. consistent if replicated).

If, for example, you were testing helpfulness, you would find it difficult to measure. However, if you operationalise helpfulness as giving directions when asked, then this is something that can be measured. Similarly, it is hard to measure aggression, but you could operationalise it as the number of times one person kicks another.

Key terms

Operationalising variables means to make your variables fully understandable; they must include exactly what is being measured.
The **independent variable (IV)** is the variable that the researcher manipulates.
The **dependent variable (DV)** is the behaviour that the researcher measures and is dependent on the way the IV is manipulated.

For example, in a study to investigate the effect of alcohol on driving:

- The IV would be the amount of alcohol given, and this might be operationalised as the number of units of alcohol consumed.
- The DV might be operationalised as the number of cones knocked over on a designed driving course.

Now test yourself

1. Making variables measurable is also known as?
2. Outline the difference between the independent and dependent variables.

Active learning

Identify the IV and DV for each of the examples below and then operationalise the IV and DV.

- A study to investigate whether lack of sleep affects school work.
- A study to investigate whether boys score higher on an aggressive test than girls.
- A study to investigate whether students who have a computer at home do better on exams than those who do not.

The influence of extraneous variables

There are some variables the experimenter can't control – these they are called **extraneous variables.**

When planning research, psychologists need to ensure that the only factors affecting the behaviour being studied are the ones that researchers are interested in. However, researchers recognise that there are many things that can affect the behaviour of participants. Extraneous variable is the term used to refer to any unplanned influences that might affect people's behaviour during research.

A **confounding variable** is a variable which has an unintentional effect on the dependent variable. It occurs when an extraneous variable has not been controlled fully and if this affects the dependent variable, we call this a confounding variable. For example, noise during an exam is an extraneous variable, which if not controlled might confound (upset) your results.

Key terms

Extraneous variables can be defined as 'any other variable apart from the IV which could influence the DV'.
Confounding variable is an extraneous variable which influences the DV.

Situational and participant variables

Situational variables can be found in the environment (situation) in which you are conducting your experiment.

Situational variables can also occur when using designs and allocating participants to conditions. Order effects can occur in a repeated measure design; these include the practice effect (improvement in performance due to repeated practice with a task) and fatigue effect (decline in performance as the research participant becomes tired or bored while performing a sequence of tasks). These order effects are a direct disadvantage of using the same participants in both conditions and can therefore skew the results.

Participant variables are characteristics and differences to do with the individuals taking part. Examples of participant variables include emotional state, sex and age. There are also the characteristics of the task that might have an influence on the results, such as the instructions and the way stimulus materials are presented.

Controlling extraneous variables

Counterbalancing is a method of controlling 'order effects' by having some participants do one task first and the rest the other task first. In repeated measures designs, the same participants will do two or more tasks. For example, if you are testing the reliability of an intelligence test, participants would take one form of the test and then the other. If everyone did test A and then test B and were found to do better on the second test, it may be due to having had practice on the first test. Similarly, if everyone did worse on test B it may be because they had become tired during the second test.

The way to control this in the above example would be for half the participants to do test A then test B, whilst the other half do test B then test A. So, if there were any order effects, they would be 'balanced' out equally across both tests. This is counterbalancing.

Randomisation is another way to control bias as much as possible. It is designed to 'control' (reduce or eliminate if possible) bias. The fundamental goal of randomisation is to make sure each participant has an equal chance of being placed in the experimental or control group/condition.

Key terms

Situational variables can be found in the environment, e.g. if you were testing memory and some participants had to cope with more noise, light and heat, etc. than others, it might affect your results.

Participant variables can be found in the participant themselves, e.g. if you were testing driving behaviour and some of your participants were tired, that might affect your conclusions.

In **randomised** controlled trials, the research participants are assigned by chance, rather than by choice, to either the experimental group or the control group.

Let's suppose you have six shopping vouchers and a total of nine friends to distribute these to. You may write down names of each of your friends on a separate small piece of paper and fold all the small pieces of paper so no-one knows what name is on any paper. Then you ask someone to pick six names and give the vouchers to the first six names. This will remove the bias without hurting any of your friends' feelings.

Now test yourself

3. Pollution levels might be an example of which type of extraneous variable?
4. Why do we have an experimental group and control group in research?

Hypotheses

Whenever psychologists carry out a study, they must start with a **hypothesis**: an intelligent guess as to what they are likely to discover.

Let's start with a hypothesis which many teachers might subscribe to: that students work better on a Monday morning than on a Friday afternoon. Now, we can use a repeated measures design to test this, i.e. we use the same students on Monday morning as on Friday afternoon, and in each case, we give them a lesson and then test their recall on the material covered. If we want to be very thorough, we can do it over several weeks and take an average score for Monday's recall and compare it with the average score for Friday's recall.

Now, when we have collected our data, we must decide between two hypotheses:

1. The experimental hypothesis, which states that students will recall significantly more on a Monday morning than on a Friday afternoon.
2. The null hypothesis, which states that there will be no significant difference in recall between Monday morning and Friday afternoon.

The experimental hypothesis is sometimes referred to as the alternative hypothesis. Remember that some studies are not experiments (they may be observations, correlations, etc.) and in this case we do not start with an experimental hypothesis but with an alternative hypothesis. When we carry out an experiment, we can use either term.

Key term

A **hypothesis** is any idea or theory which makes certain predictions, and an experiment is designed to test these predictions.

The null hypothesis says the opposite of our experimental hypothesis and our results allow us to choose between the two, i.e. to decide which one we can reject. If there really is a significant difference between the Monday morning scores, then we reject the null hypothesis. If there is no significant difference, then we reject the experimental (alternative) hypothesis.

Sometimes a hypothesis predicts the direction in which the results are expected to go – for example, 'older people will use social media less than younger people'. When a hypothesis predicts the direction of the results, it is referred to as a directional hypothesis.

If a hypothesis does not state a direction but simply says that one factor affects another, or that there will be a difference between two sets of scores without saying in which direction that difference will be, then it is called a non-directional hypothesis. For example, 'there will be a significant difference in the use of social media between older and younger people'.

Now test yourself

5. Why do we need an experimental and a null hypothesis?

Active learning

Decide if the following hypotheses are directional or non-directional:

- Lack of sleep affects reaction times.
- The speed you drive affects how likely you are to crash.
- High temperatures make tomatoes grow more quickly.
- People who sit next to each other in class at the beginning of the year are more likely to become friends.
- The quality of service in a restaurant affects its popularity.
- Age affects short-term memory.

Methods of sampling

Sampling is a technique for drawing out individuals to form a subset from the population being studied in order to observe and measure. A **target population** is then established – these are the people you want to apply your results to.

Key term

Target population means a whole collection of individuals who have the relevant criteria for the study that is to be undertaken.

Types of sampling techniques

Random

This is like the National Lottery, where every member of the target population has an equal chance of being picked, e.g. names drawn from a hat.

Stratified

The target population is divided into subsets, such as age, race and gender, and a representative sample of each is found. For example, if the target population consisted of 75 per cent males and 25 per cent females, a stratified sample of 20 would include 15 men and 5 women.

Opportunity

Whoever is available at any opportune moment, e.g. the first 20 people you find in the canteen. It is the simplest form of sampling and involves selecting anyone who is available from the target population.

Volunteer/self-selected

People volunteer to take part in an experiment, e.g. volunteers replying to a newspaper advertisement.

Strengths and weaknesses of methods of sampling

An opportunity sample is a quick, convenient and economical form of sampling in that you are gathering participants who are available at that specific opportune moment. This is positive as there is less planning and preparation required and so it leads to fewer delays in the research process and costs less. However, it is for just this reason that it tends to be very unrepresentative and the researcher may be biased by choosing participants who may be helpful or even people they know. For example, if a study in a city centre is conducted during work hours, this sample will not represent individuals who work, go to school, college, etc.

Stratified sampling can become complicated if there are lots of subsets, making it a lengthy procedure and quite difficult to carry out quickly. However, the advantage is that there is no bias in selection and every member of the target population has a chance of being selected for each subset.

Random sampling provides the best chance of an unbiased representative sample as every member of the target population has an equal chance of being picked. However, this works well for small to medium-sized samples; the larger the population, the more difficult random sampling becomes.

Volunteer sampling is ethical, as participants have chosen to take part willingly. It also means the researchers have little work to do other than advertise for the sample and then just sit back and wait. However, the sample tends to be biased on the part of the participant as they tend to be more motivated and perform better, so might be more up for it and likely to display demand characteristics.

Now test yourself

6. Which is the fairest type of sampling technique?

Experimental and research designs

Before carrying out an experiment, the researcher needs to decide whether to use the same or different participants in the different conditions of the IV. This is known as **experimental design**. The researcher wants to test cause and effect between the independent and dependent variables, so must set up experimental conditions and compare people's performance between them.

An **independent measures design** means that different participants will take part in each of the experimental conditions. The two groups of participants in this type of experimental design will be exposed to one level of the IV only. In this design, the two or more groups used in the experiment consist of different individuals. For example, you compare 20 boys with 20 girls on a reading test.

Key terms

Experimental design refers to the allocation of same or different participants.
An **independent measures design** is where participants only take part in one condition of the experiment.

A **repeated measures design** is when the same participants are tested on two or more separate occasions. So, the same participants are used in each group. For example, you test ten participants on two different IQ tests and compare the results.

A **matched-pairs design** involves matching each participant in one of the experimental conditions as closely as possible to another participant in the second condition according to variables that are relevant. So, for example, pairs of participants might be matched for age, gender, their intelligence or personality test scores.

Key terms

A **repeated measures design** is where participants take part in both (or all) conditions of an experiment.
A matched-pairs design refers to the allocation of different participants in two or more groups but who have been matched on various traits.

Table 11.1 Strengths and weaknesses of experimental and research designs

	Advantages	Disadvantages
Independent measures	No order effects; different participants in each group so less chance of practice or fatigue effects.	Uncontrollable participant variables mean individual differences affecting results.
Repeated measures	No uncontrollable participant variables so less chance of individual differences affecting results.	Order effects, as same participants in each group so more chance of practice or fatigue effects.
Matched pairs	Reduces participant variables (as far as they can be matched) so less chance of individual differences affecting results.	It requires a large number of potential participants to start with in order to get enough pairs, making it expensive and time-consuming (rarely used).

Now test yourself

7. Which design would have been used in Zimbardo's prison guard study?
8. Which design would have been used in Peterson and Peterson's study on short-term memory?

Reliability and validity of research

It is obviously true that psychological tests and other similar measures need to produce consistent, **reliable** results and need to measure what they are supposed to measure.

The participants in research, the sample, should be as representative as possible of the target population. The more representative the sample, the more confident the researcher can be that the results can be generalised to the target population.

Sampling technique such as opportunity or volunteer would be viewed as less reliable than a random sample as they are more biased, making the results less likely to be repeated in exactly the same way, as you have chosen a biased sample.

The same point applies to independent measures designs where, because the two or more groups are made up of different individuals who have varying participant variables, we are less likely to get the same results if repeating the investigation and so less reliable findings.

A **valid** test measures what it is supposed to measure. A test can be reliable but not valid. You would not think much of a psychology exam which only asked questions on physics.

Stratified samples are more likely to have high population validity because everyone in the target population has an equal opportunity of being selected and the sample is proportional to the target population, so making the sample more representative of the target population.

Repeated measures designs suffer from order effects, which means the participant may get better or worse at a given task second time around as they have had practice or are now bored. This lessens the validity of this design as we don't know whether the outcome of the task was down to the independent variable or the two order effects.

Qualitative data gathered from case studies and self-reports is very subjective in nature and so it is difficult to apply standards of reliability and validity. As the researcher gathers the data, it is not possible to replicate qualitative studies. Also, contexts, situations, events, conditions and interactions cannot be replicated to any extent, nor can generalisations be made to a wider context than the one studied with any confidence.

On the other hand, quantitative data is based on measured values and can be checked by others because numerical data is less open to interpretation. Hypotheses can also be tested because of the use of statistical analysis and so replication and therefore reliability is higher than with qualitative methods.

Key terms

Reliability refers to the consistency of a test or an observer, one which produces the same results on different occasions.
Validity refers to what extent we are testing what we set out to test.

Ethical issues in psychological research

The code is based on four ethical principles from the BPS Code of Human Research Ethics (2014):

1. Respect – psychologists value the dignity and worth of all persons of all cultural backgrounds and regarding people's rights, including those of privacy. The experience they bring to the research must be respected and other guidelines including informed consent and right to withdraw should be followed.
2. Competence – psychologists should be fully able to carry out the work assigned to them and place value on the high standards of their own competence in their professional work. They should have an awareness of their own ability and limits and work within these.
3. Responsibility – psychologists have a responsibility to themselves, their clients, the public and to the profession of psychology. They must try and ensure any research does not damage the reputation of psychology. They must ensure participants are protected from harm and always debriefed at the end of any research.
4. Integrity – psychologists should be honest and accurate in all their research and with all parties concerned. This includes honesty and accuracy when results of research are published and any conflicts of interest must be open and transparent. There should be an underlying impression of fairness carried out within all the research and with all those concerned.

Informed consent

Whenever possible, the consent of participants must be obtained. It is not sufficient to simply get participants to say 'Yes'. They also need to know what it is that they are agreeing to. You need to explain what is involved in advance and obtain the informed consent of participants. If there is difficulty in gaining consent, then presumptive consent may be sought – a similar group of people can be asked how they would feel about taking part. If they think it would be OK, then it can be assumed that the real participants will also find it acceptable.

Debrief

At the end of the study, the participant should be able to discuss the procedure and the findings. Debriefing should take place as soon as possible and be as full as possible; participants must be given a general idea of what the researcher was investigating and why, and their part in the research should be explained. They must be asked if they have any questions and those questions should be answered honestly and as fully as possible.

Protection of participants

Researchers must ensure that those taking part in research will not be caused distress and will be protected from physical and mental harm. The risk of harm must be no greater than in ordinary life. The researcher must also ensure that if vulnerable groups such as the elderly and children are used they must receive special care. Children get tired easily, so participation should be brief.

Deception

This is where participants are misled or wrongly informed about the aims of the research. The researcher should avoid deceiving participants about the nature of the research unless there is no alternative – and even then, this would need to be judged acceptable by an independent expert. However, there are some types of research that cannot be carried out without at least some element of deception – for example, in Milgram's study of obedience. The true nature of the research should be revealed at the earliest possible opportunity, or at least during debriefing. Researchers can determine whether participants are likely to be distressed when deception is disclosed, by consulting culturally relevant groups.

Confidentiality

Participants, and the data gained from them, must be kept anonymous unless they give their full consent. No names must be used in a research report. Ultimately, decisions to disclose information will have to be set in the context of the aims of the research.

Withdrawal from an investigation

Participants should be able to leave a study at any time if they feel uncomfortable. They should also be allowed to withdraw their data. They should be told at the start of the study that they have the right to withdraw. They should not have pressure placed upon them to continue if they do not want to. Even at the end of the study, the participant has a final opportunity to withdraw the data they have provided for the research.

Now test yourself

9. Which ethical guidelines did Milgram *not* break?

Understanding research methods

Experiments

The experimental method is a study of cause and effect. It involves the deliberate manipulation of one variable while trying to keep all others constant. The researcher manipulates the independent variable and measures the dependent variable.

Whether it is a laboratory or field experiment is determined by where it takes place:

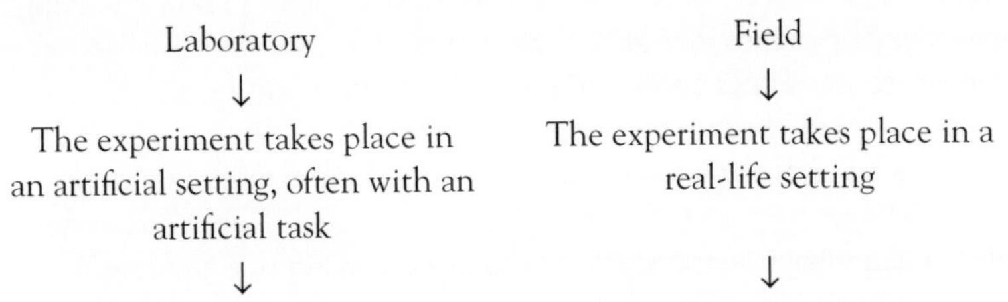

Table 11.2 Strengths and weaknesses of laboratory and field experiments

Strengths of laboratory experiments	Strengths of field experiments
The researcher has more control over situational variables, so high levels of precision are achieved. This means cause and effect can be established (the IV has caused the effect on the DV). Lab experiments are replicable, which means they can be repeated by other experiments, so are high in reliability. Procedures can be repeated easily.	There is high ecological validity as they take place in real environments, so behaviour is less artificial and more natural. There is less chance of demand characteristics and experimenter effects as participants may not have to leave their natural environment and often are unaware of being tested.
Weaknesses of laboratory experiments	**Weaknesses of field experiments**
There is low ecological validity as they use artificial environments that are different from real life; this makes it hard to apply results. Demand characteristics may be present as people may respond to features of the experiment (guess the aim). Experimenter effects may also be present as how they communicate to the participant may affect the results.	The researcher has less control over situational variables, so levels of precision are not as high. This means it is difficult to establish cause and effect. (Confounding variables could have affected the DV.) Field experiments are not easy to replicate, and procedures are not easily repeated due to low control, so are generally lower in reliability.

Natural experiments tend to be in the participants' natural setting because the independent variable occurs naturally. This is the main feature – that the IV is not something which is manipulated or set up but is found already 'out there'. A natural experiment has a naturally occurring IV, e.g. gender or school, so it is not under the strict control of the experimenter, but the experimenter can still study the effect on the DV.

For example, Charlton *et al.* (2000) wanted to see the effects of television on children and they studied a community where television was to be introduced. They studied the community both before and after and these were the two conditions of the IV. They did not introduce the television; it was being introduced in any case – it was a naturally occurring situation. Most of the time participants are aware that they are taking part in an experiment.

Strengths and weaknesses of natural experiments

They take place in a real-life context so are important for real-life application and are high in ecological validity. Natural experiments also have fewer ethical issues as the experimenter doesn't manipulate anything, like in other types of experiments. Demand characteristics are not a problem, unlike laboratory experiments, so participants are less likely to adjust their natural behaviour as they might not know they are even taking part in a study.

However, a disadvantage is the experimenter has little control over the variables so difficult to establish cause and effect as there is no direct manipulation of the IV. It also means they are difficult to replicate as there is little control so they lack any kind of testing for reliability unlike more controlled methods, like laboratory experiments.

Interviews

An interview is like a verbal questionnaire and involves asking people questions either face-to-face or over the phone/Internet. There are many ways to conduct an interview, ranging from casual chats to formal interviews using a set of questions, like a questionnaire but with the added benefit of being able to ask clarifying questions due to being in personal contact with the participant.

Different types of interviews include:

- Structured interview: a researcher works through several pre-determined questions. Participants' replies are often recorded using a tape or a video-recorder and sometimes written transcripts.
- Semi-structured interview: initially pre-determined questions are used, then the researcher develops new questions as they progress through the interview in response to the answers given by the participant.
- Unstructured interview: a researcher conducts a more relaxed conversation with the participant, aiming to finding out what the participant thinks about certain issues but without using pre-determined questions.

As with questionnaires, the same issues need to be considered in order to ensure that the research is ethical, and the responses gathered are valid and reliable. Therefore, it is a good idea to pilot the interview questions on a small number of people prior to carrying out large-scale research. That way, any amendments needed could be made before these are issued on a larger scale. Access is an issue that needs to be addressed when carrying out an interview, in terms of contacting participants. At times, researchers may need to contact another person, such as a guardian, so access can be more difficult for some participants than others.

Interviews range from being unstructured to semi-structured (e.g. like clinical interviews) to structured. The more structured interview will use a questionnaire and therefore these two methods are often difficult to separate. Some issues which researchers need to consider when designing questions include avoiding double barrelled, leading, complex, ambiguous and emotive questions. Researchers also need to decide between open and closed questions and the order in which they are asked. In more unstructured interviews, it is usually necessary to make recordings or take detailed notes.

Strengths and weaknesses of interviews

Interviews allow researchers to collect a relatively (i.e. compared to experiments) large amount of information quickly. Both interviews and questionnaires can act as a useful starting point for more controlled research.

Distortions of the truth (social desirability) may occur whereby participants may not answer truthfully/accurately either because they want to appear in the best light or because they are not interested enough to think carefully about their answers. The interviewer may also influence responses by their non-verbal cues.

Questionnaires

A questionnaire contains a number of items that are used to draw information from people, to find out what they think, feel and do. When questionnaires are being administered to a large number of participants, the research is commonly referred to as a survey.

When using questionnaires, the researcher will normally assemble a number of items, which are then posed to a representative sample of the relevant population. Participants' responses, in turn, allow the researcher to make generalisations about a particular topic. Items can be in the format of a question or a statement that the participant needs to respond to. Questionnaires need to be designed very carefully as they often ask for personal information from the participant, so they should only ask for information that is relevant to the investigation so that they remain ethical.

Strengths and weaknesses of questionnaires

Questionnaires are ethical because they allow for informed consent and allow for the right to withdraw. They are also reliable because standardised instructions tell participants what to do and are the same for everyone, which is useful as what the researcher says might influence how the participant answers.

Questionnaires are more realistic than experiments – for example, investigating dreams in a laboratory. This would be an unfamiliar setting and might not produce very valid results. A questionnaire can ask about what dreaming is like at home, so is more valid.

Response bias is an issue when participants fill in a questionnaire as they sometimes fall into patterns of answering. As participants know someone will be reading their answers, this can make them give socially acceptable answers rather than what they really believe, which is called social desirability bias.

Correlation

A correlation measures the relationship between two variables. The researcher measures the variables without manipulating them. They do not say whether one variable causes the other, only that two things occur together. For example, height and weight – taller people tend to be heavier and shorter people tend to be lighter, but your height does not actually cause your weight. A correlation can be represented visually if the form of a scatter gram, where each point represents one person's scores on the two variables being measured.

Researchers carrying out correlational analysis would typically:

- collect values measuring two (or more) different variables from the same participants
- plot each set of data on a scatter gram to see if there is relationship between them, then
- calculate the correlation coefficient to see how strong that relationship is between the variables.

If an increase in one variable tends to be associated with an increase in the other, then this is known as a positive correlation. For example, the more hours of revision you do then the higher your exam grade will be.

If an increase in one variable tends to be associated with a decrease in the other, then this is known as a negative correlation. For example, the more lessons you miss in psychology the lower your exam grade will be.

Strengths and weaknesses of correlations

Correlation can be used when it is unethical to manipulate a variable – for example, investigating smoking and lung cancer. Correlational techniques allow us to measure many relationships between variables at the same time. Thus, they can be useful in unravelling complex relationships and can suggest directions for future research. They play a big part in establishing the reliability and validity of psychological measuring instruments. For example, correlational techniques have played an important part in establishing the reliability and validity of psychometric tests of intelligence and personality.

It is impossible to establish a cause-and-effect relationship as a correlation only measures the degree of relationship between variables, and not whether one variable has caused another. We cannot draw conclusions about cause and effect, as some other factor may be responsible for the findings. For example, we cannot say that days off college *caused* poor exam results.

Case study

Case studies often involve simply observing what happens to, or reconstructing the 'case history' of, a single participant or group of individuals. They involve studying one unique individual (or small group) and gathering in-depth, rich, detailed data about them. Many methods may be used within a case study, e.g. observations, questionnaires, interviews, experiments and case histories. A case history is the 'story' of an individual using qualitative data.

Case studies generate qualitative data as researchers tend to rely on verbal descriptions of participants rather than numerical analysis. That is not to say that numerical analysis is excluded, but the main data collected consists of description rather than measurement.

Strengths and weaknesses of case studies

Case studies are useful because they are often the only way of studying a particular behaviour and they can gather data that cannot be obtained by other means. They produce valid data. This is because the data comes directly from the people concerned and is usually gathered in their natural surroundings.

Case studies are not replicable because the situation is unique. Also, another researcher at another moment in time might gather different data (cannot be tested for reliability).

Another weakness is that it is hard to use the results and say they are true of other situations. If results come from one unique individual or small group, the findings cannot be generalised.

Observation

Observations are useful when it is difficult to intervene or manipulate behaviour for the purpose of study. They are a useful first step in research for identifying areas for further experimentation. There are several types of observations, including:

- Controlled observations – this is similar to a laboratory experiment in that the study takes place in a controlled environment, but variables are not manipulated by the researcher. For example, participants in sleep labs are allowed to sleep naturally but with electrodes attached to their heads to measure brain activity.
- Naturalistic observations – this is where participants are observed in their natural environment with minimal control and manipulation.
- Participant observations – a variant of the naturalistic observation, this involves the researcher actually becoming part of the group they are observing. Participant observation is where the observer interacts with the groups of people whose behaviour is being observed. This can affect their objectivity and makes it difficult to record behaviours. This type of observation can be overt or covert (see below).

Controlled observations may distort behaviour similar to laboratory experiments because they are done in artificial environments. Observations are open to demand characteristics if participants know they are being observed. Observer bias can be a problem, especially in less structured observations. This can be overcome by the use of two or more observers, who are trained beforehand, to achieve consistency in observations. The recordings of the two observers are correlated to check consistency (inter-rater reliability).

Overt observations refer to the researcher being open about their intentions in the field and ensuring all members of the social group are aware of what is happening. Covert observations involve the researcher not informing members of the group of the reason for their presence, keeping their true intentions secret.

Strengths and weaknesses of observations

Most are carried out in natural surroundings and, therefore, if they are conducted carefully, most participants won't know they are being observed. Observations can provide hypotheses for more rigorous examination and so help in the first stage of the scientific process of gathering knowledge.

An advantage of overt observations is that they allow the researcher to be honest with the participants, thus avoiding problematic ethical issues such as deception or lack of informed consent. However, a disadvantage would be that the participants understand the aims of the observer and so there is likely to be possible observer effects (the participants changing their behaviour, acting in a way that they believe is expected by the experimenter).

In the case of covert observations, the researcher may not be protected, or may not protect others, from the risk of harm. Also, they will be deceiving the participants and will lack informed consent. An advantage of covert observation is that it allows access to social groups that normally would not provide consent to being involved in studies; therefore, allowing us to research and expand knowledge on lesser-known social groups, which in turn will widen our psychological understanding of the world. Also, this type of observation avoids problems surrounding observer effects and so may be considered to be higher in validity than overt observations.

Data analysis

When we summarise data to help reach conclusions, we are using a process called data analysis.

Arithmetic and numerical computation

Standard form is a way of writing large numbers in a shortened version

Example 1

$$4.5 \times 10^4 + 6.45 \times 10^5$$
$$= 45{,}000 + 645{,}000$$
$$= 690{,}000$$
$$= 6.9 \times 10^5$$

Here you can use the rules for multiplying and dividing powers. Remember these rules:

- To multiply powers, you add, e.g. $10^5 \times 10^3 = 10^8$
- To divide powers, you subtract, e.g. $10^5 \div 10^3 = 10^2$

Example 2

Simplify $(2 \times 10^3) \times (3 \times 10^6)$

Solution

Multiply 2 by 3 and add the powers of 10:

$$(2 \times 10^3) \times (3 \times 10^6) = 6 \times 10^9$$

Question

Simplify $(36 \times 10^5) \div (6 \times 10^3)$

Answer

$(36 \times 10^5) \div (6 \times 10^3) = (36 \div 6) \times (10^5 \div 10^3) = 6 \times 10^2$

Decimal places and rounding

Imagine you want to know the attendance at a big boxing match at Wembley stadium and are told its 38,945. But for most people who want to know the attendance figure, an answer of 'nearly 39,000', or 'roughly 38,000', is fine.

We can round off large numbers like these to the nearest thousand, nearest hundred, nearest ten, nearest whole number or any other specified number.

Round 38,945 to the nearest thousand.

First, look at the digit in the thousands place. It is 8. This means the number lies between 38,000 and 39,000. Look at the digit to the right of the 8. It is 9. That means 38,945 is closer to 39,000 than 38,000.

The rule is, if the next digit is 5 or more, we 'round up'. If it is 4 or less, it stays as it is.

38,945 to the nearest thousand = 39,000.

38,945 to the nearest hundred = 38,900.

Significant figures – decimals

Rounding 12.756 or 4.543 to 1 decimal place (d.p.) seems sensible, as the rounded figures are very close to the actual value.

12.756 = 12.8 (1 d.p.)

4.543 = 4.5 (1 d.p.)

Counting significant figures

Significant figures start at the first non-zero number, so ignore the zeros at the front, but not the ones in between. Look at the following examples:

0.0081 – in this case, the '8' is the first significant figure and '1' is the second significant figure.

0.0678 – in this case, the '6' is the first significant figure and '7' is the second significant figure and '8' is the third significant figure.

Rounding significant figures

The method for rounding significant figures is more or less the same as for rounding to a given number of decimal places.

Round 0.0961591 to three significant figures (s.f.).

To round to three significant figures, look at the fourth significant figure. It's a 5, so round up.

Therefore, 0.0961591 = 0.0962 (3 s.f.)

Ratios

A **ratio** shows how much of one thing there is compared to another and are usually written in the form a:b. If you are baking a cake and you mix one part water to four parts flour, then the ratio of water to flour will be 1:4. The order in which a ratio is stated is important. Changing the order of the numbers in a ratio changes the proportions.

Fractions

A **fraction** is a part of a whole – for example, $\frac{1}{2}$. The top number of the fraction is called the numerator. The bottom number is called the denominator. In order to compare fractions, you need to change them so they have the same denominator. Equivalent fractions are fractions that look different but show exactly the same amount, such as $\frac{1}{3}$ or $\frac{2}{6}$ or $\frac{4}{12}$.

Key terms

Ratio refers to showing the proportion of something against another.
Fractions show the proportions of something by cutting it up.

Percentages

'Per cent' means 'per 100'. If 80 per cent of the population own a car, this means that 80 out of every 100 people own a car. It is often useful to be able to find a percentage of a quantity. For example, Olivia has 60 pairs of shoes; 20 per cent of the shoes are black. How many shoes is that?

You need to find 20 per cent of 60.

1 per cent of 60 is: $60 \div 100 = 0.6$

So, 20 per cent of 60 is: $0.6 \times 20 = 12$.

Descriptive statistics, tables, charts and diagrams

There are three types of measures of central tendency:

- Mean – add up all the scores in a condition and divide by the number of participants.
- Median – put all of the scores in order and find the mid-point. There must be an equal amount of numbers either side of this point.
- Mode – the most frequently occurring score in a condition.
- Range – where you minus the lowest score from the highest score.

Drawing graphs

Draw a bar chart for the following data:

Participants were surveyed to see what type of car they drive: 2 participants drive a Peugeot, 4 participants drive a BMW, 3 participants drive a Renault and 1 participant drives an Audi.

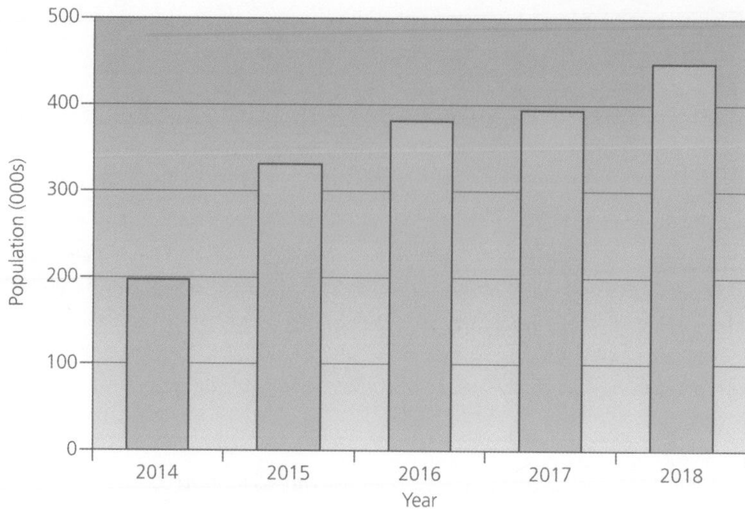

Figure 11.1 Example of a bar chart

Draw a frequency polygon and a histogram for the following data:
Participants were surveyed to see how many miles they drive in a year (see Table 11.3).

Table 11.3 How many miles participants drove in a year

Participant	Miles	Participant	Miles
1	5,000	6	4,000
2	4,800	7	25,000
3	10,000	8	26,000
4	11,500	9	6,500
5	15,000	10	30,000

The normal distribution

The **normal distribution** is a special kind of frequency distribution which is often arrived at where a large set of measures is collected and then organised into a frequency polygon.

Key term

Normal distribution refers to a distribution where the mean, mode and median are the same.

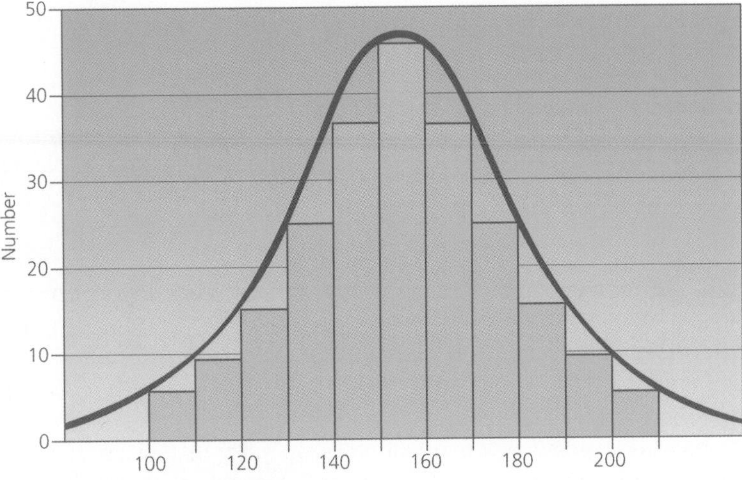

Figure 11.2 Normal distribution curve

This is a very well-known bell-shaped distribution called a 'normal' distribution. It often occurs where a large number of measurements are taken of naturally occurring phenomena, e.g. people's heights, weights, foot sizes, etc.

Characteristics of the normal distribution

- The mean, median and mode all occur at the same point (the highest point of the curve).
- It is symmetrical on either side of the central point of the horizontal axis – the pattern of scores is exactly the same above the mean as it is below it.
- A large number of scores fall relatively close to the mean on either side. As the distance from the mean increases, the scores become fewer.

Primary and secondary data

Primary data is data which is derived from original thinking or new information.

Examples of primary data include results from a questionnaire or experiment, which can be qualitative or quantitative, respectively. Data can be sets of statistics that you then input into a computer programme to construct frequency distributions or other descriptive statistics. Primary data can come from an observation you have carried out where you may have raw data like a tally chart of aggressive behaviours between boys and girls in a playground.

In contrast to secondary data, primary data comes from observations made by the researchers themselves. This often creates credibility issues that do not arise with secondary data. Researchers may be subjective in what kinds of data they look for – data that 'fits' the hypotheses they are trying to test.

The data must be gathered from scratch, which involves finding a large enough population and in turn gleans a large volume of data. This usually makes it costlier and more time-consuming (it requires direct and personal intervention – you must be there) than collecting secondary data.

Secondary data is second-hand analysis of pre-existing (primary) data, used in a different way or to answer a different question than originally intended. Secondary data analysis uses data that was collected by someone else to further a study that you are interested in completing. It means that, after performing statistical operations on primary data, the results become known as secondary data.

The Internet is a great source of secondary data. Many published statistics and figures are available on the Internet either free or for a fee.

Key terms

Primary data means original data that has been collected by those who saw an event first hand or collected data themselves.
Secondary data usually interprets, analyses, evaluates, explains or comments on primary data.

Qualitative and quantitative data

Both qualitative and quantitative data have a place in psychology. If your interest is primarily research based, e.g. cognitive psychology, then you will probably favour quantitative approaches where you have highly controlled experiments producing precise numerical data. However, if your interest is more applied aspects of psychology, e.g. if you are trying to understand what causes football violence and how to reduce it, then you are more likely to find qualitative approaches useful.

In general, quantitative methods tend to be stricter and will produce more reliable data as they can be replicated easily, which enhances their scientific status. But such approaches can be criticised for producing narrow, unrealistic information which only focuses on small fragments of behaviour. In contrast, qualitative approaches, with less control, conducted in more natural circumstances, tend to produce more valid data but are criticised for low reliability and subjectivity. Qualitative methods can be subjective because they produce information which the researcher has to organise and select from.

Quantitative (What?) = measuring by number (e.g. number of words recalled in a memory experiment or how many participants obeyed in the Milgram experiment).

Qualitative (Why?) = describing, emphasising meanings and experiences (e.g. how memory works or interviewing participants to see why they went so far on Milgram's shock generator).

Now test yourself

10. Which type of data did Peterson and Peterson find in their results on short-term memory?

Issues and debates

Understand ethical issues in psychological research

Ethical issues were discussed earlier and involve following guidelines such as informed consent and deception. In this section, we will apply these ethical issues to the content in topics 1–5.

Topic 1: Development – how did you develop?

The research by Dweck has shown that praise linked to reinforcing learners about their intelligence or talent is detrimental to their view about their abilities. It reinforces (fixed mindset) ideas that their achievements are a consequence of IQ or other innate ability. It led to students worrying that future tests might reveal their shortcomings, and that challenges were to be avoided as, again, struggling demonstrated that they weren't really as smart as their teachers had believed. This links to the ethical issue of protection of participants as children are considered a vulnerable group and should not be caused distress.

Topic 2: Memory – how does your memory work?

Case studies of brain-damaged patients are useful as it would be unethical to test using other methods, i.e. we cannot deliberately damage the brains of people just to see the effect it may have on their memory. They can therefore be used for studying unusual behaviours or circumstances which may be hard to find outside clinical settings.

Cases like that of H.M. don't use the real name of the participant. One of the ethical guidelines is confidentiality, which states you should never name your participants or let them be identified.

Topic 3: Psychological problems – how would psychological problems affect you?

There are ethical issues with therapies such as CBT as their underlying assumptions for addiction and depression may be seen as blaming the individual for his or her maladaptive thinking, which raises issues around labelling and responsibility. Methadone is highly addictive and has many side effects, such as dry mouth, fatigue and weight gain. There are also some ethical objections to heroin users being given drugs as treatment, partly because it will lead to withdrawal symptoms itself when the individual tries to stop using it.

Topic 4: The brain and neuropsychology – how does your brain affect you?

The prefrontal cortex processes feelings of empathy, shame, compassion and guilt. Damage to this part of the brain causes a reduced ability for social emotions but leaves logical reasoning intact. However, we have to be careful when making cause-and-effect conclusions from cases like the two adults who suffered prefrontal cortex damage when they were very young children. These two individuals had severe behavioural problems, including impaired decision-making ability and defective moral reasoning. It would be unethical to label individuals as criminal or violent based on links between brain and behaviour as these are only correlational.

Topic 5: Social influence – how do others affect you?

Participants in the Piliavin *et al.* (1969) study were unaware that they were taking part in an experiment. Therefore, they could not consent to take part and it was also not possible to withdraw from the study or be debriefed. Furthermore, seeing a victim collapse may have been stressful for the participants. They also may have felt guilty if they did not help, so leading to psychological harm.

Similarly, the participants are being deceived because they are unaware that it is not a genuine emergency. Participants were also not debriefed as this would have been almost impossible.

Similarly, Haney, Banks and Zimbardo (1973) lacked full informed consent from participants as the researchers themselves did not know what would happen over the two weeks. The prisoners did not consent to being 'arrested' at home. Participants playing the role of prisoners were not protected from psychological harm, experiencing incidents of humiliation and distress. However, in the researchers' defence, extensive group and individual debriefing sessions were held, and all participants returned post-experimental questionnaires several weeks, then several months later, and then at yearly intervals.

Exam questions

1. Outline three features of a laboratory experiment. (3)

Matt is carrying out psychological research into memory. He goes to the canteen in his school and asks the first 20 people he meets to be participants in his study.

2. What is the sampling method used in Matt's study? (1)
3. What would be a fairer sampling method that Matt might have used? (1)

Matt decides to test the memory of males and females in his research.

4. Which would be the most appropriate design for Matt to use? (1)
5. Explain why this design is the most appropriate one for Matt to use. (2)

Matt gathers lots of quantitative data from his research into memory.

6. What is meant by quantitative data? (1)
7. Explain one strength and one weakness of using quantitative data. You must refer to Matt in your answer. (4)

A researcher wanted to investigate how people felt about the rising use of social media amongst teenagers.

8. Explain what type of interview would be most suited for this investigation. (3)

The researcher then looks to try and find a relationship between age and use of social media.

9. Identify the IV and DV in this investigation. (2)

A positive correlation is found between the two variables.

10. Evaluate the use of correlations as they are used in psychological research. (5)

Eve wants to see whether students at her college in Chesterfield are more obedient to their teachers as compared to her friends who go to a school in Dronfield. Eve decides to use an interview to investigate levels of obedience between the two groups.

11. Explain which type of interview Eve might use in her investigation. (2)
12. Give an example of one open and one closed question Eve might use as part of her interview. (2)

Eve finds that the students in Chesterfield are more obedient than those in Dronfield.

13. Using both situational and personality factors in obedience, explain why the students in Chesterfield might be more obedient to their teachers. (6)

End of chapter summary

You should now have an understanding of all the points below:

Be able to identify:

- an independent variable (IV)
- a dependent variable (DV)
- extraneous variables, including:
  - situational variables
  - participant variables.

Understand the influence of extraneous variables and suggest possible ways to control for them, including:

- use of standardised procedures
- counterbalancing
- randomisation
- single-blind techniques
- double-blind techniques.

Be able to write a null hypothesis.

Be able to write an alternative hypothesis.

Understand methods of sampling, including strengths and weaknesses of each sampling method:

- target population samples
- random sampling
- stratified sampling
- volunteer sampling
- opportunity sampling.

Understand experimental and research designs, including strengths and weaknesses:

- independent measures
- repeated measures
- matched pairs.

Understand the reliability and validity of the following when analysing the planning and conducting of research procedures:

- sampling methods
- experimental designs
- quantitative methods
- qualitative methods.

Understand ethical issues in psychological research and how to deal with ethical issues, including:

- informed consent
- deception
- confidentiality
- right to withdraw
- protection of participants.

Understand research methods, including the features, strengths and weaknesses of the following, and the types of research for which they are suitable:

- laboratory experiment
- field experiment
- natural experiment
- interview, including:
  - structured
  - semi-structured
  - unstructured
- questionnaire, including:
  - closed-ended questions to elicit quantitative data
  - open-ended questions to elicit qualitative data
- correlation
- case study
- observation.

Arithmetic and numerical computation:

- recognise and use expressions in decimal and standard form
- estimate results
- use an appropriate number of significant figures.

Be able to understand and use, including calculations:

- mean, and finding arithmetic means
- median
- mode
- ratios
- fractions
- percentages
- range as a measure of dispersion
- the characteristics of normal distributions.

Be able to:

- construct and interpret frequency tables and diagrams
- construct and interpret bar charts
- construct and interpret histograms
- construct a scatter diagram
- use a scatter diagram to identify a correlation between two variables
- translate information between graphical and numerical forms
- plot two variables from experimental or other data and interpret graphs.

Understand, and know the difference between:

- primary data
- secondary data.

Understand, and know the difference between:

- qualitative data
- quantitative data.

Understand ethical issues in psychological research, including:

- know the term 'ethical issue(s)'
- use content, theories and research drawn from the compulsory topics to explain ethical issues in psychological research.

Now test yourself answers

1. Operationalisation.
2. The IV is manipulated and the DV is measured.
3. Situational.
4. To compare the effect of the independent variable on the dependent variable.
5. To see whether our results are due to chance or if the IV did in fact influence the DV.
6. Random sampling, as everyone has an equal chance of being picked.
7. Independent measures, as there were two groups who were independent of each other.
8. Repeated measures.
9. Debriefing and confidentiality.
10. Quantitative data.

Index

Page numbers in **bold** denote tables, those in *italics* denote figures.